Narrating Discovery

THE ROMANTIC EXPLORER IN AMERICAN LITERATURE, 1790–1855

Bruce Greenfield

Columbia University Press   New York

PS
217
.D57
G·73
1992

COLUMBIA UNIVERSITY PRESS
New York   Oxford
Copyright © 1992 Columbia University Press
All rights reserved

Library of Congress Cataloging-in-Publication Data

Greenfield, Bruce Robert, 1951–
Narrating discovery : the romantic explorer
in American literature, 1790–1855 / Bruce Greenfield.
p. cm.—(The Social foundations of aesthetic forms)
Includes bibliographical references and index.
ISBN 0-231-07996-6
1. American literature—19th century—History and criticism.
2. America—Discovery and exploration—Historiography.
3. Discoveries (in geography) in literature.
4. Romanticism—United States.
5. Explorers in literature.   6. America in literature.
7. Travel in literature.   8. Narration (Rhetoric) I. Title.
II. Series: Social foundations of aesthetic forms series.
PS217.D57G73   1992
810.9′003—dc20   92–21030

Casebound editions of Columbia University Press books
are Smyth-sewn and printed on
permanent and durable acid-free paper.

Book design by Audrey Smith
Printed in the United States of America

c 10 9 8 7 6 5 4 3 2 1

For Anne

8793

Contents

Acknowledgments
ix

Introduction
1

Chapter One
Trading and Telling: Discovery and the British Fur Trade
15

Traveling for History   15
Discovery and Narrative Structure in Samuel Hearne's
Journey to the Northern Ocean   26
Alexander Mackenzie's *Voyages*: Discovery and the Fur
Trade Entrepreneur   41
Alexander Henry's *Travels and Adventures:*
Narrating Captivity   55

Chapter Two
Early Western Travels and the American Self
71

Lewis and Clark's *History*: The Search for Authority   84
Zebulon Pike and John Charles Frémont: Pioneers of
Popular Self-Discovery   102

Contents

Chapter Three
Washington Irving: Historian of American Discovery   *113*

Irving's *Columbus*   122
Irving on the Prairies   130
Irving's Discovery of the Far West   144

Chapter Four
Poe and Thoreau: The Romantic Discovery Narrative   165

Discovery and Violence:
Poe's *Narrative of Arthur Gordon Pym*   165
Thoreau's Discovery of America:
A Nineteenth-Century First Contact   183

Conclusion
203

Notes
211

Works Consulted
233

Index
245

Acknowledgments

This book owes much to the scholarly example and specific advice of Sacvan Bercovitch, who guided its earliest stages and read a later draft. I hope it is some small credit to this gifted and generous teacher. Thanks are due, as well, to Karl Kroeber for encouragement and many helpful suggestions. Howard Lamar generously read an early chapter, offering a historian's point of view on a mainly literary project. At a later stage, Peter Antelyes and Donald Pease read the manuscript, and their perceptive comments and suggestions have undoubtedly led to a better book. Jonathan Arac and Harriet Ritvo offered helpful comments about my discussion of Lewis and Clark. Ian MacLaren read and commented upon a draft of the discussion of Alexander Henry's *Travels and Adventures*. My colleague David McNeil kindly allowed me to consult his notes and his unpublished paper, "In Search of Alexander Henry," and he read a version of my Henry discussion. Len Diepeveen's reading of the manuscript provided encouragement and invaluable guidance for which I am deeply grateful. Above all, thanks is owed to Anne Higgins, without whose advice and support at untold crucial moments this book would not have been written.

Initial research for this project was supported by the Social Sciences and Humanities Research Council of Canada. Later, fellowships from

Acknowledgments

the John Carter Brown Library, the American Antiquarian Society, the American Society of Eighteenth-Century Studies, and the Beinecke Rare Book and Manuscript Library enabled me to benefit from the rich collections and superb staff of their libraries. I have also been assisted by Dalhousie University's Research Development Fund, as well as by a sabbatical leave from Dalhousie.

I am grateful, too, for the guidance and encouragement of Jennifer Crewe at Columbia University Press and for Sarah St Onge's perceptive and meticulous editing.

Parts of chapters 1 and 2 appeared in earlier versions in *Dalhousie Review* 65, no. 1 (Spring 1985): 56–65. The discussion of Samuel Hearne first appeared in *Early American Literature* 21 (1986–87): 189–209. A version of the Lewis and Clark discussion appeared in *Macropolitics of Nineteenth-Century Literature: Nationalism, Exoticism, Imperialism*, ed. Jonathan Arac and Harriet Ritvo (Philadelphia: University of Pennsylvania Press, 1991): 12–36. An earlier version of parts of chapter 3 appeared in *Letterature d'America*, anno IX, no. 39 (1990): 113–141. Part of my discussion of Thoreau appeared in *ESQ: A Journal of the American Renaissance* 32, no. 2 (1986): 81–95. I am grateful to the editors of these journals and presses for permission to include revised versions of this work in this volume.

Introduction

Perry Miller described the "Romantic Dilemma" of the 1830s and 1840s as one in which Euro-Americans, having "identified the health, the very personality of America with Nature," watched anxiously as material expansion eroded that symbol of American self-recognition: "How could we at one and the same time establish our superiority to artificial Europe upon our proximity to Nature, and view with complacency the rapidity of our despoiling her?"[1] Having attached their sense of national identity to the idea of primordial forests and majestic mountains, Euro-Americans felt threatened by their own lumbering, mining, bridging, and railway building.[2]

Miller's focus on the American romantic's anxiety about the future illuminated the contemporary construction of the problem, but some of the cultural tensions that first prompted the emergence of "Nature's Nation" remain obscure in his discussion. The appeal of European romanticism, and Euro-Americans' avid adaptation of it to their own circumstances, was a response, at least in part, to their anxieties about the past, particularly about their relationships with those with prior claims to the land. Generations of European colonists had conducted the legal, diplomatic, commercial, and military maneuvers necessary to wrest land as it was needed from the hands of its original inhabitants.

1

But the citizens of the newly constituted United States of America, having deprived themselves of the authority of their European sponsors and institutions, needed a new basis for their continued expansion on the continent. It seems that they found one such basis in the idea of the place itself, at least once they could conceive of it as natural, empty, uncivilized, or virgin. For after America had become "natural," Euro-Americans were no longer cohabitants of a continent whose peoples they had conquered; instead, they could see the primordial land itself as the explanation and justification for their presence in it.

We are accustomed to seeing the contradictions inherent in nineteenth-century Americans' identification with nature and their energetic expansion and industrialization, thanks particularly to Leo Marx's *The Machine in the Garden*. How did the pioneering citizens of a country—every inch of whose terrain had been bought, stolen, or won from existing inhabitants—decide that what distinguished them as a people was their contact with nature? Reading narratives of discovery, in which relationships with Indian peoples are crucial, one recognizes afresh the importance of these relationships in Euro-American culture. One can also see the beginnings of the new role for American nature that developed, at least in part, as a result of the painful conflicts between Euro-Americans and the continent's first peoples.

American literary romanticism flourished and matured during the era of the nation's greatest territorial expansion and Euro-Americans' most extensive use of force against the original inhabitants of those territories. Jefferson's "purchase" of the Mississippi basin initiated the actual exploration of these lands and the subjugation of their inhabitants. The annexations of Texas and California in the 1840s and the subsequent rush of settlers to both regions also resulted in much aggression against Indian inhabitants. In the 1830s, the removal of Indian peoples from their lands east of the Mississippi to areas west of the river continued in the West until they survived mainly on reservation islands in a rising sea of Euro-Americans. The native peoples who for 350 years had been a shaping fact of European experience and rhetoric in North America had been rendered avoidable and, hence, less visible to future generations.

Arguing for the centrality of conflict with Indians in American society of the Jackson era, Michael Paul Rogin claims that, beginning in 1819, "Jackson, Indians, and westward expansion, not slavery and Negroes, structured American politics for the next generation."[3] Patricia Limerick seems to agree not only with Rogin's sense of the importance of Euro-American and Indian conflict but with his belief that it has not been properly recognized. Summarizing the reorganization of western historiography so that the new "history of the West is a study of a place undergoing conquest and never fully escaping its consequences," she notes that

> the subject of slavery was the domain of serious scholars and the occasion for sober national reflection; the subject of conquest was the domain of mass entertainment and the occasion for light-hearted national escapism. An element of regret for "what we did to the Indians" had entered the picture, but the dominant feature of conquest remained "adventure." [4]

American writers treated differently the conflicts inherent in the expansion of United States territory, but no major antebellum writer ignored them. For all, the new nation's character as a society was very much bound up in its land, and how that land was acquired was an unavoidable problem. "The preoccupation with property rights, pursued in litigation," writes Rogin of the frontier landholders of the teens and twenties, "was an effort to build a firm foundation on quicksand," for, in America, "property was theft. Title derived from force and fraud against Indians, from speculation, and from manipulation of the law."[5] Anxiety over the legality of land titles was emblematic of the more general problem of origins and destiny that nineteenth-century American writers faced.

Many scholars have dealt with the notion of an irreducible America of natural facts and virgin land. There is wide variation, however, in the extent to which they recognize that the ideas of naturalness and virginity are creations of the culture they are treating rather than responses to objective geographical conditions. Many of the influential studies of American literature and culture, in fact, fail to question—and some even promote—the idea of an empty, natural America as a crucial factor in the culture.

D. H. Lawrence, however, came very close to the idea of an empty, virgin America as a creation of the Euro-American imagination. He regarded the final disappearance of the Indian inhabitants as a prior condition to the "white" American's coming into direct contact with the "Spirit of Place": "No place exerts its full influence upon a new-comer until the old inhabitant is dead or absorbed."[6] Lawrence recognized that this condition had not yet been achieved when he wrote, but he did see it coming "within the present generation." As the situation stood, Lawrence considered the "white American soul" to be torn by "a dual feeling about the Indian": "The desire to extirpate the Indian. And the contradictory desire to glorify him [as the noble Red Man]." "Both," he said, "are rampant still, today" (36). Lawrence believed that the continuing actual presence of Indians provoked these equally unsatisfactory reactions to the unresolved conflict over the land, and he felt further that these reactions blocked the direct contact with place that would lead to the revelation of "IT. IT, the American whole soul" (8). He regarded emptying the place of its Indian inhabitants as the essential condition for a new flowering of the renovated European in America, but he was an astute enough reader of the American "classics" to recognize that such a condition, though fervently desired, had not yet been achieved and that its nonachievement had had a profound effect on American writing.

In his reading of Cooper's *Leather-Stocking Tales,* for example, Lawrence emphasized that the "blood-brother theme," while central to Cooper's myth of America, was a "wish-fulfilment vision, a kind of yearning myth" (51). Such a myth is not evident in the first appearances of Chingachgook in *The Pioneers,* where he is landless, alone, nominally Christian, and often drunk. Indeed, in the parts of the book set in town, Cooper's portrait has the air of having been drawn from life. In this state, Chingachgook is a reproach to Indians and Euro-Americans alike. Yet, if the historical relationship is a study in a common pattern of betrayal, the "new human relationship" that Lawrence said Cooper "dreamed" is specifically ahistorical: "Deeper than property, deeper than fatherhood, deeper than marriage" (54). Both Natty and Chingachgook recognize in the other "the crude pillar of a man," but across "an impassable distance" (61). Synecdoches of their respective cultures, together they are an emblem of a mutual recognition that only a few could experience, which could never have any effect on the history of the continent. Lawrence read Cooper's drawing back from the mixing of bloods, especially in *The Last of the Mohicans,* as Cooper the artist's ("trust the tale not the teller") fidelity to the integrity of the myth. But Lawrence the critic recognized "two childless, womanless men, of opposite races . . . , each . . . alone, and final to his race . . . , side by side, stark, abstract, beyond emotion, yet extremely together," as "sheer myth" (59). "What true myth concerns itself with is not the disintegrated product. True myth concerns itself centrally with the onward adventure of the integral soul" (62–63). Lawrence's insight distinguished what is culturally true as "the tale" from the complicating factors with which "the teller" must necessarily deal in his role as a writer. In his isolation of the tale or myth as the locus of truth and value, Lawrence saw the artist as creator of the "place" in which he can be at home, and he perceived that place as related to the historical place only as a kind of prophecy. He recognized that the creation of this place, which would "exert its full influence upon the new-comer," was an essential part of the cultural work of the nineteenth-century American "classics" he wrote about.

R. W. B. Lewis broadens Lawrence's childless, womanless, solitary man from the vision of a particular writer to a widely shared myth, a part of the culture. Lewis's Adam is "man himself, taken all aloof from his country and his age and standing in the presence of Nature and God."[7] Lewis sees the "American Adam" as the product of a broad dialogue within the culture, an image and corresponding narrative that focus the culture's disputed vision of itself. It is essential to Lewis's view that the terms of the dialogue are mainly temporal. He adopts Emerson's shorthand for the two poles of the debate: "the party of the Past and the party of the Future," the parties of "Memory and Hope" (7). In the hands of the latter party, the figure expresses the radical separation from the parent stock, newness, innocence, limitless possibility; in the hands of the former (and also in those writers Lewis consigns to the "party of Irony"), the new Adam is in danger of imagining himself suddenly freed from the pride, selfishness, sin, and guilt that have heretofore been components of human experience. As Lewis conceives it, the debate focuses on the extent to which nineteenth-century Americans regarded their freedom in the New World to be limited by their historical connection with the European past. In this, Lewis agrees with Lawrence's reading of the *Leather-Stocking Tales*. He, like Lawrence, views *The Deerslayer* as "the culmination of a process which exemplifies the American myth" (103). He argues that it is the trend of the *Tales* to move "away from a semi-historic authenticity . . . toward a sort of sustained fantasy, in many respects *more* authentic: a recreation in story of the dream-legend of [Cooper's] contemporaries" (102).

When Lewis examines Adamic characters in fiction, however, he brings spatial considerations into the discussion. Seeing "the evolution of the hero as Adam" as beginning with Natty Bumppo, Lewis refers to Bumppo (and his descendants) as "the hero in space," first, because he "seems to take his start outside time" and thus to be located in terms of space alone and, second, because his habitat is "spacious," "unbounded," an "area of total possibility" (91). Although Lewis recognizes that the temporal freedom of the Adamic figure is a matter of dispute, he seems to take the spaciousness, the lack of limitation on action, as a given condition of the American continent. No one disputes that America is very large, but to conceive of it as an arena in which the hero's action is without limitation is to assume that it is completely unclaimed, that the space had no history of its own, that there was no competition over its possession. Such an assumption obscures the importance of conflict over land in nineteenth-century American history, as well as noteworthy features of the world imagined in much nineteenth-century fiction, especially Cooper's.[8] The plots of all five *Leather-Stocking Tales*, for example, are built on outright violent conflict over space and complicated by profound questions concerning Euro-Americans' legal and moral rights to appropriate land in the New World.

Lewis takes pains throughout his study to keep in mind that the nineteenth century's "vision of innocence and the claim of newness were almost perilously misleading." But it is an essential part of his argument that this "illusion of freedom from the past led to a more real relation to the continuing tradition."[9] In the hands of their greatest writers, then, nineteenth-century Americans enjoyed a complex and "tragic" understanding of their culture's claims and its relation to the European tradition. They were involved in a "testing of moral and artistic possibilities." Lewis's study does not take into account, however, the extent to which the Adamic hero also embodies the conflict among the other inhabitants of his "space." He sees the American hero as needing to be different from, while remaining related to, Europe, but he does not acknowledge that this hero also needed to distinguish himself from the Indian even while he became like him by taking his identity from the same land.

Whereas Lawrence recognized that the Euro-American's "spirit of place" was still in conflict with the original American inhabitants, Lewis treats place as mere neutral space. This view seems to overlook the importance of European/Indian warfare in American narratives, not to mention in history, but it may be, of course, that the myth of an empty continent was itself a response to this intractable conflict.[10] When we remember the competition for space in history and literature, it seems possible that the appeal of the Adamic figure stemmed not only from its assertion of freedom from the European past but also from its evocation of a relation to place that cast actual conflict among competing Euro-American and Indian peoples into the background.

While Lewis defines newness in nineteenth-century American culture mainly in temporal terms, in *Virgin Land,* Henry Nash Smith took up the idea of empty space as the main determinant. In his prologue, Smith described his work as a study that "traces the impact of the West, the vacant continent beyond the frontier, on the consciousness of Americans."[11] Vacancy is understood as an objective condition to which the culture responds.

Smith himself offered the most effective critique of this aspect of *Virgin Land.* In a recent reconsideration of his earlier work, he thought that his attitudes had been more influenced than he had realized by the "basic myth or ideology of America," especially by "the pervasive interest in the frontier generated by [Frederick Jackson Turner's] work."[12] He had failed, he said, "to comprehend fully the assumptions underlying Turner's . . . declaration that 'the existence of an area of free land, its continuous recession, and the advance of American settlement westward explain American development' " (28). "I took over from Turner," he says, "the attitude that Ursula Brumm has found to be characteristic of American culture, a refusal to acknowledge the guilt intrinsic to the national errand into the wilderness" (28). He says that he had acquired "an important contagion from Turner's conception of the wilderness beyond the frontier as free land: the tendency to assume that this area was devoid of human inhabitants" (28). *Virgin Land* does take into account that ideas and images of the West were often inaccurate, and Smith is generally concerned with the way even false visions of the West could affect the way it was approached by easterners. Even so, Smith's thinking in this work sustained the notion that Euro-Americans moving westward were dealing with the land as a natural fact, rather than as a number of inhabited foreign countries.

Richard Slotkin's two important books restore the warring parties to the terrain of the frontier. On the macro–political level, he sees colonial governments as having to contend "not only with competing local interest groups, but with external centers of power: the Metropolitan government and the native tribes."[13] In the most general sense, for Slotkin, the "space" of the New World is a theater of conflict, an arena of formative violence. The Indian "was an inescapable presence to the colonists throughout their history." He was the "primitive proprietor of the land and . . . the human product of the New World" (52). Slotkin notes an early tendency among colonists to dehumanize "the Indians, by treating them simply as an aspect of the inanimate world, a natural obstacle to acquisition" (53); and the "myth of the Indian wars" (52) that he outlines

> imagines that strife as that between a fully human entity—"civilization"—and an entity that is primarily inhuman. . . . Though Indians are human, they are so much a part of "nature" as to seem only slightly different from the beasts of the forests. Thus the story of Indian displacement translates a human drama of dispossession into one in which resources are innocently appropriated directly from nature, without human cost. Nonetheless, the Indians are human, and to dispossess them provokes a sense of guilt that is a recognition of the human character of the conflict. (79–80)

According to Slotkin's reading, Cooper's *Leather-Stocking Tales* are preeminent in their vision of the frontier as the place where possession of American land is fought out. Cooper's geopolitical map "is active, with lines that break and shift as human actors cross the boundaries in both directions, pursuing a struggle that will end only when one people and one geographical realm has been eliminated from the map" (88). All five of the *Leather-Stocking Tales* are centered on the struggle for hegemony in North America, but *The Pioneers* (1823) and *The Prairie* (1827) are directly concerned with actual ownership of American land, with the legality of Euro-American expansion across the continent. In *The Pioneers*, the plot is constructed around the legalistic question of who actually owns a medium-sized piece of New York state and is couched in terms of wills, marriages, and civil contracts. As Michael Rogin points out,[14] however, all title disputes in the United States threaten to return to original transactions with native inhabitants that can rarely, if ever, comfortably be construed in terms of Euro-American law, and the specific squabble over title to the Effingham estate does, in fact, lead to larger questions of the legitimacy of the Euro-American presence in the disputed land. In *The Prairie*, where no specific land claims are staked by any of the characters, the question of ownership is played out on the macro–political level, with various characters standing for conflicting assertions of power in the region. Middleton, the official hero, wields the legal authority of the Louisiana Purchase; Ishmael Bush relies on practical ability and his de facto presence (until forced out); Inez, the kidnapped Louisiana Creole, suggests the claims of prior European groups; Natty Bumppo represents sensitivity to the land itself; and, of course, the right of the Pawnees and the Dakotas stems from having lived in the area for time out of mind. Both novels end on a strongly elegiac note, as the historical forces of Euro-American law, sheer numbers, money, and military strength appear to presage the doom of Bumppo's environmentalist quietism and Indian societies.

There is real, irretrievable loss on Cooper's frontiers. All these claims to the land cannot coexist, and no one group monopolizes virtue. Those who cede the ground are victims of those who triumph, and the victims take with them qualities that cannot be reclaimed or subsumed by those who remain. For Cooper, the defeat is all the more poignant in light of his belief that the burgeoning Euro-American society would soon reach the limits of the habitable portion of North America, a view that is made clear in *The Prairie*.

Cooper's sense of geographic space is theatrical and, above all, highly political. Formally, his historical romances do not much resemble the first-person travel genre that is the main subject here, but his fictions grapple directly and memorably with the central conflict of New World history. Indeed, although Cooper is rightly remembered for his evocative romantic landscapes, the focus of Natty Bumppo's spirituality and the forebears of later romantic narrative, nature does not obscure the primacy of this conflict in Cooper's plots. Cooper is the last (perhaps the only) major American fiction writer of the nineteenth century to deal directly with this conflict in a way that suggests its full historical scope.

Discovery or exploration narratives for the most part do not attempt Cooper's panoramic historical vision, and often they do not generalize about the contest between existing and invading peoples. By definition, their point of view is limited to that of an individual immediately engaged in circumstances he does not entirely understand or control. But in writing accounts of exploratory journeys, European travelers needed to address the same problem of authority that structured Cooper's fictions, the authority, that is, according to which the European or Euro-American lays claim to what is by generic definition alien territory. And discovery narratives do, as a matter of course, construe European action in America as being in conflict with existing peoples, even though, over the years, they developed rhetorical strategies for mitigating and marginalizing this conflict (since the late seventeenth century, they have presented themselves as scientific discourse). It now seems commonsensical to include the discovery narrative in the realm of what Peter Hulme (among others) has defined as "colonial discourse": "an ensemble of linguistically-based practices unified by their common deployment in the management of colonial relationships."[15] Reporting on an exploratory journey, especially in published form, meant casting individual activity in terms that would be recognized and valued in European and colonial power centers. To "make discoveries" was to travel and to observe, but it was also to participate in European expansionism.

As my sketch of one line of American critical discourse suggests, for the most part, it has not been common practice to understand even the early national period of American literature in terms of its continuities with colonial practices. These are rejected, in fact, as part of the European past, a past that threatens the new nation's primitive engagement with nature and its organic expansion into American space. But a second look at Cooper again shows him to be the exception that illuminates what came to be a common practice of the American Renaissance. Three of Cooper's *Leather-Stocking Tales, The Last of the Mohicans* (1826), *The Pathfinder* (1840), and *The Deerslayer* (1841), are set in the "colonial" period of American history, prior to the War of Independence, and so knowingly represent a version of "colonial discourse" from the perspective of a son of the early United States. In these novels, Britain and France openly fight for control of North America, and Indian peoples are variously engaged as allies, enemies, and, ultimately, as victims in the contest. Euro-American colonials are not directly identified with the British—in fact, they are engaged unconsciously in distinguishing themselves from the British institutions that prosecute the war—but they, too, have interests at stake. In *The Pioneers* and *The Prairie*, though Cooper sets his action after the Revolution, the contest is still over control of the land, and the same issues of legitimacy prevail. Cooper shifts the same basic plot structures and some of the same characters back and forth across the revolutionary divide, implicitly recognizing that the actions of United States citizens and government were of a piece with those of the "colonial" period. *The Prairie* begins, in fact, by contemplating what the United States will do as the new proprietor of Louisiana, in other words, as an imperial nation.

Cooper's direct approach to the basic conflicts of American history, and to the way American colonies were themselves becoming imperialist, though praised and admired in his day, was not widely imitated. One might say, in fact, that one of the distinguishing features of the romantic literature of the American Renaissance is (with the exception of Hawthorne) a lack of interest in colonial subjects and a strong tendency to treat indirectly the contemporary conflicts of an expansionist society. It is perhaps a measure of the success of one stream of American Renaissance rhetoric that spatial freedom became a common assumption of American culture and that awareness of how it was gained receded to such an extent.

The discovery narrative was particularly germane to the Euro-American identity because it linked individual experience to corporate significance. The conditions of exotic travel dictated that individuals would be privileged as sources of knowledge; as the spokesman for, at most, a small group of fellow Europeans who had visited an unfamiliar region, a writer's account had undeniable authority. Yet it was only the widely shared understanding that Europeans and Euro-Americans were fundamentally concerned with, even defined by, their global expansion that enabled the traveler to undertake his mission and to gain a public hearing when he returned. Through the well-established conventions of the discovery narrative, individual adventurers, often dimly if not selfishly motivated, allied themselves with the power of European and Euro-American institutions. To validate individual suffering and expense in the face of imminent physical danger and/or social oblivion, travelers sought to transform adventures into history. Even the fictional adventure stories of this period, as Martin Green has shown, "reflected and served the West's cult of expansion—political and economic and military expansion, material and spiritual."[16]

A reading of the English-language accounts of North American exploratory travel written during the period (the later eighteenth and earlier nineteenth centuries) when a new state was created in the New World suggests that there was a qualitative change in the ways in which the newly constituted American state justified its presence in and, more importantly, its growth toward the bounds of the continent. The narrative of exploration that developed in conjunction with the new political authority was more than the expression of the new government's pretensions: it was part of the new state's creation of itself.

In his study of the earliest period of European expansion into the New World, Edmundo O'Gorman attempts to recover the contemporary context of Columbus's voyages in order to demonstrate how the idea of discovering America has profoundly affected our understanding of the European engagement with the New World. O'Gorman argues that the way one conceives of the history of the earliest European contacts with the Americas depends fundamentally on how one understands the intentions of those discoverers, explorers, soldiers, and settlers who left accounts of their activities. His complaint about the traditional historiography of European expansion into the New World is that its practitioners revise the record by imposing the intention to "discover" America on an earlier period, when "America" had no being, because it had not yet been "invented." O'Gorman's critique of "the foundations of American historiography" focuses on the way America, a creation of history, is conceived as transcending history, as an essence that determines the accidents of its own history: "The traditional idea of America as a thing in itself, and the no less traditional idea that because of this previous notion we are dealing with an entity endowed with a 'discoverable' being, which in fact was discovered, are, respectively, the ontological and hermeneutical premises on which the truth of that historiography depends."[17] In this historiography, the place, stripped of its role in native lives, reveals itself in its essential, timeless being to those sent to behold it. Discovery takes place "irrespectively of any opinion or intention of the person who carries it out" (43). But, as O'Gorman insists, Columbus's accidental collision with the islands adjacent to the continent cannot logically be regarded in terms of an intention imposed by Americans of later centuries.

O'Gorman's goal is to show how the idea of the "substantialist America" is itself a historical phenomenon, and he investigates sixteenth-century documents in order to show how the concept of America came to be invented and what it meant to its earliest users. My study picks up the literature of exploration in North America in the later eighteenth and earlier nineteenth centuries, when the idea of "discovering America" had been an operative concept for three centuries but the understanding of the idea in the United States was undergoing an important transformation. In it I have tried to get at the distinctiveness of the concept of discovery and the role it played in the early national period of the United States through reading United States narratives against contemporary and slightly earlier British examples of the genre. The second half of the study looks at examples of discovery narrative by Washington Irving, Edgar Allan Poe, and Henry David Thoreau, focusing on the way these American romantic writers managed the cultural conflicts, and the rhetorical strategies for dealing with them, that were inherently part of the genre.

This is throughout a study of narrative strategies in relation to historical conflict. My main approach is to offer readings of individual narratives and, through comparisons, to trace the development of what was implied in narrating discovery up to the middle of the nineteenth century in the United States. As already indicated above, I am particularly concerned with the construction of a certain kind of natural space as the site within which the expansion of the new nation could be seen as occurring, and I end by singling out Thoreau's "Ktaadn" as a striking example of how the discovery narrative could be used to displace history with nature. My method is suggestive rather than exhaustive, and what follows is not intended as a definitive history of the discovery narrative genre. Neither am I asserting that "narrating discovery" should be understood as the central concern of Irving, Poe, or Thoreau. Finally, in attempting to define and understand one development within the vast body of American travel writing and to suggest its importance to the literature and society of the United States in the mid-nineteenth century, I am not claiming that it was the only rhetorical mode of dealing with that society's expansion. I argue that it achieved a certain cultural centrality, and I suggest why this came to be so, but I am not pretending that there were not other voices, other discourses.

CHAPTER ONE

Trading and Telling: Discovery and the British Fur Trade

Traveling for History

The defeat of French forces in North America in 1760 opened the way for the British and Anglo-Americans into the basin of the Great Lakes and initiated an era of exploration by English speakers entering the interior of the continent. Aside from soldiers, the earliest Anglophones in the interior were the fur traders who had quickly taken over the trading network that the French had built up. The elimination of the barrier of French claims to the west and north of the English seaboard colonies opened the way for their rapid commercial expansion. Colonial traders such as Alexander Henry, who was born in New Jersey and took a cargo of goods from Montreal over the Ottawa–French River route to Michilimackinac,[1] were able to take over much of the infrastructure of the French trade by learning French and hiring French assistants, but the new ventures nevertheless exposed the English to many unfamiliar territories and peoples, and a major effort of reconnaissance was necessary for them to prosecute the trade successfully.[2] The English-language literature on the exploration of these territories that developed in response to this need constitutes the first set of narratives studied here. In addition to the narrative of Alexander Henry, this group includes those by Samuel Hearne and Alexander Mackenzie; all three were widely read by Euro-Americans interested in the competitive exploration of the continent.

The independence of the United States split Anglo-American interests into two groups, one to the north and one to the south of the Great Lakes and the St. Lawrence valley, a split formalized at the conclusion of the War of American Independence in 1783. At that time, British traders in Montreal and at Hudson's Bay had access to territories as far west and north as their supply and transportation systems could reach. In fact, they had established a trading network that extended to the Rocky Mountains and as far south as the Missouri River basin. Traders working under the new flag of the United States, however, were hampered in the Far West until the Louisiana Purchase of 1803 opened the territory beyond the Mississippi. Thus, in 1804, it was with a sense of urgency that President Jefferson organized an expedition up the Missouri under the command of Meriwether Lewis and William Clark to initiate official United States exploration of this territory. A second major group of narratives, recounting this first wave of American exploration, begins with Lewis and Clark's *History* and includes the published narratives of Zebulon Pike, Stephen Long, and John Charles Frémont. These record the expansion of United States interests up to their firm establishment on the Pacific, in the Oregon country, in the 1840s. Frémont's volume includes an account of the route to the Oregon country that facilitated popular movement into a territory that had previously been known only to the commercial and military vanguard. It marks the point at which information in an easily obtainable book enabled the average individual to reach the western ocean. What had been the goal of hundreds of years of exploration was now the terminus of a mass movement, and Frémont's 1845 report, a truly popular book, signaled the end of an era of exotic travels.

These two groups of explorations, separated by colonial politics, form one large group when they are considered in terms of their subject matter. The lands and peoples they deal with were interrelated, and the anglophone movement into the Northwest was conceived by the competing factions as one movement. All the various expeditions, whether they were financed governmentally or commercially, were ultimately concerned with the commercial and strategic possibilities of the unknown region, and knowledge of the land, its peoples, and its resources was necessary for establishing control. Writing from and to different centers of control, however, American and British explorers developed characteristic ways of relating their experiences and findings. At the beginning of the nineteenth century, citizens of the United States confronted contradictory demands as they wrote of their travels in the western part of the continent; on the one hand, like their somewhat earlier British counterparts, they were exploring unfamiliar lands inhabited by many different peoples, and, practically speaking, they were abroad among foreigners. At the same time, however, Euro-Americans needed to conceive of themselves as native to the Americas, distinct from their European cousins. Eighteenth-century British explorers could speak of themselves as abroad in exotic regions, but nineteenth-century Euro-Americans had to devise ways to claim even distant, unfamiliar lands as part of America, their home.

The eighteenth- and nineteenth-century explorers of North America wrote of voyages and travels for a large international readership that had been cultivated by writers and publishers since the sixteenth-century compilations of Hakluyt and Purchas. Exploration reports from 1760 to 1845 are heirs to a tradition of discovery narratives that exhibited many similarities to nonfactual literary narrative and appealed to an audience far beyond the circle of those materially interested in exploration.[3] According to G. R. Crone and R. A. Skelton, "With the opening of the eighteenth century the vogue of travel literature . . . was outrun in popularity among the reading public only by theology . . . , and was to be sustained throughout the century."[4] Eighteenth-century England's interest in narratives of exploratory travel peaked with the publications resulting from James Cook's three voyages to the Pacific in the 1770s. The highest levels of the British government and scientific community participated in the planning and support of Cook's expeditions, making them the most prestigious of their kind in English history. This support, together with Cook's own remarkable talents as a navigator and observer, the high quality of the scientific personnel who accompanied him, and the care and expense lavished on the reports, set Cook up as the standard for all who followed him. His reports, particularly that of the second voyage, which he wrote himself, became models for anyone who undertook to publish a report of exploratory travels.[5]

Very briefly rendered, this is the context in which Samuel Hearne, Alexander Mackenzie, Alexander Henry, Meriwether Lewis and Wil-

liam Clark, Zebulon Pike, and John Charles Frémont wrote their accounts of North American travel. In fact, it was this established tradition that enabled obscure fur traders and junior army officers to assert
the importance of their actions; the public understanding of discovery
as a central theme of European history offered these men, and others
like them, the means with which they could claim the attention of the
reading public.

Published narratives were derived from the records that all serious
eighteenth- and nineteenth-century explorers kept as they traveled. The
elaboration of these records varied considerably, but the basic form was
that of a log in which the location and progress of the expedition were
recorded, along with important events, observations of the terrain,
climate, natural resources, peoples, animals, and so forth, and the explorer's own thoughts as he went along. Post-Enlightenment Europeans, moving inland through the vast forests and plains of North America, adapted the instruments and methods of maritime navigation and
record keeping, and regardless of the local reckoning of distances, direction, or present position, they ultimately referred to the quadrant,
telescope, and chronometer to construe their "true" positions on a grid
of longitude and latitude. Their attitudes toward time were similarly
centered in their own culture. They recorded particular events and their
general progress through the country with reference to a calendar and
often noted their daily rising and retiring according to a mechanical
timepiece.

It is essential to recall that a journal, while establishing chronology,
is not necessarily, or even usually, narrative. The events of one day do
not necessarily stem from or lead to those of the next. The extent to
which such a record can be cast as narrative is fundamentally related to
the writer's ability to connect daily experience to conscious intentions
and goals. The journal, as a testament to authentic experience, imposes
its linearity of time and movement on the final account, determining its
overall form, but the writer can reshape these records by condensing,
deleting, adding, foreshadowing, and commenting upon them. The success with which a journal or log has been transformed into a narrative
is potentially one index of a traveler's achievements as a discoverer. In
the field, the journal is the tool the explorer uses to extend to the
"trackless" forests and prairies the order that he, the "civilized" traveler, has sustained within himself. The narrative's published form is an

assertion of the power the explorer exerts over new lands and peoples, portraying them as part of his own story. By means of his journal, the traveler writes himself into and out of the unknown country; by means of his narrative, he makes his journey a significant event.

The transition from journal or log to published narrative was often assisted by pens other than that of the traveler himself. It is known that the journal manuscripts of Samuel Hearne, Alexander Mackenzie,[6] and Lewis and Clark differ in significant, though mainly stylistic, ways from the accounts published under their names, and the account of John Charles Frémont's first expedition was to some extent a collaboration with Jessie Benton Frémont, his wife. As Ian MacLaren points out, "One must not underestimate the changes that could occur when a travel journal metamorphosed into a publishable commodity."[7] Such changes can tell us a great deal about the differing assumptions of a traveler in the North American hinterland and a metropolitan writer or publisher. As MacLaren notes with respect to Paul Kane (85–92), it is wise not to assume that all the attitudes and views expressed in published accounts are those of the traveler himself. At the same time, however, it is the published narrative produced with the travel-reading market in mind that influences subsequent travel writers. I am mainly interested in the public discourse of exploratory travel, and while I shall compare journal and published versions of some journeys, I shall for the most part be offering readings of the published books, not journals, even when the latter are available.

The explorer/writer modified the order of events recorded in his journal in light of the actual outcome of the journey and his understanding of its meaning, making the record of his observations into the story of his discoveries. Things randomly occurring and promiscuously noted are recognized as leading toward, or stemming from, a revelation. In a narrative, to use Hayden White's phrasing, events are "revealed as possessing a structure, an order of meaning, which they do not possess as mere sequence."[8] The process of discovery becomes one with the process of narratization, which, on every level, involves standing back from experience or placing it in a larger context in order to see what has been achieved. The meaning I attribute to the word *discovery* in relation to eighteenth- and nineteenth-century exploration accounts differs from the concept developed by Wayne Franklin in his *Discoverers, Explorers, Settlers: The Diligent Writers of Early America*. I define *discovery* with reference to the economic and political contexts in which journeys were planned and accounts written. The verb *to discover* thus implies anticipation, and later knowledge, of an object that has already been defined or allowed for in the contemporary discourse about where the traveler has been. One should not imagine that the traveler-turned-writer was free to ignore the authorities that sanctioned his original voyage when it came time to plot his account. For Samuel Hearne and his contemporaries, the word implied practical, goal-oriented travel. Eighteenth-century explorers thought of themselves as "making discoveries," and it is with this sense of official public purpose that they undertook to mount expeditions and write narrative accounts.[9]

For Franklin, however, the object of discovery accounts, which he distinguishes from narratives of exploration and settlement, is relatively unspecific, and so it is "an absolute necessity rather than an anomaly" that such accounts "lack a true narrative interest."[10] In "discovery narratives" as Franklin defines them, the discoverer stands "in silence before a purely present landscape," with which he communes in a "ritualistic, even eucharistic" way (23). Franklin's discovery narrative highlights wonder and "timeless delight," rendering features of the terrain in long catalogs rather than as objects of transitive verbs (23, 69). But Franklin is also aware that "the discoverer, to be sure, exists in a world of plots and actual journeys, and [that] in this sense the discovery account has temporal and spatial implications" (21). And he goes on to point out that publicizing the idealized moment of discovery implicates it in the economy and politics of imperialism and that the subsequent action of exploration "is the hunter's . . . locating of a desired commodity, the catch of a usable quarry" (71). Yet, for Franklin, the prose of discovery (as opposed to that of exploration or settlement) can crop up in any century; it is like a recurring attitude, or rhetorical stance, adopted by traveler/writers, along with a set of characteristic tropes.

Franklin's categories reflect some of the features of an enormous group of travel accounts having to do with America, but it is somewhat misleading to detach, even for the purposes of description, accounts that emphasize mystical wonder and static appreciation from the dynamic context that drove Europeans across the ocean and into unfamiliar countries. Like Marvell's lover speaking to his coy mistress, some of

of the Hudson's Bay Company, at whose "request and expense" the journey was undertaken. Then, in his introduction, he defends the officers of the company from charges that they "were avers to making discoveries of every kind; and . . . did not want to increase their trade." With this, he clearly links exploratory expeditions with the expansion of trade, the latter being the obvious motive of such an institution as the Hudson's Bay Company undertaking to make "discoveries." " The following journey," he says, "together with the various attempts made . . . to find a North West passage, are recent proofs that the present members of the Hudson's Bay Company are as desirous of making discoveries, as they are of extending their trade."[13] Later in his introduction, Hearne reproduces the "Orders and Instructions" that initiated and guided his undertaking. They begin:

> Whereas the Honourable Hudson's Bay Company have been informed of the report from Indians, that there is a great probability of considerable advantages to be expected from a better knowledge of the country by us, than what hitherto has been obtained; and as it is the company's earnest desire to embrace every circumstance that may tend to the benefit of the said company, or the nation at large, they have requested you to conduct this expedition. (lxvi)

Hearne's explanation of the company's motives established the authority of his expedition, with reference to which his narrative would be shaped.

Of all the British explorers, Alexander Mackenzie had the most developed vision of large-scale commercial possibilities in the North American fur trade, and not surprisingly, his *Voyages* is the most coherent narrative of those examined here. His purpose in journeying, first down the Mackenzie River to the Arctic Ocean and then over the western cordillera to the Pacific Ocean, was to develop a trade route across North America linking the North American and Oriental trades.[14] "By opening this intercourse between the Atlantic and Pacific Oceans," he says in the concluding pages of his *Voyages*, "the entire command of the fur trade of North America might be obtained. . . . To this may be added the markets of the four quarters of the globe."[15] "The general utility of such a discovery," he says in the preface, "has been universally acknowledged; while the wishes of my particular friends and commercial associates . . . contributed to quicken the execution of this favourite project of my own ambition" (57). Of the journeys discussed in this chapter, Mackenzie's were the most free of the need to turn an immediate profit, but they were nevertheless conceived in a definite relation to trade, and Mackenzie's narrative reflects a single-minded effort to achieve his goal to which all other concerns were subordinated.

The manner in which discovery narratives both assert and require significant public goals can be clarified through reference to Hegel's theory of historical narrations, according to which events only emerge in conjunction with the authority of the state. For Hegel, "history" implies that the teller has recourse to an institutional authority, with a transpersonal existence, that provides a context in which individual actions assume a meaning. Hegel's view of history is that "historical narrations" appear "contemporaneously with historical deeds" and that "it is the State which first presents the subject-matter that is not only adapted to the prose of History, but involves the production of such history in the very progress of its own being."[16] History as conceived by Hegel "denotes quite as much the *historia rerum gestarum*, as the *res gestae* themselves; on the other hand it comprehends not less what has *happened*, than the *narration* of what has happened" (60). Hegel obviates any question of whether events are worthy of historical narration by asserting that it is really a matter of whether they are subject to it through their nature. The condition he isolates for the historical subject is the existence of the state, for "only in a State cognizant of Laws, can distinct transactions take place, accompanied by such a clear consciousness of them as supplies the ability and suggests the necessity of an enduring record" (61).

According to this view, one would say that the mere rambler in unfamiliar lands can discover nothing; the traveler becomes a discoverer through an act of narration that implicitly asserts his links to a higher authority. It is in the act of writing for a transpersonal end that the event is constituted. One might say, conversely, that the imperialist traveler's need for authority in the "discovered" land elicits the written account in the first place. Having read, and read about, the writers of exploration narratives in North America, one cannot help being impressed by the pains they took to record their experiences as they traveled—often in the face of terrible hardship—and perhaps more by the trouble they endured afterward as aspiring writers. In some cases, the journey itself seems incidental to the struggle to express it; violence, physical privation, and loneliness are raw data that only assume the character and dignity of events in narration. The traveler arrives home with a heavy burden of experience that he must carry until he can put it down in a form that others will recognize and respect. It is often hard to write, because his legitimate business in the new lands is not always obvious; but because it is not obvious, he *must* write.

Far from wishing to assert that there is some transcendent purpose (a Hegelian "Spirit") in the history of European expansion across the Atlantic or seeking to validate the state-sanctioned versions of European intrusion, I have tried to analyze North American discovery rhetoric in the decades before and after the American colonies' independence to show how a romantic discourse of discovery became part of the discourse of American identity. The relationship Hegel suggests between the self-consciousness of agents acting within the culture of a state and their ability to recount their actions in the form of a narrative bears directly upon the documents that form the primary public record of European expansion into North America. His understanding of history as the coming together of event and narrative reminds us that the "discovery of America" was not simply the location of a previously unknown land mass but rather a series of events that occurred as much in language as in a canoe or "Silent, upon a peak in Darien." And it further reminds us that the precondition of such a series of events is the consciousness of a social center, a seat of authority, a basis of legitimacy, that both "supplies the ability and suggests the necessity of an enduring record" (61).

Much of what is recounted of European expansion, from Columbus's letters through accounts of Canada's or Brazil's present-day exploitation of hinterland resources, requires the justification that individuals act in the service of an entity with claims to a historical being. Individuals acting for the good of the state are often publicly authorized to act in a manner that would otherwise be condemned. The debates over the validity or sincerity of the various religious, moral, and national authorities that have been advanced for the European expansion into the Americas have continued as long as that expansion itself. The narrativity of discovery accounts, partial or fully achieved, is in response to the moral, political, and armed conflict that was acute at the leading edge of

European expansion and endemic in the culture. Narrativity is a key aspect of the writer's appeal to authority, a way to situate his individual actions in a national history.[17]

A fully achieved narrative has been defined as one in which events seem "to tell themselves" and the role of external authority recedes from view.[18] One of the interesting features of exploration accounts is that they rarely realize such a state of affairs. As texts, they characteristically betray the uncertainty of their relationship to fully realized history, retaining many signs of their origins as writers grapple with conflicting versions of their own intentions. Approached as aspiring but only partially achieved narratives, exploration accounts offer a rich ground for a renewed understanding of the conflicts inherent in European expansion into America and the perhaps even more extreme ideological stresses upon the new society of native Euro-Americans. The efforts toward narrative coherence in an explorer's account should not be regarded as indicating that the writer merely witnessed a series of events that appear "to tell themselves" but as betraying where the stresses of the conquering and colonizing venture were greatest and thus where the need for authority was most keenly felt.

Discovery and Narrative Structure in Samuel Hearne's *Journey to the Northern Ocean*

Samuel Hearne, an Englishman, received some education in Beaminster, Dorset, until, at the age of twelve, he joined the navy as a captain's servant. Hearne spent six years in the navy before being paid off with the peace in 1763. In 1766, he joined the Hudson's Bay Company as a seaman and served in the fleet that went whaling and trading every summer from Churchill up the western coast of Hudson's Bay. Then, in 1769, he was chosen by the governor of Prince of Wales Fort to undertake an expedition in search of the source, somewhere far to the north, of the copper that Indians had brought to the fort.

Hearne, like other important explorers, developed an inventory of experience that could not easily be rendered into a simple narrative of discovery. As much in their respect for the facts as in the derring-do of their travels, these men elaborated what could be recognized or discovered by those who followed them. They contributed more to the long-term process of invention than they celebrated any single moment of discovery. In this way, their narratives complicated rather than simply confirmed public perception of their subjects.

The conflicts between publicly espoused goals and the recorded experiences of the actual travelers are the basis of the rhetoric of the narratives these explorers composed. This tension is evident in *A Journey from Prince of Wales's Fort in Hudson's Bay to the Northern Ocean in 1769, 1770, 1771, 1772* (first published in London in 1795), as Hearne tries to deal with the expectations of his employers, backers, and home audience, on the one hand—what we might call the facts of the imperial context—and the specific demands of life and travel in the remoter regions of eighteenth-century North America on the other— the facts of the local context. It pervades Hearne's narrative (and others like it), whether he is describing the day-to-day conduct of the expedition or discussing the formulation of its ultimate goals. Hearne experienced it as he attempted to carry out the instructions he had accepted at the beginning of his journey, and he experienced it again as he attempted to write his account of his journey, when he had to keep in mind both the initial concept of his journey and what actually happened. This tension is inherent in any experiment, because results may invalidate the assumptions upon which the experiment was conceived. However, Hearne and men like him were not operating in the context of experimental science but that of business and politics. Powerful interests paid for their journeys, and what had urged them on to discover what was needed and desired did not simply melt away when they sat down to write their reports. An employee of the Hudson's Bay Company was not free to become the creature of his own experiences; his story remained, at least in part, that of his sponsors. Thus, even though Samuel Hearne's achievement seems to recent readers to have more to do with his personal adaptation to the Northern culture that sustained him on his travels, this very ability to change was what most threatened his success as the author of his own discovery narrative.

In the broadest terms, eighteenth-century Europeans regarded the exploration of America as a matter of assimilating it into their world. They did not expect their experiences to invalidate the ideas they brought with them to the new continent. On the level of actual experience in the unknown land, however, Europeans learned to adapt themselves to the ways of its inhabitants. Hearne got to the mouth of the Coppermine River on the Arctic coast of North America because, after two unsuccessful expeditions, he attached himself to a group of Dene (Chippewa, or "Northern," and "Copper" Indians) who went there in the course of their normal migrations, just as Alexander Mackenzie crossed the continent to the Pacific by purchasing supplies and information from the Indian nations along the way. Both learned from the local context what made their journeys possible. Their accounts of the day-to-day details of life and travel in unknown regions reveal knowledge that often has little to do with the object of discovery, but often it is at this level of reporting that the account makes its most lasting contribution to knowledge of America.

When Hearne and others like him came to write about their travels, their task was to translate what they had learned from experience and from Indian peoples into knowledge that was comprehensible and useful to European imperialists. Hearne, for example, had to determine what a source of copper that was important to the local Indians would mean to the Hudson's Bay Company and whether the Indians' journey to the Coppermine River would be feasible for Europeans. He had to translate his invention of the Indian north (by means of which he had reached his destination) into a European discovery that would in some way justify the trouble and expense of its undertaking. The vitality of Hearne's narrative springs from the conflicts between his role as a Hudson's Bay Company employee—a semiofficial envoy of an expansionist England—and his remarkable ability to understand and adapt to the mundane realities of Northern nature and society, quite apart from their potential usefulness to his employers and government. We find in the end that, although Hearne's narrative retains the form of the myth of discovery with which he set out and with which readers would approach his text, he was unable to give much substance to that form. To the extent that he retained the terms according to which he initiated his journey, Hearne really discovered nothing. Nonetheless, all the distractions from and obstacles to his success survive as the fascinating content of a competing story.

A fairly straightforward example of such a conflict between European expectations and local experience can be seen in Hearne's account of the Chippewas' method of impounding deer. By driving small herds of deer into a prepared enclosure, certain groups were able to support all the members of their community comfortably, in one place, for a good portion of the winter. The problem with this practice, from the trader's point of view, was that these Indians had neither the need nor the inclination to hunt fur-bearing animals and so they had nothing to trade. Hearne was aware of this problem, but his account of these Indians begins with a long and detailed description of the ingenuities of their method of capturing deer and, because he was an avid and astute observer of wildlife, an equally complete analysis of the habits of the "poor timorous deer" that render them vulnerable to this mode of attack. Moreover, he observes that this method "is an easy way of procuring a comfortable maintenance in the Winter months" and that it is "wonderfully well adapted to the support of the aged and infirm" (51). Hearne clearly admired the wisdom that kept these people comfortable and secure throughout the worst months of the year. He says that, compared to those who organize their lives around the pursuit of fur-bearing animals, they are "by far the greatest philosophers, as they never give themselves the trouble to acquire what they can do well enough without." They are seldom, he says, unable to satisfy their "real wants" (52).

Hearne's admiration of this way of life was not a case of literary primitivism. He had received little formal education and had himself experienced from early youth the hardships of the navy and the fur trade. As a trader and traveler, he knew well the Indian groups northwest of Hudson's Bay, and he had personally suffered terribly from hunger and exposure in their company. His estimate of what constituted a "plentiful subsistence" was made in the context of the local economy, about which he knew a great deal, and in comparison to other Indian groups of which he had knowledge. He would have known, for example, that, while those who lived off the pounds were able to care for the sick and aged members of the group, others, following the furs, were often forced to leave behind those who could not keep up.

As soon as he brings the Indians' way of life into the context of the fur trade, however, Hearne's tone undergoes a radical shift. "It cannot be supposed," he says, "that those who indulge themselves in this indolent method of procuring food can be masters of anything for trade," whereas "the more industrious" are able to "procure furrs during the Winter to purchase a sufficient supply of ammunition, and other European goods, to last them another year" (51). In this context, those who hunt for furs, disregarding what Hearne has just defined as their own best interests, are suddenly "industrious," while those who were the intelligent "philosophers," careful of the aged and infirm, are suddenly seen as "indolent," self-indulgent, and "unambitious." Similarly, when these latter Indians do make a trip to the trading factory, "with three or four beaver skins," he says they generally "beg and steal" more than the furs they bring in are worth. The "philosophers" of the wilderness become the beggars of the trading post.

Nevertheless, because of his extensive experience with Indian peoples and his extraordinary ability to apprehend the logic of unfamiliar cultures, Hearne could not help recognizing that most Indians could best satisfy their "real needs" without recourse to the traders:

> It is undoubtedly the duty of every one of the Company's servants to encourage a spirit of industry among the natives, and to use every means in their power to induce them to procure furrs and other commodities for trade, by assuring them of a ready purchase and good payment for every thing they bring to the Factory: and I can truly say, that this has ever been the grand object of my attention. But I must at the same time confess, that such conduct is by no means for the real benefit of the poor Indians; it being very well known that those who have the least intercourse with the Factories, are by far the happiest. As their whole aim is to procure a comfortable subsistence, they take the most prudent methods to accomplish it; and by always following the lead of the deer, they are seldom exposed to the griping hand of famine, so frequently felt by those who are called the annual traders. (52)

This willingness to express his ambivalent feelings about his role as go-between exposed Hearne to the criticism of some readers, who perceived his adaptability as moral laxness or want of courage and questioned whether he sufficiently maintained the sense of the original purpose of his travels while he was submerged in Indian life. He has even been called "timorous" by John Bartlet Brebner, a twentieth-century historian of North American exploration.[19]

Hearne's near-total submersion in the logic and process of an alien land and culture created many rhetorical difficulties when he assumed the persona of the adventurer relating the story of his discoveries. The actual means by which he achieved his end were troublesome for him to write about, for the conventional and desirable image of the explorer was that of a man mastering the unfamiliar, uncooperative lands and peoples that lay in his path. The journey of discovery conventionally connoted independence and aggressiveness, the knowledge-gathering process as preparation for outright conquest. Hearne's narrative, in contrast, is full of situations in which he is a passive dependent on the strangers he is investigating. He achieved the ultimate goal of his travels mainly because the Indians themselves had their own reasons for going where he wanted to go. His actual role was that of an observer being led to his destination.

Hearne made two unsuccessful attempts before his third expedition finally reached the mouth of the Coppermine. His accounts of the two failures prepare the reader to accept the nearly nugatory results of his third "successful" voyage. He begins his account of the first attempt by describing the formal send-off he received at Prince of Wales's Fort, "under the salute of seven cannon." Almost immediately, however, two of his Indian "crew" desert, and it soon becomes apparent that "Captain Chawchinahaw," the main guide, "had not the prosperity of the undertaking at heart." Chawchinahaw often, Hearne continues,

> painted the difficulties in the worst colours, took every method to dishearten me and my European companions, and several times hinted his desire of returning to the factory: but finding I was determined to proceed, he took such methods as he thought would be most likely to answer his end; one of which was, that of not administering toward our support.[20]

Noncooperation soon became outright rebellion as Chawchinahaw and his crew "packed up their awls, and set out toward the South West, making the woods ring with their laughter," leaving Hearne and his companions to make their own way back to the factory (4).

There is a sharp incongruity in this account between the images of order and hierarchy suggested by the send-off with cannon salutes and the numerous references to the chain of command and the actual conditions Hearne encountered once away from the fort. Hearne, the commander, in possession of his orders, plans, and instruments of navigation, seconded by his European assistants and guided by the duly subordinate Indians, set off on a mission that would be guided by his judgment and subject to his will. Hearne was the head, his subordinates the limbs. His was the consciousness that would extend European rationality to the wilderness. Once on his own, however, Hearne found that he was subject to the whims and wishes of his Indian guides, without any real means of enforcing his will. Hearne expressed the problems in terms of an inversion of hierarchy, noting with concern that his European assistants were treated even more carelessly than he, because the Indians knew that they were of low social standing at the factory (9). The "clanship" of the Indians, he says, put any Englishman at a disadvantage when he was "at such a distance from the Company's Factories as to entirely depend on them for subsistence" (6). Hearne's determination to proceed, which he takes pains to portray, comes to nothing in face of the Indians' loss of interest in the undertaking, and he and his companions were lucky to be able to return to the factory, where he immediately began to organize another expedition.

The second attempt compounded the errors that led to the failure of the first, in that the changes made were in accord with a European view of efficiency. Hearne dispensed with his two European companions, and the governor forbade any women to accompany the expedition. This second change, as Hearne himself points out, was very ill-advised, for it was Indian women who hauled the baggage and prepared the clothing, food, and fire, thus leaving the men free to hunt. Rather than streamlining matters, leaving them behind proved to be a step away from a workable organization for Hearne's purposes. Hearne portrays himself, at the beginning of this second expedition, as having been ready to relinquish any useless formalities in the interest of a more realistic approach to the achievement of his goal. His description of the ceremony at his departure is a good example of his attitude:

> The snow at this time was so deep on the top of the ramparts that few of the cannon were to be seen, otherwise the Governor would have saluted me at my departure, as before; but as these honours could not possibly be of any service to my expedition, I readily relinquished everything of the kind; and in lieu of it, the Governor, officers, and people, insisted on giving me three cheers. (10)

Hearne appears increasingly uncomfortable with a grandiose view of exploration, and he attempts to wean his readers from expectations based on past great voyages of discovery. The plot of the second expedition is basically the same as that of the first: he sets off in command of a party with the intention of directing it to the discovery of the Coppermine River. This intention is again blunted and finally defeated by the difficulties that nature and the Indian inhabitants throw up in its path.

Hearne's account of his second attempt is longer and more elaborate than that of the first, and the crisis that precedes his return to the fort a second time is more intense and threatening. Much of this part of his story concerns his struggle to obtain food and the suffering all endure during periodic shortages. In this context, Hearne expresses his impatience with the Indians' practice of eating everything when food is plentiful, instead of preparing for future famines. This struggle with climate and the lack of food goes on throughout the trip, increasing Hearne's anxiety:

> None of our natural wants, if we except thirst, are so distressing, or hard to endure, as hunger; and in wandering situations, like that which I now experienced, the hardship is greatly aggravated by the uncertainty with respect to its duration, and the means most proper to be used to remove it, as well as by the labour and fatigue we must necessarily undergo for that purpose, and the disappointments which too frequently frustrate our best concerted plans and most strenuous exertions: it not only enfeebles the body, but depresses the spirits, in spite of every effort to prevent it. (21)

A cycle of hunger and anxiety, followed by the killing of animals and subsequent feasting, develops in Hearne's account of his second expedition. This cycle evokes a feeling of timelessness that, combined with the lack of variety in the landscape, suggests Hearne's difficulty in maintaining a sense of progress. Hearne has the instruments with which to construe his advance in space toward his goal, and he also has a chronometer and a diary with which to maintain his awareness of the passage of time. However, his desire to reach a certain place in a certain amount of time, his abstract sense of progress, is increasingly frustrated by the reality of the Indian world in which he must live.

In this situation, Hearne increasingly perceives Indian behavior as sinister, until he arrives at the point of despair, worn down by hardships and frustrations in the company of people who appear not to recognize his common humanity:

> The very uncourteous behaviour of the Northern Indians then in company, gave me little hopes of receiving assistance from them,

any longer than I had wherewithal to reward them for their trouble and expense. . . . So inconsiderate were these people, that wherever they met me, they always expected that I had a great assortment of goods to relieve their necessities; as if I had brought the Company's warehouse with me. Some of them wanted guns; all wanted ammunition, iron-work, and tobacco; many were solicitous for medicine; and others pressed me for different articles of clothing: but when they found that I had nothing to spare, except a few nick-nacks and gewgaws, they made no scruple of pronouncing me a "poor servant, noways like the Governor at the Factory, who, they said, they never saw, but he gave them something useful." It is scarcely possible to conceive any people so void of common understanding, as to think that the sole intent of my taking this fatiguing journey, was to carry a large assortment of useful and heavy implements, to give to all that stood in need of them; but many of them would ask me for what they wanted with the same freedom, and apparently with the same hopes of success, as if they had been at one of the Company's Factories. Others, with an air of more generosity, offered me furs to trade with at the same standard as at the Factory; without considering how unlikely it was that I should increase the enormous weight of my load with articles which could be of no more use to me in my present situation than they were to themselves.

This unaccountable behaviour of the Indians occasioned much serious reflection on my part; as it showed plainly how little I had to expect if I should, by any accident, be reduced to the necessity of depending on them for support; so that, though I lay me down to rest, sleep was a stranger to me that night. (27–28)

Unable to articulate his goals in a way meaningful to his Indian companions, Hearne's exploring expedition had turned into a mere exercise in survival.

At this point, Hearne breaks his quadrant, the main instrument with which he measured and objectified the fruits of his efforts. Having taken one observation, he lets the instrument stand a few moments while he eats dinner. Unfortunately, he says,

to my great mortification, while I was eating my dinner, a sudden gust of wind blew it down; and as the ground where it stood was very stoney, the bubble, the sight-vane, and venier, were entirely broke to pieces, which rendered the instrument useless. In consequence of this misfortune I resolved to return again to the Fort, though we were then in the latitude 63° 10′ North, and about 10° 40′ West longitude from Churchill River. (29)

This incident, recounted at the end of a long chapter of trials and hardships, effectively signals the moment of Hearne's second defeat. The broken instrument seems an objectification of the feelings that have been building in Hearne. Perhaps it is also a way for Hearne to suggest that his defeat was a result of external factors, not of any lack of courage or application on his part. Moreover, the quadrant very handily serves as a symbol for the European intentions and rationality that are supposed to guide the mission, and its breakage as an index of the wilderness's resistance. When the quadrant breaks, it becomes impossible to maintain abstract standards of measurement of the expedition's progress, and so it seems pointless to proceed.

At this low point in his narrative, Hearne is, as it were, rescued by the "famous leader," Matonabbee, a Chippewa who arrives on the scene with his entourage. Matonabbee was well known to the English and of very high standing among the Indians themselves. He speaks the languages of both the Chippewas and the Cree ("Southern Indians"), as well as a fair amount of English. He carries on a trade between the fort and the Indians in the distant West, and he does well enough at it to support six wives. He is young, strong, intelligent, and handsome, and he appears to understand both Hearne's goal and his mistakes:

He attributed all our misfortunes to the misconduct of my guides, and the very plan we pursued, by the desire of the Governor, in not taking any women with us on this journey, was, he said, the principal thing which occasioned all our wants: "for," said he, "when all the men are heavy laden, they can neither hunt nor travel to any considerable distance; and in case they meet with success in hunting, who is to carry the produce of their labour? Women," added he, "were made for labour; one of them can carry, or haul, as much as two men can do. They also pitch our tents, make and mend our clothing, keep us warm at night; and, in fact, there is no such thing as travelling any considerable distance, or for any length of time, in this country, without their assistance." (35)

Matonabbee offers to serve as Hearne's guide on a third attempt to reach the mouth of the Coppermine, and Hearne readily accepts this relation with Indian culture that will lead him to his goal. He develops a sympathetic relation with Matonabbee in which the two of them appear to understand each other sufficiently to allow them to proceed, each for his own distinct reasons, to a common destination. Although Hearne initially refers to Matonabbee as his "guide," he actually joins Matonabbee's entourage as an honored guest, adapting himself to the society and mode of life that he finds there. In this situation, Hearne is very much a bird on the buffalo's back, happy enough with his position but hardly in control of the direction he is moving. Matonabbee's competence allows Hearne to devote himself to his astronomical observations and his journals, and the long intimacy with Matonabbee's family must have contributed to his remarkably detailed and sympathetic descriptions of Indian life in this region. During this part of his journey, his narrative takes on an almost domestic tone, as he concerns himself more and more with the daily routines of a well-managed society. He frequently makes remarks that suggest contentment: "As to myself, I had little to do, except to make a few observations for determining the latitude, bringing up my journal, and filling up my chart up to the present time" (56).

This happy symbiosis persists throughout many months. However, as they near their goal, it becomes increasingly apparent that Hearne and his hosts are going there for utterly different reasons. In fact, Hearne learns that his companions are going to the Coppermine River "with no other intent than to murder the Esquimaux [i.e., "Copper" Inuit], who are understood by the Copper Indians to frequent that river in considerable numbers" (74). This news upsets Hearne, and he at first tries to dissuade them from their "inhuman design." The Indians, however, interpret his objections as cowardice, and he is obliged to protest that he will certainly kill as many "Esquimaux" as is necessary "for the protection of any one of my company," knowing that his "personal safety depended in a great measure on the favourable opinion" the Indians entertained of him (74–75). He decides that there is nothing he can do to alter the Indians' intentions and that he must simply go along and attend to his own business. "Indeed," he says,

> when I came to consider seriously, I saw evidently that it was the highest folly for an individual like me, and in my situation, to attempt to turn the current of a national prejudice which had subsisted between these two nations from the earliest period. (75)

The irony of Hearne's situation is bitter. He finally has a group of Indians doing what is necessary to get him to the mouth of the Coppermine, but upon learning of their reasons for doing so, he would like to stop them. Moreover, the recounting of this situation is a major rhetorical problem for Hearne. In relating the circumstances of this part of his journey, he must convey that he was successful in attaining his goal and yet avoid any appearance of complicity in the Indians' designs. After having spent so much time and energy trying to get to the Coppermine, he must now appear to be going there against his will. The difficulties of this problem contribute to making Hearne's account of his experiences at the river mouth the emotional climax of his narrative. In it, we see Hearne finally realizing his own and his backers' discovery plot, while, at the same time, we see him in a situation that epitomizes the difficulty of his relations with the Indians. As an explorer, he finds what he set out to find, but in doing so he also confronts facts of life in North America that make his original goals and his actual discovery seem rather trivial. He retains the story of discovery as his basic plot, but the supposedly ancillary events and characters suggest that a quite other and perhaps more powerful story remains to be told.

Approaching the mouth of the Coppermine after twenty months of travel, Hearne's attention is divided between observations of the terrain and his geographical position and of the Indians' preparations for their attack on the Inuit. He begins the chapter by noting his surprise when the Coppermine differed "so much from the description which the Indians had given of it at the Factory; for, instead of being so large as to be navigable for shipping, . . . it was scarcely navigable for an Indian canoe" (94–95). He was able to proceed with his "survey," over the next two days, as they approached the river mouth. However, when "spies" returned with the information that a small group of Inuit were camped in a position where they might easily be surprised, "no further attention was paid to [his] survey" (96).

At this point, Hearne turns all his attention to the activities of the Indians. He describes the preparation of their weapons, the painting of their shields and bodies, the removal of their clothes, and how they approached the encampment in complete silence, keeping out of sight behind some low hills. He charges his diction with disapproval of the "bloody design" and the "horrid occasion." Skillfully he creates a feeling of suspense as he leads the reader closer and closer to the encampment, into a position "within two hundred yards of the tents" from which the Indians would spring in ambush. Yet in the thick of these preparations, his rhetorical dilemma surfaces, and he feels obliged to assure the reader that he was simultaneously performing his role as surveyor of the river:

> Our course . . . on this occasion, though very serpentine, was not altogether so remote from the river as entirely to exclude me from a view of it the whole way: on the contrary, several times (according to the situation of the ground) we advanced so near it, as to give me an opportunity to convince myself that it was as unnavigable as it was in those parts which I had surveyed before. (97)

He was, he wants to remind us, not there as an assassin but as a representative of the legitimate interests of the Hudson's Bay Company. In this situation, when he notes that "the number of my crew was so much greater than that which the five Esquimaux tents could contain" (98), one feels that he has lost control of the ironies, for here he is trying to cast himself as the leader of his "crew," at the very moment they are about to embark on a massacre he is powerless to prevent.

Hearne describes the victims of the slaughter as "unsuspecting creatures," "poor unhappy victims," clearly indicating his sympathy for their misfortune. His account of the killing is long and graphic, with details of particular cruelties and examples of suffering. He mentions a young girl pinned to the ground with spears and an old man whose body was "like a cullender."

> My situation and the terror of my mind at beholding this butchery, cannot easily be conceived, much less described; though I summed up all the fortitude I was master of on the occasion, it was with difficulty that I could refrain from tears; and I am confident that my features must have feelingly expressed how sincerely I was affected at the barbarous scene I then witnessed; even at this hour I cannot reflect on the transactions of that horrid day without shedding tears.[21] (100)

The Inuit are creatures to be pitied, but in the thick of events his "crew" become "barbarians" and "savages," beings whose actions remove them from the circle of humanity Hearne's sentiment draws around himself and the Inuit. Up to this point Hearne has never distanced himself from his companions in this way. He had simply distinguished Indians according to rough ideas of nationality, while referring to himself as "English." But now he clearly feels the need for an absolute distinction.

When the killing was finished, they sat down and "made a good meal of fresh salmon." "When we had finished our meal," Hearne continues,

> which was the first we had enjoyed for many hours, the Indians told me that they were again ready to assist me in making an end of my survey. . . . I therefore set instantly about commencing my survey, and pursued it to the mouth of the river, which I found all the way so full of shoals and falls that it was not navigable even for a boat, and that it emptied itself into the sea over a ridge or bar.[22]

Thus Hearne immediately picks up the thread of the story he had intended to tell, the story of his "discovery" of the Coppermine River.

Hearne concludes the story of the voyage out by explaining how he calculated the latitude he assigned to his location and noting that "for the sake of form, . . . I erected a mark, and took possession of the coast, on behalf of the Hudson's Bay Company" (106). The irony of this gesture was probably not lost on him. In going through this ceremony, he identified himself with a central image of the European age of discovery and conquest, that of the heroic discoverer planting his flag or cross in the land of which he has taken possession for his ruler and god. The gesture is presumptuous even when made by a Cartier on the mere fringes of a new land, within reach of his ships and weapons. Here, however, Hearne is beyond even presumption, hundreds of miles from any means to buttress his authority. He is, in effect, the possession of what he pretends to possess. In making this gesture, Hearne means to call attention to his original reasons for undertaking the journey and to the "form" of the story he wants to tell—the journey out, the triumphant discovery, and the return to the context that gives meaning and value to the whole effort. However, when he says that he made it "for the sake of form," he is clearly aware that his possession of the Coppermine region is merely formal; first, because he has learned that it is effectively beyond the range within which any European power can enforce its will and, second, because he has found nothing of what he originally hoped for, no copper to speak of, and no navigable harbor.

Hearne everywhere takes pains to show his readers that he has done whatever possible to fulfill his obligations to the original form of his undertaking, but it nevertheless becomes increasingly evident as his story unfolds that the real fruits of his labors consist of his invention of the land and people in and of themselves. It seems that the real contents of his expedition lie in the partially suppressed account of his interaction with the Indians and environment of the region. The plot of his story, rather than one of conquest or discovery, involves dependence, apprenticeship, and adoption, voluntarily or not, of a new system of values.

This "apprenticeship" is immensely threatening to Hearne's original intentions, to the conventional expectations of his readers, to his identity as a European explorer, and therefore to the overall design of his narrative as a story of discovery. Were he to cease distinguishing himself from the Indian society around him, he would, of course, cease to exist as the narrator of the tale. He would disappear into the cycles of famine and feasting, struggle and repose, into the daily routine of Indian life as it appears to the outsider. He would suppress or relinquish the consciousness that conceived the journey in the first place and leave behind the identity based on the European understanding of his errand. Instead of discovering a new world, he would disappear from view within an existing one. The drama of his story arises from his getting close enough to an unfamiliar reality to obtain some insight into it, without getting so close as to be completely absorbed. Though Hearne relaxes into the daily domestic surroundings of Chippewa society, he somehow retains enough sense of his public intentions to continue the purposeful motion toward his goal and back to his home. The original plot persists even as the second story emerges around it.

It was difficult, nonetheless, for Hearne the storyteller to sustain his sense of purpose and his discovery plot. His journey kept him away from the factory two years, seven months, and twenty-four days. Undoubtedly he became very well acquainted with his Indian hosts, and he devoted most of his energy to the same daily chores as his Indian companions. Though it is unlikely that he ever considered remaining with the Indians (as many European traders did), it was nevertheless difficult for him to portray his own sense of purpose and progress as distinct from these shared activities and problems. Most of Hearne's days were taken up with repetitious tasks, in which the landscape—at least to the unfamiliar eye—changed very little, in which the narrator lacked knowledge of where he was going, and in which he had no

European companions with whom to communicate. And ultimately, of course, the original goal proved illusory, and Hearne's only discovery was the negative one of confirming that the Hudson's Bay Company would have to look elsewhere for a supply of copper, a navigable harbor, a Northwest Passage.

Hearne dealt with this problem, perhaps in part unconsciously, by summoning the taxonomic categories of eighteenth-century science. With their ambitions to collect, categorize, and catalog, scientific conventions offered one means whereby Hearne could portray the growth of his knowledge as a legitimate substitute for the copper and furs his employers originally sought.[23] They also gave him a way to appear in control of his experiences with the Indians; whatever he suffered in their hands, he was able to render his observations of them as scientific knowledge, a form of power that, in the long run, was the European's most effective weapon in the conquest of the continent. Hearne the scientist, though largely a product of his own writing desk, was able to assert European intentionality in spite of his many concessions to the Indian world he explored and the revelation that the original objects of discovery, though scrupulously pursued, were founded on misinformation. Knowledge of the country based upon Hearne's first-hand experience emerges as a more worthy objective.

Alexander Mackenzie's *Voyages:* Discovery and the Fur Trade Entrepreneur

Alexander Mackenzie was born in Stornoway, Scotland, in 1763. In 1775, after his mother's death, his father brought him to New York. Mackenzie was sent to school in Montreal in 1778, but in 1779 his school career ended, and he entered the "counting house" of Mr. Gregory, a partner in a fur-trading concern. He spent five years there as a clerk until, in 1784, at the age of twenty, he set out on a trading mission to Detroit for the same firm. Soon after he arrived in Detroit, however, he was offered a partnership in the firm if he would proceed farther west to the Indian countries as a wintering trader. He spent his first winter as a partner at Ile-à-la-Crosse, in what is now northern Saskatchewan.[24]

Though the expeditions recounted in his *Voyages from Montreal, on the River St. Lawrence, through the Continent of North America, to the Frozen and Pacific Oceans; in the Years 1789 and 1793* (London, 1801) were at least as arduous as Hearne's, Mackenzie's task as a writer was more straightforward. Hearne had to make many compromises with his companions and the northern environment, and his account of his journey struggles to represent this process of adaptation without appearing to have betrayed the European motivations of his journey. Mackenzie, by contrast, portrays himself as overcoming obstacles, whether mountains, raging rivers, or Indian nations, never allowing them to alter substantially the original goals of his expedition. In his account of his voyages to the "Frozen and Pacific Oceans," his persona is that of a man always in control of himself, his men, and his movements, in spite of whatever the unknown territories might offer by way of resistance.

The actual circumstances of Hearne's and Mackenzie's journeys were very different, quite apart from the different personalities of the two men. Hearne was a salaried employee of the Hudson's Bay Company who was selected to undertake a journey not of his own imagining or planning. The Hudson's Bay Company of this period did most of its trading from its "factories" on the coast, waiting for hunters to bring their furs to them; they did not have a system of travel in the interior upon which Hearne could have called for his extraordinary trip. Hearne made his journey almost entirely on foot, through country in which he could neither supply nor guide himself. Mackenzie, however, was a partner in the North-West Company, operating more or less under his own direction in the Far West. His voyages were of his own imagining, based on his own experience in the Northwest and on his study of such contemporary reports and surveys as those of Hearne, Cook, and Vancouver. Mackenzie's mode of travel was an extension of the means that the North-West Company used regularly to carry on their trade in the Far West—large canoes manned by Canadian voyageurs and guided by native Indians with which they annually transported large quantities of goods back and forth between Montreal and the foothills of the Rocky Mountains.

Most important for Mackenzie's style of narration was his vision of his undertaking. While Hearne and his employers had only vague notions about finding a source of copper and forging relations with distant Indian groups, Mackenzie imagined establishing an overland route that would link the fur trade of North America with the luxury trade of the Far East. By means of this new route, furs from North

America, instead of moving east, would go west to the Pacific coast and thence to China, where they would replace precious metals as payment for Chinese goods. As Mackenzie says at the end of his account of his journey to the Pacific,

> by opening this intercourse between the Atlantic and Pacific Oceans, and forming regular establishments through the interior, and at both extremes, as well as along the coasts and islands, the entire command of the fur trade of North America might be obtained, from the latitude 48 to the pole, except that portion of it which the Russians have in the Pacific. To this may be added the fishing in both seas, and the markets of the four quarters of the globe.[25]

These commercial ambitions pervade Mackenzie's narratives, always hurrying him along toward his goal and subordinating the details of the actual passage to the discovery of the end. Hearne at times seemed to be in danger of losing all forward momentum in the complexities of life around him; Mackenzie, on the other hand, though a remarkably acute observer, was so devoted to his plan that, with a few exceptions, he only reported those details that impinged directly on the safety and progress of his expedition. In his preface, Mackenzie himself explains his preoccupations:

> My thoughts were anxiously employed in making provision for the day that was passing over me. I had to encounter perils by land and perils by water; to watch the savage who was our guide, or to guard against those of his tribe who might meditate our destruction. I had, also, the passions and fears of others to control and subdue. Today I had to assuage the rising discontents, and on the morrow cheer the fainting spirits, of the people who accompanied me. The toil of our navigation was incessant, and oftentimes extreme; and in our progress over land we had no protection from the severity of the elements, and possessed no accommodations or conveniences but such as could be contained in the burden of our shoulders, which aggravated the toils of our march, and added to the wearisomeness of our way. (58–59)

Mackenzie seems at no time to have assumed the mentality of a captive. No matter how threatening and difficult his situation, he keeps his ultimate purpose in view, regarding his present circumstances merely as steps on the way to the achievement of his goal.[26] While Hearne's rhetorical problem lay in giving the narrative of his protracted journey a sense of direction, Mackenzie's lay in giving the reader a sense of the particular nature of the lands and peoples he encountered as he rushed along. It is generally true in the case of these two writers that one's strength is the other's weakness: where Hearne renders a detailed, rounded invention of the peoples, animals, and lands he observed during his travels, Mackenzie engages the reader, moment to moment, in the ceaseless toil and danger of his trips down the Mackenzie River and across the western mountain chains to the Pacific Ocean, the goal of his voyage of discovery.

Of the two voyages Mackenzie recounts in his book, the one to the Pacific is the longer and more interesting as a narrative. In its published form, Mackenzie's account of the Pacific voyage was preceded by his "General History of the Fur Trade," especially as carried on by representatives of the North-West Company, and his account of his voyage to the mouth of the Mackenzie River. His "History of the Fur Trade" establishes the economic context of his efforts to find a route across the continent, and his account of his earlier voyage establishes him as a leader with a long-standing commitment to western exploration. Mackenzie ends the volume with his proposals for a reorganization of the fur trade based on the discoveries he has made.

Given this background, the account of the Pacific voyage has a unity of plot quite unlike anything that Hearne was able to manage. The close agreement between Mackenzie's stated intentions and the journey that he actually completed meant that he was able to portray the journey as the fulfillment of his wishes. The narrator is simultaneously engaged with his ambitious vision and with the moment-to-moment events of the journey. Though Mackenzie rarely records his feelings, his narrative has a marked personal quality, because of the way his constant, intense desire to reach his goal colors his responses to events. In his narration, Mackenzie always knows where he wants to go, and through the exercise of amazing stamina and intelligence, he is able to make reality accord with his wishes.

The extent to which this unity of motive, character, and execution is the result of Mackenzie's own pen is hard to determine. It is known that William Combe worked over the manuscript of the original edition of Mackenzie's *Voyages*. Mackenzie's journal of the Pacific voyage is not known to have survived, but the journal of the earlier voyage down the Mackenzie River does exist, and as Ian MacLaren's comparison of it to the published version has shown, one main effect of Combe's editing is an "aesthetic rendering of generally unaesthetic observations."[27] Approaching the mouth of the Mackenzie River, "Mackenzie's concern lies chiefly with the discovery of the river's debouchement on an ocean: anything appearing to preclude that frustrates him. . . . Combe's phrasing [however] suggests that the prospect of the blocked river disappoints the explorer only on aesthetic grounds" (144). If the very few aesthetic responses in the published version of the Pacific voyage are similarly due to the added touches of Combe, MacLaren's characterization of Mackenzie as "relentlessly commercially-minded" (141) would seem to be justified. Again, it is Mackenzie's single-mindedness that distinguishes the structure of his narrative from that of Hearne.

The plot of the narration of the Pacific voyage is simple. In the fall of 1792, Mackenzie and his crew set off from Fort Chipewyan, on Lake Athabasca, and headed up the Peace River to Fort Fork, which Mackenzie had selected in advance as the wintering spot as far along his proposed route as he could get before the river froze. He spends the first two chapters of his narrative describing the trip as far as the fort and the events of the winter passed there. His focus is on his relations with the Indians who traded out of the fort (a subject that would be of importance throughout his narrative) and on his preparations for the spring departure, which included especially his attempts to gather information about what lay to the west. For example, he deduced from the warm winds that periodically brought temperatures above freezing that the Pacific Ocean could not be far away, "the distance being so short, that though they the winds pass over mountains covered with snow, there is not time for them to cool."[28] More particularly, one report from Indians who came from the west suggested that the course of the Peace River was "interrupted, near, and in the mountains, by successive rapids and considerable falls" and also that "there is another great river towards the mid-day sun, whose current runs in that direction, and that the distance from it is not great across the mountains" (250). Finally, at the moment of departure on May 9, 1793, he sets the stage for the voyage proper by ascertaining the exact position of the fort, regulating his navigational instruments, describing the twenty-five-foot canoe and its three thousand pounds of lading, naming his crew of eight voyageurs and two Indian hunter/guides, and noting that those he left behind "shed tears on the reflection of the dangers which we might encounter in our expedition, while my own people offered up their prayers that we might return in safety from it" (257).

Mackenzie portrays his journey as one action, from this beginning on May 9 until July 22, when he painted his famous message on the rock in Dean Channel.[29] Indeed, Mackenzie only stopped his party when absolutely necessary, after long days or particularly shattering experiences, and then only just long enough to recuperate and decide on the next move. In the words of a contemporary reviewer of Mackenzie's *Voyages,* he

> went steadily forward, without knowing where he was to issue, amidst the roaring of cataracts, and the solitude of the mountains; exposed to the daily hazard of shipwreck, and famine, and mutiny; and to the danger of treachery or assault from the melancholy savages that roamed across his course, or reluctantly agreed to direct it.[30]

Mackenzie never raises the possibility of defeat, except when events themselves nearly succeed in blocking his progress. And at no time does he admit that his own will to proceed ever faltered. He recounts, for example, how one of his men walked with a lighted pipe over eighty pounds of gunpowder spread out to dry in the sun. "I need not add," he remarks, "that one spark might have put a period to all my anxiety and ambition."[31] As if to establish his own determination, he also dramatizes several situations in which he had to shame his men into proceeding with him by declaring it his "fixed and unalterable determination to proceed alone in spite of every difficulty that might oppose, or danger that should threaten me" (333). He shows himself making such declarations at moments when the men have concluded, perhaps reasonably, that the extreme difficulty of their circumstances would make it impossible to continue.

The conflict between Mackenzie's will to proceed and the incomprehension, reluctance, and resistance he meets along the way provides the structure of his narrative. Thanks to the introductory framework of Mackenzie's volume, his readers understand the source of the narrator's strength in such discouraging circumstances. His vision of a world trade route across the continent motivates him in spite of the most extreme dangers and punishing labors. Mackenzie's men, however, accustomed merely to the predictable dangers and hardships of regular fur trade voyages, frequently lose confidence and need Mackenzie's encouragement, even coercion, to keep going. The Indians whom Mackenzie employs as guides and interpreters have little understanding of his goals and less commitment to his success. And, of course, the peoples he encounters along the way are completely ignorant of his purposes.

One of the ways by which Mackenzie conveys a sense of his determination is in his recording of the passage of time. While his men and the Indian guides thought of time in terms of days, moons, and seasons, Mackenzie carried a chronometer and measured time in half-hours. In his narrative, he customarily notes the hour at which they embark in the morning (usually before sunrise), and he measures the difficulties encountered during the day in terms of hours lost. If the party retires at night earlier than normal, Mackenzie records it with the loss of hours.

He accounted for distance and direction with comparable care, using a compass, estimating the ground covered in half-miles, and taking as many observations for latitude and longitude as possible. An uneventful day comes out sounding like this:

> The weather was clear, and the air sharp, when we embarked at half past four. Our course was South by West one mile and an half, South-West by South half a mile, South-West. We here found it necessary to unload, and gum the canoe, in which operation we lost an hour; when we proceeded on the last course one mile and an half. I now took a meridian altitude, which gave 56.11.19 North latitude, and continued to proceed West-South-West two miles and an half. Here the Bear River, which is of a large appearance, falls in from the East; West three miles and an half, South-South-West one mile and an half, and South-West four miles and an half, when we encamped upon an island about seven in the evening. (262–263)

Mackenzie clearly wanted his route to seem as clear and credible as possible to those who might choose to follow in his steps.

This mode of reckoning time and distance was of little use to the "Canadians" who paddled for him or to the Indians who guided him. His voyageurs were inclined to reckon that a day had elapsed when they were exhausted by the difficulties of the route, even if this was at noon, and, for his guides, their position relative to the longitude of the beginning and end of the journey was of no meaning at all. What had meaning for them was their awareness that, at a certain point, they were leaving their homeland and entering that of strangers and enemies.

Near the beginning of his journey, Mackenzie describes the expedition's departure from the guides' relatives:

> The weather was cloudy, with an appearance of rain; and the Indians pressed me with great earnestness to pass the day with them, and hoped to prolong my stay among them by assuring me that the winter yet lingered in the Rocky Mountains: but my object was to lose no time, and having given the chief some tobacco for a small quantity of meat, we embarked at four, when my young men could not conceal their chagrin at parting with their friends, for so long a period as the voyage threatened to occupy. When I had assured them that in three moons we should return to them, we proceeded on our course. . . . The apprehensions which I had felt respecting the young men were not altogether groundless, for the eldest of them told me that his uncle had last night addressed him in the following manner:- "My nephew, your departure makes my heart painful. The white people may be said to rob us of you. They are about to conduct you into the midst of our enemies, and you may never more return to us. Were you not with the Chief Mackenzie, I know not what I should do, but he requires your attendance, and you must follow him." (261–262)

The "apprehensions" Mackenzie alludes to here have to do with the reluctance of his guides and interpreters to accompany him at all, a problem he faced throughout his journey. Mackenzie and the reader have quite a precise sense of the position and progress of the party in relation to its ultimate goals, but the other members of the expedition were to a large extent participating in a meaningless venture.

Unlike Hearne, who, because of his complete dependence on local Indians, was obliged to tell two parallel versions of his trip to the mouth of the Coppermine River, Mackenzie could largely ignore the Indians' view of his undertaking and allow their participation in it to go largely unrepresented. Regardless of the considerable amount of help he received along the way, Mackenzie could plausibly represent himself as being solely responsible for the venture. When views other than Mackenzie's are registered, it is in terms of their resistance to his own. His original ideas are challenged but never defeated or substantially changed. Hearne's narrative includes his account of the new approaches he was forced to adopt to the territory he was exploring; Mackenzie's narrative confirms the notions with which he began. By a combination of good planning, force of character, and good luck, Mackenzie's narrative makes the unknown lands and peoples conform to his original vision of them. He knows what he wants to find and is able to discover it to his readers.

The overcoming of difficulties is an often-repeated pattern within the overall plot of Mackenzie's narrative. Obstacles causing fatigue and anxiety are surmounted, yielding a moment of repose and a sense of progress; then the struggle resumes, as Mackenzie urges his party on to the next challenge. This pattern applies to encounters with both natural and human obstacles. Among the former were the many dangerous rapids and falls that they had laboriously to ascend and descend as they crossed two major mountain ranges going and returning. Human difficulties included the numerous villages along the Bella Coola River through which they were also obliged to pass twice. Each encounter with a village meant a process of mutual investigation, including diplomatic formalities, negotiations for food and guides, and miscellaneous trading, always with the possibility of serious misunderstanding. Though Mackenzie was a wonderfully astute observer and negotiator in these situations, he mainly took note of what was likely to contribute to the friendly and swift passage to the next village. In general, his approach to negotiating his way through a village was not unlike the manner in which he forged a difficult part of the river; both required his strict attention for the moments during which he was involved with them, but upon emerging his mind was already moving on to the next hurdle.

Mackenzie's narrative thus represents the progress of his expedition as a series of successful encounters with the lands and peoples in his path. These episodes are linked end to end in space and time, but they are also unified by the way each of them calls the ultimate viability of Mackenzie's vision into question. Each difficulty requires a reassertion of the consciousness that imagined the journey in the first place, because each problem threatens the narrator's resolve to proceed. Each "adventure" is interesting not only for its own sake but also because, after emerging successful from the challenge, the narrator is one step closer to the goal he continually holds before himself and the reader. Here, for example, is Mackenzie's account of a particularly harrowing passage down some rapids:

At an early hour this morning the men began to cut a road, in order to carry the canoe and lading beyond the rapid; and by seven they were ready. That business was soon effected, and the canoe reladen, to proceed with the current which ran with great rapidity. In order to lighten her, it was my intention to walk with some of the people; but those in the boat with great earnestness requested me to embark, declaring, at the same time, that, if they perished, I should perish with them. I did not then imagine in how short a period their apprehension would be justified. We accordingly pushed off, and had proceeded but a very short way when the canoe struck, and notwithstanding all our exertions, the violence of the current was so great as to drive her sideways down the river, and break her by the first bar, when I instantly jumped into the water, and the men followed my example; but before we could set her straight, or stop her, we came to deeper water, so that we were obliged to re-embark with the utmost precipitation. One of the men who was not sufficiently active, was left to get on shore in the best manner in his power. We had hardly regained our situations when we drove against a rock which shattered the stern of the canoe in such a manner, that it held only by the gunwales, so the steersman could no longer keep his place. The violence of this stroke drove us to the opposite side of the river, which is but narrow, when the bow met with the same fate as the stern. At this moment the foreman seized on some branches of a small tree in hope of bringing up the canoe, but such was their elasticity that, in a manner not easily described, he was jerked on shore in an instant, and with a degree of violence that threatened his destruction. But we had no time to turn from our own situation to inquire what had befallen him; for, in a few moments, we came across a cascade which broke several large holes in the bottom of the canoe, and started all the bars, except one behind the scooping seat. If this accident, however, had not happened, the vessel must have been irretrievably overset. The wreck becoming flat on the water, we all jumped out, while the steersman, who had been compelled to abandon his place, and had not recovered from his fright, called out to his companions to save themselves. My peremptory commands superseded the effects of his fear, and they all held fast to the wreck; to which fortunate resolution we owed our safety, as we should otherwise have been dashed against the rocks by the force of the water or driven over the cascades. In this condition we were driven several hundred yards, and every yard on the verge of destruction; but, at length, we most fortunately arrived in shallow water and a small eddy, where we were enabled to make a stand, from the weight of the canoe resting on the stones, rather than from any exertions of our exhausted strength. For though our efforts were short, they were pushed to the utmost, as life or death depended on them. This alarming scene, with all its terrors and dangers, occupied only a few minutes; and in the present suspension of it, we called to the people on shore to come to our assistance, and they immediately obeyed the summons. . . . All the different articles were now spread out to dry. The powder had fortunately received no damage, and all my instruments had escaped. Indeed, when my people began to recover from their alarm, and to enjoy a sense of safety, some of them, if not all, were by no means sorry for our late misfortune, from the hope that it must put a period to our voyage, particularly as we were without a canoe, and all the bullets sunk in the river. It did not, indeed, seem possible to them that we could proceed under these circumstances. I listened, however, to the observations that were made on the occasion without replying to them, till their panic was dispelled, and they had got themselves warm and comfortable, with an hearty meal, and rum enough to raise their spirits. (297–298)

With calm reestablished, Mackenzie proceeds to show the men how it is still possible to proceed onward toward their goal and to argue why it would be a "disgrace" to return home "without having attained the object of the expedition" (299).

While his men take a more moderate view, preferring to retreat when they feel the risks have become too great, Mackenzie's heroic narrator restricts his alternatives to success or destruction. With the "object of the expedition" always in clear view, Mackenzie can clearly focus his reporting on the business at hand. Reaching the Pacific is a synecdoche for the system of world trade that he outlines at the beginning of his account, and even such pure action reporting as the foregoing passage registers as part of the struggle toward the ultimate purpose. There is conflict and resistance in Mackenzie's narrative, but no ambiguity. He shapes his engagement with the lands and peoples of the West by the kinds of questions he asks about them. His narrative establishes a binary relationship with the environment, centering on the narrator's constant questioning as to whether he will be able to proceed safely or whether a certain fall or a certain people will put an end to his expedition. Mackenzie asks questions that can be answered yes or no: Can these rapids be negotiated without a portage? Is there a waterfall around the next bend? Do these people intend to let us pass without trouble? His method is to make his best judgment based upon appearances and then to test this judgment by proceeding appropriately.

The anxiety of this recurrent dilemma resembles that of the gambler, who examines the possibilities, makes his choice, and then waits for the result. It is not like the scientist's curiosity about unfamiliar surroundings or the ordinary man's fear of the unfamiliar. Mackenzie does not establish a discourse in which the object of inquiry can be revealed; he merely demands whether it will allow him to continue. For example, he speculates on the nature of the river ahead:

> In the last course the rocks contracted in such a manner on both sides of the river, as to afford the appearance of the upper part of a fall or cataract. Under this apprehension we landed on the left shore, where we found a kind of foot-path, imperfectly traced, through which we conjectured that the natives occasionally passed with their canoes and baggage. On examining the course of the river, however, there did not appear to be any fall as we expected; but the rapids were of a considerable length and impassable for a light canoe. We had therefore no alternative but to widen the road so as to admit the passage of our canoe. (307)

Mackenzie's attention to the rock formations alongside his route is not aesthetic or scientific. He is concerned only about what they portend for his passage. In this case, he wagers that it is worthwhile for him to interrupt his progress—perhaps to lose an hour—because the rocks suggest dangerous water ahead.

Similarly, he must judge the intentions of unfamiliar Indians by what he can observe of their behavior. In one instance, something happens to disturb a group with whom Mackenzie has been treating for several days, causing them to take flight and leaving him to determine whether they will attack his party. On the one hand, he relates that he has just passed one of the houses "which appeared in a state of perfect tranquility"; on the other, some of his men have encountered Indians who "appeared to be in a state of extreme rage." Resisting his men's desire to flee, Mackenzie determines to await the issue of "this mysterious business." Meanwhile he explains that, though "a general panic had seized all round him, and any further prosecution of the voyage was now considered by his men as altogether hopeless and impracticable," he himself determined to stay until appearances yielded a better understanding of their situation:

> These perplexing circumstances made a deep impression on my mind, not as to our immediate safety, for I entertained not the least apprehension of the Indians I had hitherto seen, even if their whole force should have been combined to attack us, but these untoward events seemed to threaten the prosecution of my journey; and I could not reflect upon the possibility of such a disappointment but with sensations little short of agony. (325–326)

In this instance, the path clears for him, and his concern for the nature of the obstacle diminishes rapidly as he goes on to the next problem.

Since Mackenzie does not allow the possibility of simply turning back to figure in his narrative, however much he may have entertained it in reality, he usually represents the possibility of the frustration of his intentions in terms of his personal destruction. With him, of course, would go the very idea of the journey. Defeat would not lead to a different plot, the product perhaps of a dialogue with his surroundings such as Hearne's, but to the disappearance of the narrative itself, leaving the Northwest Passage still to be discovered. This threat is always present and frequently felt. In one instance, as Mackenzie begins his return trip up the Bella Coola River, he finds that the villages of the valley have been turned against him by an enemy who is preceding him:

> When we had quitted the wood, and were in sight of the houses, . . . I was surprised to see two men running down towards me from one of the houses, with daggers in their hands and fury in their aspect. From their hostile appearance, I could not doubt of their purpose. I therefore stopped short, threw down my cloak, and put myself in a posture of defense, with my gun presented towards them. Fortunately for me, they knew the effect of fire-

arms, and instantly dropped their daggers, which were fastened by a string to their wrists, and had before been held in a menacing attitude. I let my gun also fall into my left hand, and drew my hanger. Several others soon joined them, who were armed in a similar manner; and among them I recognized the man whom I have already mentioned as being so troublesome to us. . . . Until I saw him my mind was undisturbed; but the moment he appeared, conceiving that he was the cause of my present perilous situation, my resentment predominated, and, if he had come within my reach, I verily believe, that I should have terminated his insolence for ever.

The rest now approached so near, that one of them contrived to get behind me, and grasped me in his arms. I soon disengaged myself from him; and, . . . why he did not avail himself of the opportunity which he had of plunging his dagger into me, I cannot conjecture. They certainly might have overpowered me, and though I should probably have killed one or two of them, I must have fallen at last.

One of my people now came out of the wood. On his appearance they instantly took flight, and with the utmost speed sought shelter in the houses from which they had issued. It was, however, upwards of ten minutes before all my people joined me; and as they came one after the other, these people might have successively dispatched every one of us. If they had killed me, in the first instance, this consequence would certainly have followed, and not one of us would have returned home to tell the horrid fate of his companions. (381)

If Mackenzie does not regard land formations with the eye of a geologist, neither does he engage in ethnographic discourse. In describing his experiences with the peoples along his route, there is no attempt to imagine motives nor to construct a local context for actions. "Daggers in their hands and fury in their aspect" is effective, if rather telegraphic, action writing; it conveys the nature of the immediate situation. Mackenzie summons the telling details of who held which weapons, who had the advantage and how, what his own exact movements were. And as in the description of the wreck in the rapids, the action signifies only in relation to the narrative framework that Mackenzie controls. Absolute defeat is a possibility in Mackenzie's narrative, but the possibility of a story different from the one he sets out to tell is never recognized.

Mackenzie remains determined to discover what he has hypothesized; he will tell that story or none at all.

In a sense, Mackenzie writes the purest kind of discovery narrative. All actions and events signify in terms of the traveler's stated intentions, and, what is more, these intentions are defined in relation to a global vision of European trade and power. Who Mackenzie is as a traveler and what happens to him are understood unambiguously in relation to the history of an expanding Europe-centered trade network. Conflict with native peoples is openly a part of this history, but interactions with them are not seen as likely to modify the discoverer's original vision. The native peoples that Mackenzie encounters are not individualized in his narrative, even though they would be necessary supporting players along any future trader's supply lines. Similarly, the lands that Mackenzie passes through do not alter the nature of his intentions or deflect his narrative. Mackenzie's descriptions of his struggles with the rivers and mountains in his path may fill the reader with awe, but this emotion is not shared by the writer, for whom everything is a stage in his progress toward his final destination. It is as if the reader entertains the possibility of Mackenzie's defeat in a way that the writer himself seems unable, or unwilling, to admit. Ironically, however, the roughness of the terrain and the hostility of some local peoples, against which Mackenzie's bravery and energy show to such advantage, seem to preclude the routine passage of goods that is implied in his vision of a major trade route. Mackenzie presumed that his discovery would lead to the next stage of European endeavor in northwestern America, but the directed energy of his journey and the clarity of his narrative fail sufficiently to recognize the complex relationships with native peoples and environments that had been required of the European fur trade empire up to that point.

Alexander Henry's *Travels and Adventures:* Narrating Captivity

Alexander Henry's *Travels and Adventures in Canada and the Indian Territories* (New York, 1809) can be seen as an allegory of the same kinds of conflict that occupied Cooper in his *Leather-Stocking Tales*. His narrative spans the years during which took shape the political division of North America that we now know: a functioning French colonial society forced into a relation subordinate to British colonials, who soon thereafter split themselves into loyalist and independence-minded factions, with none of the three colonizing groups allowing much thought for the sovereignty of Indian societies. Henry's account of his sixteen years as a trader among the Indian peoples north and northwest of the Great Lakes begins in 1760, "when British arms, under General Amherst, were employed in the reduction of Canada."[32] Henry recounts his peripheral involvement with the lifting of Pontiac's siege of Detroit (1764) and ends with his arrival in Montreal in 1776, where he lived the rest of his long life and where he found "the province delivered from the irruption of the colonists, and protected by the forces of General Burgoyne" (337–338). Focused on the trading hinterland, mostly beyond the reach of large European armies, his "adventures" take place among groups that were vital, dangerous competitors, as yet unrestrained by the new regimes of the settled areas.

A New Jersey–born Anglo-American, Henry (b. 1739) was among the earliest British traders to enter the French fur-trading center of Michilimackinac, and his story shows how he and other traders like him took over the trading infrastructure established by the French, retaining the hundreds of skilled canoe men, interpreters, and bourgeois traders who had made the trade profitable.[33] Henry's narrative also describes how the Indian peoples who formed the other half of the trading relationship worked for their own interests in a new and confusing situation. Most of those whom Henry met at Michilimackinac had sided with the French during the war, but beyond the hostility toward the British that that alliance generated, these Indian peoples asserted their independence from both European powers. Their reliance on European trade was very real, however, and acted as a powerful brake on the momentum of the Indian independence movement that was sometimes suggested in the rhetoric of Pontiac.[34]

Henry's memoir self-consciously connects the travels and adventures of his early years with the formation of his character and fortune.[35] For Henry, the word "adventure" refers both to the active and dangerous life he led in the West and to venture capitalism, the risking of his property in the hope of gain. The successful Montreal merchant who tells the story presents himself as the product of the unstable conditions of the trading frontier. An American-born Anglophone, he adapts himself to the conditions of the French fur trade, learning the language and assuming the garb and appearance of a "Canadian" at various points.[36] Later, he is formally adopted by a Chippewa Indian, spending the winter with his family and contemplating such a state for the indefinite future. Henry's final role is that of a member of the British-oriented, colonial elite of post-conquest Canada, distinct from the Canadian French, from the Indians, and from the Anglo-Americans of his birthplace.

Henry's *Travels and Adventures* is a remarkable example of the discourse articulating the Anglo-Canadian identity that was emerging during Henry's lifetime; the character and fortune he achieves can be understood as the products of the particular politics of eighteenth-century colonial North America. Henry's narrative is also exemplary, however, in the broader field of colonial discourse, within what has been described by Peter Hulme as an ensemble of discursive practices. This discourse did not simply record European expansion beyond the borders of Europe; it played an active role in managing colonial relationships or, as Hulme has put it, "*produced* for Europe . . . large parts of the non-European world."[37] Without detaching *Travels and Adventures* from its specific historical context, I shall focus on Henry's narrative as it "produces" for its readers the Indian, French, and English identities of colonialism after the Seven Years' War. To this end, I shall argue that *Travels and Adventures* is to a remarkable extent overtly about discourse and that it stresses the competition of discourses among native peoples and European colonialists.

In this last respect, Henry's account differs from the three major contemporary travel narratives about Canada and the fur trade. Most of Henry's traveling came before that of Samuel Hearne and Alexander Mackenzie, but Henry published his *Travels and Adventures* last, after having read Hearne's *Journey from Prince of Wales's Fort* and Mackenzie's *Voyages*. Henry also knew Jonathan Carver's influential *Travels through the Interior Parts of North-America, in the Years 1766, 1767, and 1768* (1778), the account of another Anglo-American's journey on the upper reaches of the Mississippi River and the upper Great Lakes.[38] Henry's narrative, which came out forty-nine years after the initial events of his story, is, not surprisingly, more of a memoir and less of an exploration report than are the other three.[39] In 1809, Henry could not claim much strategic importance for what he had to tell of his early career trading around the Great Lakes and northwesterly into what is now Manitoba and Saskatchewan, and at no time could he claim "first white man" status anywhere. Henry has nothing to offer that bears comparison with Hearne's and Mackenzie's overland journeys to the Arctic and Pacific Oceans. However one assesses their achievements as explorers, the published accounts of Mackenzie's, Hearne's, and Carver's journeys all present their activities in strategic, geographic terms. These three men wanted to be read as having traveled to "make discoveries." Mackenzie's *Voyages* begins with a long "General History of the Fur Trade from Canada to the North-West," and the preface explains the purpose of his journeys as being "to determine the practicability of a commercial communication through the continent of North America, between the Atlantic and Pacific Oceans."[40] Mackenzie imagines the North American trade as part of British commerce with the Far East. Hearne's *Journey* is linked to the same concern with Asia-bound passage through or around the American continents, in this case via the Northwest Passage.[41] Likewise, Carver's *Travels* claims that his intention was "to ascertain the breadth of that vast continent," and "to establish a post . . . about the Straits of Annian." "This," he says, "would greatly facilitate the discovery of a Northwest Passage . . . [and] open a passage for conveying intelligence to China."[42]

Nevertheless, despite its unique position, Henry's *Travels and Adventures* owes much to the mode of Anglo-American colonial discourse exemplified by Mackenzie, Hearne, and Carver. His narrative retains the journey as its most basic structuring device—even though there are many short trips around the lakes, the most distant destinations come last, and the story ends with Henry's return to Montreal. Especially in the second book, which deals with Henry's far western travels, much of the subject matter is classic exploration narrative material: the difficulty and excitement of travel, the appearance and resources of the country, the behavior and culture of local peoples, the measurement of distances traveled, and the plotting of topography. But since Henry's book is more of a personal memoir than the other three, invoking exotic experiences as shapers of his personality, one might think that *Travels and Adventures* is less an assertion of colonialist power than are their narratives, which are all consciously oriented toward geographical discovery and the claiming of territory. In fact, however, in its dramatization of the struggle among Indian societies and French and British colonial factions, Henry's *Travels and Adventures* is equally concerned with the marshalling of power.

Indeed, Henry emphasizes the inseparability of power and its manifestations in discourse. Whereas it might be argued that geographically focused narratives such as the other three tend to mask the assertion of European power, presenting it simply as the acquisition of objective knowledge of land or space, Henry's narrative defines the power of colonizers in terms of their ability to manage the behavior of those already present in the land.[43] It presents European colonialism as a conflict of discourses, a conflict among attempts to articulate the meaning of lives lived at the intersection of three societies. Ultimately, it claims the status of "history" as a record of the events through which this three-way conflict was resolved in the favor of the successful Montreal merchant, who tells the story from his elite station amid what had become the British colonial status quo.

One notices a strong tendency in the discovery literature of the eighteenth and nineteenth centuries to write of unknown lands, as opposed to conquered peoples. In answer to the implied question "Where did you go?" writers spoke in terms of longitude and latitude, of leagues or miles traveled along a particular compass bearing, rather than in terms of visits to the places of indigenous societies. They filled in the cartographic outline by means of the discourses of other disciplines of knowledge: certain species of plants and animals, certain types of soils and minerals, certain kinds of weather, certain groups of languages, certain patterns of marriage and funerary practices were located on the map. The narrative of discovery takes its form as a story of travel in the service of other discourses of abstract knowledge and thereby tends to distance itself from the extension of power over indigenous peoples that was part of the European expansion. From the later eighteenth century, the disinterested observer becomes a preferred pose for travelers aspiring to the status of explorer. The land is rendered in terms of well-established categories of knowledge, and American peoples are increasingly sequestered within the discourses of ethnography, treated in relation to an abstract notion of the human family, rather than as competitors for the use of the land.

Of the accounts by Mackenzie, Hearne, and Carver, Mackenzie's is the most restricted to a plot of geographical discovery. Mackenzie begs to be excused from the role of naturalist, but, as we have seen, his ambition to fill in some of the blank spaces on the map seems clear. On the one hand, Mackenzie is aware of the conventions of scientific discourse that his genre demands, but, he says, "I do not possess the science of the naturalist; and even if the qualifications had been attained by me, its curious spirit would not have been gratified. I could not stop to dig into the earth, over whose surface I was compelled to pass with rapid steps; nor could I turn aside to collect the plants which nature might have scattered on my way."[44] On the other hand, his claim to have labored in the service of geography is very clear, as is that labor's connection to imperialism. He relates, he says, "the successive circumstances of my progress . . . without exaggeration or display." And he indulges the hope "that this volume . . . will not be thought unworthy of the attention of the scientific geographer; and that, by unfolding countries hitherto unexplored, and which, I presume, may now be considered as part of the British dominions, it will be received as a faithful tribute to the prosperity of my country" (59–60).

Mackenzie delivers what he promises in this introductory passage to his *Voyages*. His accounts of his journeys to the mouth of the Mackenzie River and to the Pacific coast are plotted in terms of his progress toward these goals, and for all his energetic telling of the events of his travels, the linearity of Mackenzie's narrative limits reflection on the implications of his journey as one reads. Despite Mackenzie's obvious familiarity with the native peoples of the West and his dependence upon them, his linkage of narrative and cartographic plotting directs attention away from the political and social complexities of extending "British dominion" from sea to sea, instead registering success more in terms of geographical and legal abstractions.

Henry's *Travels and Adventures*, as I have said, owes something to this kind of narrative. The author does his best to organize the activities of sixteen years in the fur trade as a single long journey. But his account also shares the concerns and form of the narrative of Indian captivity, another important kind of personal narrative in America and one that construes the colonial experience in America in terms of conflict among societies. In the narrative of Indian captivity, the mission of European colonists is threatened and the colony's vulnerability emphasized when one of their number is removed and forced to live with a competing group. Some captives regarded their captors as utterly alien, even demonic, agents of a providential design to test and strengthen the pilgrim/colonist. Others so assimilated the language and customs of their captors that they accepted new identities and never returned to their colonial homes.[45] The captivity narrative cannot accommodate this ultimate changing of identities, and there is no narrative written by someone who stayed with his or her captors for good. But the stories of returned captives demonstrate the possibility of such a change and so point to the existence of the discourses of other societies in "American" space, even as they assert the dominance of the European discourse.[46]

The first book of Henry's *Travels and Adventures* presents a complex competition over whose law, language, trading system, and religion would end up defining the relationships among British, French, and Indian groups in the interior of North America. Much of this contest is focused on, or expressed in terms of, the definition of the young Alexander Henry's identity as he moves into a contested area of the continent, in what he himself calls "a premature attempt to share in the fur-trade of Canada."[47] As a lone English trader, Henry is both sustained and threatened by the French and native contexts within which he is bound to live. After the massacre of the English garrison at Michilimackinac by a confederacy of "Chipeways" (Chippewas) and "Saakies" (Sauks), Henry is captured, and he describes the death and cannibalistic mutilation of the body of one of his compatriots. Subsequently, Henry enters another, benign form of captivity as an adopted member of a Chippewa family, a status that preserves his life because it alters his relationship to local natives.

Cannibalism and adoption are ritual actions in *Travels and Adventures*; more specifically, they are discourses of identity, competing with that which Henry can marshal, at the intersection of Indian and European cultures at Michilimackinac in the 1760s. Henry's cannibals exact retribution and inspire courage in themselves as warriors; they assert their vitality as dangerous opponents. The victim is chosen because of who he is, or rather who he is not, and in this sense cannibalization is the ultimate assault against someone's identity, as not only the consciousness of the victim but his very flesh is absorbed into an alien ritual system. Adoption is a less deadly analogous threat to English identity. It, too, asserts the integrity of Indian society and its ability to retain its own agenda and co-opt intruders. In other words, cannibalization and adoption are equally intolerable threats to the dominant English identity that tells the story.

Henry begins the story of his western travels with his departure from Montreal. His laden canoes, with their crews of Canadian voyageurs, head up the Ottawa River and along the well-established route to Lake Huron. His account of the first part of this journey is a description of scenes and events that are new to him but routine for his voyageurs and guides. The journey proceeds according to their knowledge and customs, but Henry, as a citizen of the conquering nation and as a source of capital to fuel the existing commercial machine, is at its head.

When Henry leaves behind the British armies, however, he reenters, in effect, the preconquest power structure where Englishmen are ene- mies and English goods subject to seizure. As he approaches Michili- mackinac, he is told repeatedly that the Indians there "will certainly kill him" (23). He decides to relinquish outward evidences of his nationality and command:

> The hostility of the Indians was exclusively against the English. Between them, and my Canadian attendants, there appeared the most cordial good will. This circumstance suggested one means of escape, of which, by the advice of my friend, Campion, I resolved to attempt availing myself; and which was, that of putting on the dress, usually worn by such of the Canadians as pursue the trade into which I had entered, and assimilating myself, as much as I was able, to their appearance and manners. To this end, I laid aside my English clothes, and covered myself only with a cloth, passed about the middle; a shirt, hanging loose; a molton, or blanket coat; and a large, red, milled worsted cap. The next thing was to smear my face and hands with dirt, and grease; and, this done, I took the place of one of my men, and, when Indians approached, used the paddle, with as much skill as I possessed. I had the satisfaction to find, that my disguise enabled me to pass several canoes, without attracting the smallest notice. (34–35)

This is the first of several occasions when Henry resorts to changes of costume in order to preserve himself among Indians hostile to the English. As he proceeds with his narrative, he relates further instances of disguise and adaptation, which, though pragmatic responses to dan- ger, threaten more seriously the identity with which he entered the hostile territory. In fact, Henry's adaptations to his circumstances move beyond mere disguise to become some measure of acceptance of the false identity he has adopted, endangering his very sense of self.

Upon his arrival at Michilimackinac, he attempts to continue conceal- ing his identity: "Here, I put the entire charge of my effects into the hands of my assistant, Campion, between whom and myself it had been previously agreed, that he should pass for the proprietor; and my men were instructed to conceal the fact, that I was an Englishman" (39). Within the confines of the fort, however, Henry's secret is soon common knowledge, and he must negotiate in his own person.

As a trader with much-needed goods, Henry was a boon to the inhabitants of the region. The problem was not his function as a merchant but his identity as an Englishman, which made him a symbol of a recently encountered enemy and therefore a target of vengeance. In this connection, he relates how he was formally enlightened as to the customs of the local Indians regarding retribution for slain friends and relatives. Minavavana, a Chippewa chief, addresses him upon his arrival at Michilimackinac: "Englishman, our father, the king of France, employed our young men to make war upon your nation. In this warfare, many of them have been killed; and it is our custom to retaliate, until such time as the spirits of the slain are satisfied" (44–45). Minavavana further explains that "making presents" may be substituted for blood retribution, and Henry makes a deal that satisfies everyone for a time. However, as the situation around the fort deteriorates, Henry is informed more frequently that he is going to be killed to satisfy various people's needs to avenge lost relatives. The crisis comes with the massacre of the English soldiers and traders at Michilimackinac by Indians participating in Pontiac's campaign against the English. Henry's narrative is well known as the principal account of this massacre and as the source of the story of Henry's adoption by Wawatam, a Chippewa, through whose help he escapes the general destruction.[48] In Henry's account the two stories are intertwined; Henry escapes from the massacre only because he is taken into the family of Wawatam.

Henry first encounters Wawatam a year before the massacre:

Shortly after my first arrival at Michilimackinac, in the preceding year, a Chipeway, named Wa'wa'tam', began to come often to my house, betraying, in his demeanor, strong marks of personal regard. After this had continued for some time, he came, on a certain day, bringing with him his whole family, and, at the same time, a large present, consisting of skins, sugar and dried meat. Having laid these in a heap, he commenced a speech, in which he informed me, that some years before, he had observed a fast, devoting himself, according to the custom of his nation, to solitude, and to the mortification of his body, in the hope to obtain, from the Great Spirit, protection through all his days; that on this occasion, he had dreamed of adopting an Englishman, as his son, brother and friend; that from the moment in which he first beheld me, he had recognized me as the person whom the Great Spirit had been pleased to point out to him for a brother; that he hoped that I would not refuse his present; and that he should forever regard me as one of his family. I could do no otherwise than to accept the present, and declare my willingness to have so good a man, as this appeared to be, for my friend and brother. I offered a present in return for that which I had received, which Wawatam accepted, and then thanking me for the favour which he said that I had rendered him, he left me, and soon after set out on his winter's hunt. (73–74)

Just days before the massacre, Wawatam returns and, without exactly betraying the intentions of his countrymen, tries to warn Henry, saying that he had been "disturbed by the noise of evil birds" and asking him to depart immediately with Wawatam's family on a trip to a neighboring settlement (75). (Henry says that he had insufficient grasp of Wawatam's language, or he should perhaps have grasped the warning that the latter was trying to convey to him in various indirect ways.) Then, having failed to get Henry to leave the fort before the massacre, Wawatam returns afterward to ransom him, arguing that since Henry is his brother, it is unfitting for him to be enslaved or sacrificed. An arrangement is made, and Henry departs with Wawatam to join the latter's family, where he is welcomed with food and clothing and generally made to feel at home.

His formal adoption into a Chippewa family preserves Henry from possible slavery, murder, or being "made into broth," the last a threat that Henry says was repeated several times and an action that he claims to have witnessed when, shortly after his rescue by Wawatam, seven of the remaining English prisoners are killed and one of them butchered and cooked. Invitations are sent round for a ritual feast, and even Wawatam attends the ceremony, taking his dish and spoon with him to the "place of entertainment." Henry relates that

> after an absence of about half an hour, he returned, bringing in his dish a human hand, and a large piece of flesh. He did not appear to relish the repast, but told me, that it was then, and

always had been the custom, among all the Indian nations, when returning from war, or on overcoming their enemies, to make a war-feast from among the slain. This, he said, inspired the warrior with courage in attack, and bred him to meet death with fearlessness. (103)

Henry's account of the act of cannibalism is unequivocal. He describes the butchering of the dead body and its division into five pieces, each of which is placed in a separate kettle (102). If Henry is a reliable witness, then his account is a serious challenge to the argument of Peter Hulme that cannibalism, apart from "eating to survive *in extremis*" and "an occasional mouthful in revenge," has never been proven to exist as a social practice and that cannibalism is the invention of colonial discourse, beginning in the Caribbean, whence the word comes.[49] It may be impossible to determine the degree to which the Henry narrative reflects actual practices in the northern woodlands in the eighteenth century, but Hulme's main point regarding the function of cannibalism within colonial discourse applies nonetheless to Henry's narrative and is enlightening. Within the context of colonial discourse, Hulme argues, cannibalism means "the image of ferocious consumption of human flesh . . . used to mark the boundaries between one community and its others" (86). For all Henry's sympathetic interest in the lifeways of Wawatam and his people, this act of cannibalism asserts the difference between the narrator's consciousness and values and those of the woodlands Indians he depicts. *Travels and Adventures* even has these Indians proclaim their own aggressive sense of distinctness by singling out particular targets and boldly announcing that they are to be "made into broth."

Henry's adoption as a member of Wawatam's clan rescues him from these horrific prospects, but humane and friendly as his new family members are, the very integrity of their society is a threat that cannot be tolerated by the English identity at the center of the text. The seriousness of the threat is indicated by the imagery of death and transformation that accompany Henry's entrance into Chippewa society. Soon after witnessing the cannibal feast but before he describes how he assumed the dress of one of Wawatam's clan, Henry recounts an episode that seems designed to symbolize a liminal phase between the two identities. In order to preserve Henry from the violence Wawatam anticipates upon the arrival of canoes with a lot of liquor,

Wawatam leads him to a cave on the high land in the middle of the island of Michilimackinac. This eminence, Henry notes, is named for the *Michilimackinac* or Great Turtle, the "chief spirit" of the region.[50] Henry spends one night in the cave and then discovers it is full of human bones. He spends the second night outdoors but awakes "hungry and dispirited, and almost envying the dry bones" (109). Wawatam returns and leads Henry back to his new family, where he assumes Indian dress. His hosts advance various theories as to the origin of the bones, but Henry says that he was "disposed to believe that this cave was an ancient receptacle for the bones of prisoners, sacrificed and devoured at war-feasts" (110).

Faced with two choices, both defined in relation to discourses of Indian power, Henry opts for survival. He describes his transformation:

> My hair was cut off, and my head shaved, with the exception of a spot on the crown, of about twice the diameter of a crown piece. My face was painted with three or four different colours; some parts of it red, and others black. A shirt was provided for me, painted with vermilion, mixed with grease. A large collar of wampum was put round my neck, and another suspended on my breast. Both my arms were decorated with large bands of silver above the elbow, besides several smaller ones on the wrists; and my legs were covered with *mitasses*, a kind of hose, made, as is the favorite fashion, of scarlet cloth. Over all, I was to wear a scarlet blanket or mantle, and on my head a large bunch of feathers. I parted, not without some regret, with the long hair which was natural to it, and which I fancied to be ornamental; but the ladies of the family, and of the village in general, appeared to think my person improved, and now condescended to call me handsome, even among Indians. (111–112)

For the following year, Henry lives as a member of Wawatam's family, accompanying the group to their winter hunting grounds, learning much about their daily life, language, religious customs, and hunting techniques. His preoccupation with dress and appearance continues throughout this portion of his narrative, and there is an undercurrent of amazement that, looking and acting like an Indian, he can come to the point of being one. Henry says that he "felt [him]self more at liberty than before" (112), and he immediately adopts the first person plural to relate what happened during the succeeding year. "We were often for twenty-four hours without eating," he says, "and when in the morning we had no victuals for the day before us, the custom was to black our faces with grease and charcoal, and exhibit, through resignation, a temper as cheerful as if in the midst of plenty" (113). When one last attempt to retrieve his trade goods from the captured fort fails, he says that "nothing, or almost nothing, I now began to think, would be all that I should need, during the rest of my life. To fish and to hunt, to collect a few skins, and exchange them for necessaries, was all that I seemed destined to do, and to acquire, for the future" (112). Here and elsewhere, Henry's "goods" or "property" serve as a metonymy of his English self. One senses some self-pity in this vision of his destiny, but at other times, his account of his daily routine in the hunting camp conveys interest and contentment:

> By degrees, I became familiarized with this kind of life; and had it not been for the idea of which I could not divest my mind, that I was living among savages, and for the whispers of a lingering hope, that I should one day be released from it—or if I could have forgotten that I had ever been otherwise than as I then was—I could have enjoyed as much happiness in this, as in any other situation. (127)

In the climactic episode in Henry's story of his adjustment to Indian life, he goes out hunting alone and gets lost. This episode seems to have a symbolic function analogous to that of his night among the bones. After wandering for three wintry days without food or fire, he resigns himself "into the hands of that Providence whose arm had so often saved me." Almost immediately afterward, he stumbles upon one of the groups' previous encampments, from which he is able to deduce the present location of his friends. "An hour before," he says, "I had thought myself the most miserable of men; and now I leaped for joy, and called myself the happiest" (134). Life with Wawatam's family emerges on this, as on previous occasions, as a welcome alternative to destruction; indeed it becomes under Henry's pen an increasingly appealing image of human society.

Henry's narrative presents a threshold of eighteenth-century European and Indian cultures, describing it in the crossing. He claims to render an inside view of Chippewa life, and he at least conveys that a coherent "inside" exists independent of European awareness. Like all captivity narratives, and more sympathetically than many, Henry's *Travels and Adventures* depicts actions and agendas directed by groups other than the writer's compeers. But to acknowledge the existence of the Other is not to accede to his claims to dominate or even to be left alone. The emphasis in Henry's narrative is on the competition of societies, and his story is finally one of winners and losers. Henry leaves Wawatam as the latter sings a prayer for his safe journey; the two never meet again (154). Wawatam's story ends with Henry's departure.

In the most obvious sense, Henry narrates the origins and growth of the branch of the British fur trade that became the North-West Company, an organization that extended British influence across the continent. In a less direct manner, however, Henry appropriates French-Canadian and Indian lives to the British colonizing errand. In Henry's account of his relationship with the Others of the region, ritual cannibalism and cultural adoption are discourses analogous in social function to the narrative incorporation performed in his account. The contest is a matter of who will serve as the signifier in whose discourse. As a member of a successful group, Henry creates the French and Indians who will serve the interests of British colonialism in North America.

Henry's *Travels and Adventures* differs from some of the geographically plotted narratives of discovery written by contemporaries in the region in that it includes more actions initiated by Indians, along with the social codes and practices that guide these actions, so that the Indian peoples of Michilimackinac appear as independent, reasoning agents rather than parts of the landscape. As a captivity narrative, *Travels and Adventures* emphasizes conflict about who will set the agenda for life in the region north of the Great Lakes, and as a "captive" who is relatively sympathetic to his hosts, Henry presents Indian actions as deriving from intentions that, while in competition with those of the colonial English, are nonetheless comprehensible. But in the end, having for years operated within parts of the continent where much of life was still articulated by Indian and French languages, Henry returns to a center where English colonial discourses define who is who. In this context, "the Indian Territories" come into being as a later aspect of Henry's identity, a dimension of his character that would not have emerged had he not suffered capture at Michilimackinac and then lived as an adopted member of Wawatam's family. Writing in Montreal, Henry lays claim to an insider's understanding of North American peoples, adding their "wilderness" to the map of his own personhood. The young man who entered the "Indian Territories" in 1760 was not the same man who returned to Montreal sixteen years later. However, it is he who ultimately assimilates the "Indian Territories," not the other way round.

Henry's storytelling, in other words, represents his "reaggregation" into the world of his readers.[51] Henry manages his relations with Ottawas, Chippewas, and Frenchmen in order that he may be accepted by his compatriots. Despite the degree of sympathy with Chippewa society that Henry feels, other authorities, loyalties, and auditors guide his pen. These are specified by Henry himself in his only direct criticism of Chippewa life, a complaint that is made in passing but goes to the heart of why his assimilation into Chippewa society is reversed. "My companions in the lodge," says Henry, "were unaccustomed to pass the time in conversation. Among the Indians, the topics of conversation are but few" (148). Henry goes on to explain that "the causes of taciturnity among the Indians, may be easily understood, if we consider how many occasions of speech, which present themselves to us, are utterly unknown to them; the records of history, the pursuits of science, the disquisitions of philosophy, the systems of politics, the business and the amusements of the day, and the transactions of the four corners of the world" (148). Henry's list serves very well to indicate the discourses within which his own book was written and to which it subordinates the world of Wawatam and his family. Like other travelers and captives, Henry had his audience in mind, and even though his story allows other voices to be heard, he ultimately asserts his own authority in the struggle for colonial power.

CHAPTER TWO

Early Western Travels and the American Self

Setting out in 1804, Meriwether Lewis and William Clark led the first of a series of expeditions sponsored by the United States government into the recently acquired Louisiana Territory and across the mountains into the Columbia River valley, carrying the banner of scientific knowledge and asserting American sovereignty west of the Mississippi. Strategically, these American expeditions were in direct competition with British interests, which were represented in the Far West by the fur companies, but the narratives that reported them appealed to essentially the same scientific and literary audience as the British fur trade accounts by Hearne, Mackenzie, and Henry. Aware of this common audience and familiar with the accounts of the somewhat earlier British travelers, American writers adhered to the conventions of the international genre of exploration reportage of which Cook's *Voyages* was a primary example: they restricted themselves to reporting on what they themselves actually saw and experienced; they told their stories from the observer's point of view; they focused on regions that were "unknown" to their readers; they organized their narratives around a journey: and they held out the advancement of scientific knowledge as a concern transcending their more immediate practical goals. These conventions, which had enabled fur traders with little education to view their experiences in a context larger than that of the fur business and thus to write accounts of enduring general interest, also provided American military travelers with a model of "enlightened" discourse about the western lands and peoples recently come under their control. Under the direction of President Thomas Jefferson, Lewis and Clark, as edited for the 1814 *History* of their expedition, established the standard of reportage for the American expeditions and narratives that followed during the first half of the nineteenth century.

One of the main assertions of this chapter is that, by the time of John Charles Frémont's account of his 1842 expedition to the Rocky Mountains, discovery narratives written by United States nationals had developed a rhetoric different from that present in accounts by eighteenth-century colonial or British-born travelers. The distinctiveness of early-nineteenth-century American discovery narratives has to do with the way they construed the relationship of Euro-American citizens with the "unknown territories" of the Far West, more particularly, with whether they presented the western lands as inhabited countries or basically empty, politically unmodified, spaces. The three British narratives discussed so far deal with New World lands that are sparsely populated and subject to the imperial attentions of British commerce, backed up by the army in some instances, but Hearne, Henry, and Mackenzie openly acknowledge the resident populations of the areas through which they travel, and they rely on their help in order to survive. A resident population is essential, in fact, to the main purpose of their explorations: they are traders, and they need people to supply pelts in exchange for European goods, as well as to help transport the same. The "discovery" of the lands these traders explored includes the inhabitants, and the relationship with European societies implied for Indian peoples as a result of their "discovery" does not imply a radical disruption of their relationship with their lands. There is no suggestion that the regions traveled through will see many more Europeans in the foreseeable future; as far as most readers in the late eighteenth century were concerned, the Far North, the Far West of what is now Canada, and the areas north of the Great Lakes would remain exotic. Journeys into these regions were narrated as trips into distant, foreign lands, not very susceptible of being thought of as home. The plots of their discovery narratives include the crossing and recrossing of a threshold or boundary, a voyage out and a return.

This sense of the boundedness of English colonies in North America in the eighteenth century seems to have been true as well for those that became the United States, despite their bordering on lands that were attractive for settlement and despite Anglo-Americans' having had clear ambitions to acquire control of Indian lands to the west or, at least, to limit the ability of the French and Spanish to do so. John Juricek, in the course of tracing "American Usage of the Word 'Frontier' from Colonial Times to the Present," concludes that "until about the mid-nineteenth century most Americans would have agreed that the United States, like the English colonies before it, did not border on emptyness [*sic*] in the West. Rather, like European nations, it bordered on other countries— Indian Countries."[1] According to Juricek, "In colonial and early national times, when Anglo-Americans spoke about frontiers, they usually were referring to the more or less fortified outer edges of the colonies, states, or nation." And he goes on to note the important fact that "most of their peripheral settlements adjoined those of Indians" (14). Thus, Juricek shows that until nearly the mid-nineteenth century there was little difference between American and European usage of the word "frontier"; in both cases, it was mainly used to signify a border area or a boundary line separating two distinct countries or nations.

This meaning is not that of Frederick Jackson Turner's famous "frontier thesis," of which Juricek offers a critique. In *The Frontier in American History*, Turner had argued that "the American frontier is sharply distinguished from the European frontier—a fortified boundary line running through dense populations. The most significant thing about the American frontier is, that it lies at the hither edge of free land."[2] The American frontier, according to Turner, is the "outer edge of the wave" of advancing American settlers" (3); there is no other country or nation on the other side of this advancing line. Juricek's main quarrel with Turner is that the latter did not distinguish this late-nineteenth-century use of the word, which Juricek confirms, from the substantially different usage of the preceding three hundred years of colonial and early-national history, when "the term 'Indian Country' meant a territory which the Anglo-Americans recognized as belonging to an Indian 'nation' by natural right."[3] The American narratives I look at in this chapter belong to the period during which Americans began to believe that what lay on the other side of the frontiers was not other countries (albeit ones that might be subordinated to American policies) but Turner's "free land." My research confirms Juricek's finding that the sense of the West as "free" or "empty" land is a phenomenon of the early to mid-nineteenth century.[4]

Before looking at examples of far western discovery accounts in which this change can be observed, however, I should like briefly to discuss an eighteenth-century Anglo-American narrative that resembles those of the British fur trade in recognizing the inhabitants of the lands traveled through but in which the conflict between European agricultural settlers and Indian inhabitants is evident. *Observations on the Inhabitants, Climate, Soil, Rivers, Productions, Animals, and Other Matters Worthy of Notice Made by Mr. John Bartram, in his Travels from Pensilvania to Onondago, Oswego and the Lake Ontario, in Canada* (1751) recounts Bartram's 1743 journey with Conrad Weiser through Pennsylvania and New York as far as Fort Oswego on Lake Ontario. Published in England, *Observations* includes a preface, seemingly written in England by someone other than Bartram, that links Bartram's journey to the struggle between England and France in North America: "We are indebted to our most dangerous rivals for the little we do know [about the interior of the continent], who will, if possible, repay themselves by excluding us from all we do not actually cultivate."[5] The writer has French expeditions on the Mississippi and the upper Great Lakes in mind, and it is into this context of continental strategic thinking that he places Bartram's journey:

> Knowledge must precede a settlement, and when Pensilvania and Virginia shall have extended their habitations to the branches of the Mississippi that water these provinces, on the west side of the Blue Mountains, we may reasonably hope to insure a safe and easy communication with the most remote known parts of North America, and to secure the possession of a dominion unbounded by any present discoveries. (iii)

Bartram himself is much less grand in the scope of his rhetoric, but the steady stream of topographical description, his primary mode of conveying his progress, highlights features in terms of their potential usefulness to Euro-American settlers. One example among the many possible reads as follows:

> Now we came to most excellent level ground, than which nothing can be more fruitful, full of tall timber, sugar, maple, birch,

linden, ash, and beech, and shrubs, as opulus, green maple, horn-
beam, mama m elis [*sic*], solamum, goosberries and red currants
triphilum in abundance. Here we dined by a pleasant creek and
choice land. After dinner we soon began to mount up a pretty
steep hill, covered with oak, birch, ash, and higher up abundance
of chestnut and some hickery. This is middling land, the produce
the same for three miles as our land bears with us. It lies very
high, and when cleared will have an extensive prospect of fertile
vales on all sides. (35)

Bartram's interest in the land's potential value to agricultural settlements contributes on a somewhat smaller scale to the imperial planning
that is set forth in the preface to *Observations*. It was commonplace
during this period to contrast the self-sufficiency and growth of the
English colonies with the dependency and demographic marginality of
New France, while at the same time noting how the French had charted
the interior of the continent and extended the fur trade to the Rocky
Mountains, whereas the English seemed content to huddle near the
coast. In this context, Bartram's agricultural vision is directly related to
a vision of what the English colonies' strength had been and upon what
they would base their future growth. Bartram's account is, in other
words, clearly expansionist.

At the same time, however, Bartram's account also registers the
inhabited character of the lands through which he traveled, even though
he does not ultimately seem to regard these inhabitants as insuperable
obstacles to further English settlements. Bartram travels with Delaware
guides, who "were perfectly acquainted with that part of the country,
and being of the six Nations, they were both a credit and protection"
(17). Their route lies along the way between what Bartram calls a series
of "Indian towns," and even between these towns, Bartram's typical
topography registers the local history: "Our way . . . lay through an
old Indian field of excellent soil, where there had been a town, the
principal footsteps of which are peach-trees, plumbs and excellent grapes"
(19). Arriving at "Onondago," they descend "into the fine vale where
this capital (if I may so call it) is situated" (40). Bartram includes several
stories told to him by his guides having to do with the local history of
the places through which they pass. He makes frequent mention of the
houses at which they are entertained with food, noting with approval
that he and his party were the beneficiaries of long-standing traditions

of hospitality (15). Bartram ends his narrative "by reflecting on their manners, their complexion so different from ours, and their Traditions: this led me to conjecture at their origin, or whence they came into America, and at what time" (74). The exploration narratives of this period often reserved the last pages, after the story of the journey had been told, for some such general discussion of the peoples through whose lands the traveler had passed. Bartram's way of introducing his discussion of the history and customs of the people he met encapsulates both his sense of having traveled through foreign countries, not empty space, and his vision of a future founded on a change of ownership: he refers to his "journey into the heart of a country, still in the possession of it's [sic] original inhabitants" (74).

Despite some rhetorical strategies that tend to abstract space from history, *Observations* is both the story of Bartram's growing acquaintance with these "original inhabitants" and the story of the Anglo-Americans who would displace them from the countries through which Bartram's narrative takes us. From the point of view of the narrator and reader, the interests of the native inhabitants and those of the Anglo-Americans are clearly at odds. This opposition of interests is registered in the text, and there is no rhetorical or narrative solution offered. The resolution of this conflict, as far as Bartram is concerned, will be a matter for historical events. In this sense, Bartram's *Observations* exemplifies "the intersection of ethnic diversity with property allocation" that Patricia Limerick says "unifies Western history," and Bartram's projection of a Euro-American sense of property onto the Six Nations' lands through which he travels seems very close to the way Limerick defines "conquest" as far as the American West was concerned:

> Conquest involved the drawing of lines on a map, the definition and allocation of ownership . . . , and the evolution of land from matter to property. . . . Western history has been an ongoing competition for legitimacy—for the right to claim for oneself and sometimes for one's group the status of legitimate beneficiary of Western resources.[6]

In keeping with his relatively low estimate of Indian societies, Bartram appears to have no doubts that subsequent events will put English farmers in charge of the "rich bottoms" that he includes in his inventory, but for the moment the incompatible claims embodied in his narrative remain unresolved. This confidence makes Limerick's "conquest" seem the appropriate term here, one with which Bartram would be unlikely to quarrel. Nevertheless, despite his sense of superiority, Bartram, like Hearne, Henry, and Mackenzie, recognizes that there are conflicting claims.

American western narratives of the first half of the nineteenth century begin to project a different relationship with the lands through which their writers traveled, and we can see in them some of the changes in thinking that led to a sense of the frontier as the threshold of an unbounded region of "virgin land" in which individual Americans could operate more or less freely. There is little sense that Frémont in the 1840s was traveling in foreign countries, despite the fact that, like most other travelers in America, he met many different groups of its native inhabitants. Somehow, by this time, Indians were no longer a part of what was discovered in America, and the far western lands, despite their dramatic, difficult, or downright alienating topography were immanently part of the "America" these travelers brought with them. This new relationship with discovered lands was only just beginning to emerge in the Lewis and Clark *History*, however, where trans-Mississippi lands are the site of the same collision between aboriginal and Euro-American peoples that figures in Bartram's *Observations*, but where signs of a new rhetorical strategy for representing this archetypical American conflict are nonetheless evident.

The American discovery narrative of the nineteenth century is the product of a different kind of author, who had a different relationship with the sponsoring institutions of the United States than the British and Anglo-American colonial writers had with the analogous institutions of their day. We have discussed the relatively humble circumstances of Hearne, Henry, Mackenzie, and their peers in the fur trade. It is worth mentioning in this connection that the author of the preface to Bartram's *Observations* calls it a "misfortune to the publick, that this ingenious person had not a literal [sic] education, . . . and that his style is not so clear as we could wish," recalling the kinds of apologies that the fur trade writers wrote on their own behalf and indicating similarly that Bartram was beholden to better-educated and better-placed patrons.[7]

The Americans who undertook the government-sponsored expeditions of the early nineteenth century and later wrote about them, came from relatively privileged positions in their society and were much more overtly identified with the ideology and public institutions of the new nation than either the British fur trade authors or John Bartram, despite the latter's eventual renown as a botanist. Meriwether Lewis and William Clark were the sons of substantial landed Virginia families. Lewis was President Jefferson's private secretary before he undertook to lead the expedition up the Missouri. Clark was the younger brother of General George Rogers Clark, leader of the revolutionary army against the British and their Indian allies in the Ohio and Illinois regions. Lewis received scientific and technical training from the faculty of the University of Pennsylvania prior to departing on his expedition. Neither Lewis nor Clark was really dependent on his army pay in order to live. Stephen Long, leader of an expedition to the Rocky Mountains in 1820, was a graduate of Dartmouth College, an army engineer and sometime teacher at West Point. One of his companions on that expedition, Edwin James, who actually wrote the published account, was a medical doctor with considerable scientific training. Zebulon Pike, who led and wrote the accounts of expeditions to the sources of the Mississippi and to the southern Rockies was the son of a general in the revolutionary army. Though Pike was not particularly well educated, he managed to teach himself military tactics, elementary science and mathematics, as well as Spanish and French. John Charles Frémont earned a B.A. degree from the College of Charleston, obtained a post as teacher of mathematics to navy midshipmen, and later was commissioned in the U.S. Corps of Topographical Engineers. He accompanied the famous French scientist and explorer, Joseph Nicollet, on one of his expeditions to the plateau between the Missouri and Mississippi rivers. He was further trained by Nicollet in topography, navigation, and the natural sciences. Frémont married Jessie Benton, daughter of enthusiastic westerner Senator Thomas Hart Benton, and collaborated with the senator on various western ventures.

The type of narrative the American explorers wrote was also influenced by the authors' official connections as army officers with the federal government and its western policymakers. Whatever their personal needs and ambitions, they all undertook their travels at the behest and expense of the United States government, the primary reason for their entering unknown territory being the execution of government policy, not the pursuit of personal or commercial goals. Lewis and Clark traveled with letters of recommendation in Jefferson's own hand; they and the later United States explorers were authorized to treat with Indian groups and to assert the United States's territorial claims in the face of British and Spanish competition.

The American explorer's personal background and his official connection with government policy were reflected in the personality and tone he assumed as a narrator. In recounting the story of his travels, the typical American explorer kept in mind that he was representing the American government and that his actions and the results of his expedition were open to the view of officials, politicians, and United States citizens. It is not surprising then that the narrator assumed, and rarely relinquished, an official character consistent with his military rank and his status as a governmental envoy.

As the nineteenth-century American explorer's presence in unknown territory was the result of governmental direction, so his entry into the domain of literary and scientific discourse was a fulfillment of another official requirement: to record and publish what he observed. In fact the matter and manner were prescribed in considerable detail at the outset. Jefferson instructs Meriwether Lewis that: "Your observations are to be taken with great pains and accuracy; to be entered distinctly and intelligibly for others as well as yourself."[8] Furthermore, several copies of all notes, including one on birchbark, are to be made, "to guard . . . against the accidental losses to which they will be exposed" (xxvii). Similar instructions show up in the orders of Pike and Long. John C. Calhoun, the secretary of war at the time of the Long expedition, instructed Long that "the object of the Expedition, is to acquire as thorough and accurate knowledge as may be practicable, of a portion of our country, which is daily becoming more interesting, but which is as yet imperfectly known. With this view, you will permit nothing worthy of notice to escape your attention."[9]

In addition to their strategic interest in such information, officials such as Calhoun and Jefferson intended that the general public should share the results of these explorations. Thus Jefferson—in the same prefatory note that included his initial instructions—recounts how the return of Lewis and Clark to St. Louis on September 23, 1806, excited more joy than had any similar event in the United States. "The humblest of its citizens," he says, "had taken a lively interest in the issue of the journey, and looked forward with impatience for the information [the published journal] would furnish."[10] Similarly, though not quite reaching out to the "humblest of citizens," the compiler of the Long *Account* avers that "our design had been to present a compendious account of the labors of the Exploring Party, and such of their discoveries as were thought likely to gratify a liberal curiosity."[11]

Fortunately, the American expeditions included some of the resources required to fulfill such intentions. Although the Lewis and Clark party bordered on starvation throughout much of its journey, it was yet a large, well-supplied group compared to Mackenzie's or any of the other earlier British expeditions. Because their expeditions were relatively well equipped, the writers of the American narratives compiled a lot of detailed information, so their accounts, especially those of Lewis and Clark and of Long, are longer than the earlier British ones, and their observations are arranged in better-established categories. Lewis's training in the natural sciences and Long's specialist observers were responsible for the most detailed scientific reporting of the four narratives discussed here.[12] With the exception of Pike, who baldly states that he had neither the "education nor taste" for the pursuit of botany or zoology, the authors of the American accounts include, without apology, lengthy sections of relatively technical description, and they apparently regarded such passages as fulfilling an aspect of their official duties. With the possible exception of Pike, they could not explain away skimpy scientific reporting with their British counterparts' caveat that science had not been part of their purpose in setting out.

As the official representatives of a young, growing nation, the narrators of the American exploration accounts projected a different personality from that in contemporary narratives by the British fur traders with whom they competed in the West. While the latter certainly betrayed no desire to sell themselves short, they did not see themselves as the official representatives of king and country, with a need to behave in an exemplary manner on all fronts. The Americans, in contrast, regarded themselves as models or embodiments of what the young country was capable of bringing to the lands and peoples of the western territory, and they felt a need to reward their countrymen's expectations when they wrote of their undertakings. The following, for example, is what Jefferson said of his protégé Lewis in the "Memoir" he wrote for the beginning of Lewis and Clark's *History*:

Of courage undaunted; possessing a firmness and perseverance of purpose which nothing but impossibilities could divert from its direction; careful as a father of those committed to his charge, yet steady in the maintenance of order and discipline; intimate with the Indian character, customs, and principles; habituated to the hunting life; guided by exact observation of the vegetables and animals of his own country, against losing time in the description of objects already possessed; honest, disinterested, liberal, of sound understanding, and a fidelity to truth so scrupulous that whatever he should report would be as certain as if seen by ourselves—with all these qualifications, as if selected and implanted by nature in one body for this express purpose, I could have no hesitation in confiding the enterprise to him.[13]

A similar ideal, if from a perhaps less trustworthy source, is conjured up in this publisher's characterization of John C. Frémont:

Possessed of more than an average share of bodily vigor, and mental energy and capacity; qualified by scientific attainments, and an ardent love of nature; and imbued with a taste for investigating the arcana of the mineral, vegetable, and animal kingdoms, firm, yet conciliatory in his intercourse; modest, yet dignified in his manners; utterly regardless of self, but feelingly alive to the comforts, the rights and the privileges of others; blending the decision and the vigor of a strict disciplinarian, with the kindness and consideration of a friend, to all who shared with him the perils and privations of his arduous journeyings—with this combination of qualities, his success is not to be wondered at. Seldom have so many accessories to success been united in the leader of such expeditions.[14]

It is important to recognize in these descriptions that the ideal nineteenth-century American explorer is not only capable of "investigating the arcana of the mineral, vegetable, and animal kingdoms"—of getting results, so to speak—but of doing so in a seemly and honorable way, in keeping with the public ideals of his sponsors. When he composed his narrative, the American military explorer kept in mind that he was an exemplary character, often portraying himself as a representative citizen of the nation. The following, for example, is from Frémont's narrative of his 1842 expedition:

Yesterday evening we reached our encampment at Rock Independence. . . . Here, not unmindful of the custom of early travellers and explorers in our country, I engraved on this rock of the Far West a symbol of the Christian faith. . . . It stands amidst the names of many who have long since found their way to the grave, and for whom the huge rock is a giant gravestone. . . . I obeyed the feeling of early travellers, and left the impression of the cross deeply engraved on the vast rock one thousand miles beyond the Mississippi, to which discoverers have given the national name of *Rock Independence!* (71–72)

Focusing on the cross and "Rock Independence" as symbols, Frémont aligns himself with the self-conscious Christianity and republicanism of the nineteenth-century United States, presenting his trip west as a part of a general movement of these values into the western territories. Frémont and the other American explorer/writers try not only to introduce the new lands and peoples to readers back home but also to show how, in their persons, the values of United States society are being manifested in territory whose cultural relation to the states was still largely putative in the early 1800s.

These writers anticipated a continental empire, but then so did Mackenzie and even John Bartram and his anonymous editor. But Mackenzie's empire did not require, or even favor, large-scale settlement of the distant lands of his travels, and for Bartram the settlement of the Six Nations lands of his *Observations* remained the project of an unspecific future, while, for the present, they were the countries of their first peoples. Frémont, by contrast, went west thinking of himself as part of an impending mass movement. Earlier colonial and British narrators' adventures occur in alien lands that none but a handful of readers will ever see, whereas the Americans describe experiences in lands that they believe are immanently, and will soon be actually, part of the average American reader's world. If the British narrators' experiences are remarkable because they are exotic and unique, the Americans' claim the reader's attention by proclaiming themselves both unprecedented and typically American.

Thus, whereas earlier narratives are plotted as round-trips, there is a strong tendency in those of nineteenth-century America not to distinguish between "home" and what lay beyond the western frontier. Traveling west was not so much a journey into foreign lands as a trip into the future of the United States. Manifest Destiny, a phrase from the 1840s, expresses this collapsing of spatial and temporal distinctions in the way it makes the nation's "destiny"—something of the future— somehow real or manifest—that is, present—to contemporary observers. Lee Clark Mitchell notes how in the nineteenth century this sense of the western continent came to be a part of American identity: "Americans felt more than a proprietary interest in the continent. . . . The land formed a kind of collective self-extension, defining Americans even as it continued to be defined by them."[15] While Samuel Hearne may have seen some future for the Hudson's Bay Company in the barren-ground regions he explored, he in no sense imagined them as the future home of the English people. And while Mackenzie focused on the potential usefulness of his route to the Pacific, he thought of it only as a new conduit for the existing trade involving England, North America, and the Far East. In his mind, this route would remain a passage among foreign peoples, however subservient to the purposes of trade they might become.

In nineteenth-century American narratives, journeys are on the verge of becoming one-way. Rather than representing exotic experiences with regions forever beyond the threshold of the common reader's experience, they suggest that the traveler is pushing this threshold ahead of him on a journey that thus represents national expansion into the lands visited. Early national narratives invite the nation to move with the narrator, making his actions prototypes for the actions of the countrymen who will follow and his experience one that will be relived historically and with the same meaning. One should note in this regard that all the explorers discussed here—except for Pike, who was killed in the War of 1812—remained in the West after their journeys were over: Lewis as governor of Louisiana, Clark as Indian agent and then governor of the Missouri Territory, Long on further exploring and engineering projects, and Frémont as a landowner and politician in California and Arizona. These four lived out their lives and made their fortunes in the "unknown territory" they initially undertook to explore. They did not realize the fruits of the journey by returning to the metropolitan hub; rather, they saw its main significance in the initial westward movement. In place of a plot of liminality that expressed a society's sense of its own (present) limits, Euro-American explorers began to construct a plot of identity in which traveling Americans discovered themselves in the lands beyond the western frontier and in which the native peoples of the west played increasingly marginal roles.

Lewis and Clark's *History:* The Search for Authority

The *History of the Lewis and Clark Expedition* (1814) was assembled by Nicholas Biddle mainly from the journals and records of the two commanders. It is a complex document, in terms both of how it was derived from its journal sources and of how it undertook to mediate the westering ideology of its American audience and the western conditions encountered by Lewis and Clark. The second complexity is the subject of this essay, but the first, the complexity of the text's creation, needs to be explained briefly for my approach to the *History* as a document to be understood.

The Biddle *History* was the only published account based on the two commanders' journals available during most of the nineteenth century.[16] Consequently, except for the few who had seen the holograph journals, people only knew of the explorers' experiences and achievements through Biddle's collation and abridgement of the expedition records, and, as Gary E. Moulton, editor of the recent *Journals of the Lewis and Clark Expedition,* points out, "Many readers believed that in it they were reading the actual journals of the captains."[17] Biddle, however, omitted much of the scientific information contained in the journals, although it was conventional, even in narrative accounts, to include it, but he retained the journal format in which the narrative proceeds day by day and is divided into sections headed by a date. According to Moulton, Biddle is credited with scrupulous accuracy when he summarized and rewrote (37), and in many sections, especially when he is following Lewis's entries, his version is taken almost verbatim from his source. Both Lewis and Clark habitually used the plural "we," referring variably to the two commanders and to the whole group, so Biddle, who retained the first person plural, could mask his shifts back and forth between the journals of the original writers. (In fact, Moulton's account of Lewis and Clark's journal-keeping methods reveals such extensive collaborating and copying between the two that it seems clear they had a collective sense of their reportorial function [8–34].) The result is an oddly impersonal but nonetheless fairly unified narrative voice, one that keeps the experience of traveling in the foreground and has invited many readers' imaginative participation in the progress of the expedition. The continuity of this voice and its attendant point of view is largely Biddle's creation, but its character clearly derives from the events, factual details, and occasional personal reactions recorded in the journals themselves. Despite the complexity of the *History*'s creation, I think it is fair to say that, for its original audience especially, it was presented and perceived as the coherent story of the two leaders' journey, their representation of themselves in relation to the lands and peoples they encountered.[18] I refer in some places to the original journals, but my main concern is the text that nineteenth-century readers knew.[19]

The *History*'s mediation of westering ideology and western experience is guided and propelled by the military, diplomatic, scientific, economic, and symbolic errands with which the authors were charged. Moreover, underlying such specific categories of responsibility was the pervasive sense that these men were approaching the republic's future as they departed into western space. Jefferson's projected information-gathering expedition, although planned before the Louisiana Purchase, took on even greater political importance after that clear signal of the nation's western designs. But predating this legal claim to lands west of the Mississippi, there are many indications that the Pacific Ocean was seen as the natural boundary of the republic and that Euro-Americans imagined themselves in the West more as the result of an unfolding of, than an addition to, the nation, that they anticipated not a transformation but an expansion of their polity.[20] In a 1786 letter, for example, Jefferson asserts that "our confederacy must be viewed as the nest from which all America, North and South, is to be peopled."[21] Presumably Americans anticipated something like what Timothy Dwight prophesied in *Greenfield Hill* (1794): that there would be "white spires . . . imaged on the wave" after America's "sons across the mainland roam; / And claim on far Pacific shores their home."[22] "Roam" is rather a casual verb to denote the taking possession of an entire continent—Dwight apparently envisioned few obstacles—and "claim," as opposed to "make" or "build," suggests that the "home" already in some sense existed and only awaited taking up.[23]

To say that the Lewis and Clark expedition both grew out of and served the view that the ultimate boundaries of nation and continent were congruent is not to make any new claim for Lewis and Clark. If anything, subsequent commentary on their journey has magnified its historical significance by routinely locating it within a national teleology in which their "first sight" of the western lands began the process that culminated in statehood within the federation.[24] Lewis and Clark have become icons of an America at last ready to discover itself; they are seen both as acting for the nation and as individuals identified with the nation, which, through them, is in turn identified with the land it was undertaking to incorporate. Yet the habit of identifying continental America and the discovering American tends to conceal the tenuousness and difficulty of Lewis and Clark's relationship with western lands and peoples and the conflicts and contradictions that permeate their report. Reading the *History* with the ensuing decades of conflict among the United States, British, Spanish, and Indian competitors in mind, one is able to recover something of how difficult it then was to write a narrative that would fulfill these kinds of national expectations. The Lewis and Clark expedition was more or less successful, depending on how one defines its goals, but despite its achievements, the *History* did not manage univocally to prophesy the realization of the United States's continental errand, even though it is full of evidence that such a story is what its authors would have liked to have told, and even though subsequent generations have tended to view their report in these terms. The author/heroes of the *History*, in trying to be the American people's proxies in the West, ended up displaying in a particularly vivid way the contradictions inherent in Euro-Americans' developing imperialist relationship with the continent, and in this sense their narrative is a valuable resource for understanding an ideology that later would assume a much more coherent literary expression. The Lewis and Clark legend, as opposed to the *History*, is a particularly clear example of what Wayne Franklin calls "those bland fictions which later generations . . . have projected onto earlier times." "Too often," Franklin argues, the "plotting of the American past . . . stresses the abiding realization of original design," eliding "the plain discontinuities, the terminations of American experience."[25] The *History* itself, by contrast, retains clear evidence of the discontinuities and terminations that were part of Euro-American expansion into the West, terminations not only of indigenous ways of life but of modes of Euro-American experience, which gave way as a dominant western rhetoric emerged.

It is important to distinguish between contradictions in the way

Euro-Americans understood the West and the actual conflicts that arose in the course of establishing their presence. Their conflicts were very like those of other Europeans expanding into inhabited lands, but their contradictions were particular to their own sense of destiny. The conflicts stemmed from the United States's competition with Britain, Spain, the descendants of the French, and most importantly, the Indian peoples present in the West for control of land. The *History* itself, as an official publication, was an assertion of the United States's presence and power; it was also an account of many instances in which that presence and power were wielded against groups with conflicting claims. In this sense, it typified accounts of numerous contemporary American and British expeditions that understandably met with resistance. The overt or implied story of most such accounts of early expeditions to the West is the surmounting of obstacles, both natural and human, to the imperial ambitions of the sponsoring society. Conflict is a normal part of these accounts, and thus when we read of Lewis and Clark prevailing over the Sioux[26] or of Alexander Mackenzie evading the violent designs of villagers on his route through the Bella Coola valley,[27] our responses are guided by our knowledge of both imperialist politics and literary conventions. Our view of the history of the continent and our sense of literary convention lead us to expect the resolution of these conflicts through the use of the European's superior power.

The contradictions in the way Euro-Americans imagined the West, however, could not be resolved through action. As both Jefferson's and Dwight's comments suggest, many thought it natural that Euro-Americans would inhabit the West. For many, it was already in some sense American, and increasing contact with the land would make manifest a condition that was as yet but immanent.[28] Actual conflict over possession, however, raised doubts about this fundamental identification with the land, doubts that did not necessarily disappear after physical possession had been secured. The very existence of conflict contradicted the underlying assumption of American identification with continental integrity, that the land was a vacant entity waiting to be discovered. History could not proceed as a development of this identity of people and place if the process itself turned up evidence that conflicted with its assumptions. Because the Lewis and Clark *History* presented a remarkably copious and conscientious inventory of the West, more evidence than any other American exploration narrative provided that the western continent was a mosaic of peoples and not an empty landscape, it embodies the contradiction at the heart of American continentalist ideology.

In this discussion of how the Lewis and Clark *History* functions as a text, this contradiction can be construed as a problem of authority, as, in fact, one voice competing with another for influence. Cultural contradictions are internal to the individual as well as to his society, so the resolution of competing authorities is a matter of choosing the voice that is somehow more fundamental and reliable as a basis for one's sense of integrity and direction. American explorers needed to be able to establish how, as Americans, they were entitled to assert their claims on western lands. As writers, perhaps more than as men of action, they confronted directly the complexities of the relationship between their subject (the lands they explored) and their audience (the society that sponsored their travels). They needed to find a way of speaking that would allow them to proclaim most effectively the link between "unknown territory" and themselves, their sponsors, and their readers.

The conflict inherent in any imperial initiative required that the recounting of officially sanctioned exploration demonstrate clearly the writer's authority. Without such authority, the writer's ability to portray his assertion of power in what were by definition unknown territories was compromised, and heroic action in the face of resistance appeared as simply foolhardy or selfish individualism.[29] In part to establish its historical authority in the terms Hegel described,[30] the typical exploration narrative of the period was dedicated to a respected public figure, prefaced by copies of the traveler's instructions, and clearly identified with an official sponsoring government or legally constituted body such as the Hudson's Bay Company.[31] It was as an agent of such public figures and institutions that the explorer was able to act aggressively in what were—and until the mid-nineteenth century were consistently portrayed as—inhabited lands. The exploration narrative's conventional "I" speaks from faraway lands as the sanctioned representative of its audience and expects to be judged according to public criteria. The rhetoric of the exploration narrative asserts a relationship between the sponsoring group or society and what is being explored in which the former's power is seen to be both effective and legitimate.

Logistically and politically, the Lewis and Clark expedition was very ambitious, and for that reason alone its authority was very unstable.

Only Alexander Mackenzie's party was known previously to have crossed
the continent north of Spanish territory, but as a fur trader acting more
or less as a private citizen, Mackenzie could not really be said to have
had a nation behind him as Lewis and Clark had. Even with such
backing, Lewis and Clark's assertion of the United States's relation to
the Far West strained even the traditionally hyperbolic rhetoric of
European exploration writing. As self-conscious representatives of a
self-conscious new society, their presence in the West bristled with
possibilities, and they invoked every means to buttress their authority.
Because the United States's claims on these western lands were so large,
yet Euro-Americans' presence in them so recent, the explorers' presentation of the sponsoring society's relation to the western lands and
peoples is remarkably variable, even contradictory. The first-person
"we" suggests coherence in the explorers' point of view, but the text in
fact shows us different and unreconcilable modes of linking Euro-American society and the western territories that harbor the contradiction at
the core of American national life: whereas the explorer turned to his
role as representative of national institutions to authorize his interven-
tion in the western countries, the nation itself was turning increasingly
to its sense of identity with the western lands to justify its authority. A
circular pattern of institutions existing to discover the basis of their own
being thus emerges.

In spite of the first-person voice and chronological plotting typical of
the travel adventure narrative, there is nothing of the picaresque in
Lewis and Clark. Their *History* is a solid thatch of purposes and responsibilities. I have identified four modes of discovery rhetoric, defining
each in terms of the authority it invokes. The first mode invokes the
official authority arising from their sponsorship by a nation. In this
mode, Lewis and Clark undertake to show themselves advancing their
country's legitimate interests in the West. In a second mode, they
present themselves as servants of scientific knowledge, disinterested
data gatherers relying on the authority of European categories of learning to impose order on western lands and peoples. A third mode of
authority develops from Lewis and Clark's reporting of their exchanges
with western peoples, what I have called their "local" authority. Last,
and less conventionally, Lewis and Clark speak from their feelings about
the landscape, invoking their own aesthetic responses as an authority
for their presence in what they know are inhabited lands. I shall argue

that this rhetoric of personal, primarily aesthetic, appropriation becomes privileged because it offers a way of obviating the conflict between imperial authority over the land and the cooperative relationship Lewis and Clark developed with local peoples during their twenty-nine months in the West.

However, the earliest and clearest basis upon which to approach western lands and peoples was the official. Captains Lewis and Clark led a military expedition and were authorized to treat with the Indian peoples they encountered, and in their writing they go to some trouble to show themselves behaving as empowered envoys. They record, for example, that on July 22, 1804, "we camped [on the Missouri, ten miles from the mouth of the Platte] intending to make the requisite observations, and to send for the neighboring tribes, for the purpose of making known the recent change in the government [from French to American], and the wish of the United States to cultivate their friendship."[32] At the subsequent meeting with six chiefs of the Ottoes and the Missouris, the entire Lewis and Clark party "paraded for the occasion. A speech was then made announcing to them the change of government, our promise of protection, and advice as to their future conduct" (65). Lewis and Clark never show themselves slighting the formalities on such occasions or understating their authority. From such a basis, they feel secure in characterizing western peoples in terms of their friendliness or hostility, their potential usefulness in trade, their amenability to settled patterns of land tenure, and their attachment to competing European powers. The explorers had clear instructions to assert United States legal authority in Louisiana, and their narrative makes such assertions unequivocally.

An equally clear basis of authority lay in their roles as natural scientists and ethnographers. The collection of scientific data had long been understood as part of the explorer's role, and formalized categories of knowledge had been established to organize the traveler's reporting.[33] Whatever the immediate economic or political motives of the venture, scientific description was an accepted mode of reporting and an implicit assertion of the traveler's power over lands and peoples. Jefferson carefully defined Lewis's responsibilities to science in his written instructions to him, insisting that his observations were "to be taken with great pains and accuracy; to be entered distinctly and intelligibly for others as well as yourself."[34] Lewis was to observe and record the longitude and latitude of the places visited; the possessions, relations, languages, traditions, monuments, occupations, food, clothing, shelter, diseases, moral and physical circumstances, laws, customs, dispositions, commerce, morality, and religion of the peoples who inhabited the western countries; the soil and face of the country; the growth and vegetation; animal life; remains of extinct animals; mineral productions; volcanic appearances; and climate (xxvii–xxviii).[35] These instructions were referred to by later American explorers as a model of how to conceive of their role.

The linkage of knowledge and power is especially apparent in the *History's* ethnographic observations, and the writers did not really try to disguise it. Whereas later anthropological writing would shift toward a stance of disinterested objectivity, the political context of Lewis and Clark's ethnography is explicit.[36] Thus Jefferson ends his list of ethnological categories by asserting "the interest which every nation has in extending and strengthening the authority of reason and justice among the people around them," concluding that knowledge of these people "may better enable those who may endeavor to civilize and instruct them, to adapt their measures to the [people's] existing notions and practices."[37] For example, the narrative up to the expedition's winter with the Mandans on the upper Missouri contains frequent mentions of land "susceptible of cultivation" or "better calculated for farms," as well as of sites for trading forts, towns, and mills, and the explorers used the extent to which Indian groups relied on agriculture as a rough index of the difficulty they would present to United States citizens moving west (5, 28, 30, 35, 117). Indian peoples who stayed in one place could be isolated and avoided. The Mandans, who lived in semipermanent villages and who relied to some degree on corn and vegetables, presented few problems. Similarly, the Osages, "residing . . . in villages, and having made considerable advance in agriculture [are] less addicted to war" (12); but the "Kaninaviesch [an offshoot of the Pawnee nation] . . . have degenerated from the improvements of the parent tribe, and no longer live in villages" (57).

While considering an agricultural life as a possible future for the Missouri peoples, Lewis and Clark also, less optimistically, adverted to the widely held view that Indian societies in general faced inevitable decline. The Missouri section of the journey seemed to provide abundant support for this notion. "The history of the Mandans . . . illustrates more than that of any other nation the unsteady movements and tottering fortunes of the American Indians" (196–197). Similarly, the story of the "Chayennes [*sic*] . . . is the short and melancholy relation of the calamities of almost all the Indians" (147). The reasons for the "tottering fortunes" and the "calamities" are left unspecified, although Lewis and Clark certainly knew that they and their countrymen were deeply implicated. Yet here and elsewhere their descriptions of Indian cultures show a strong tendency to coalesce around theories that view their decline as inevitable and the whole process as a natural rather than a political phenomenon.

The United States's legal claims and the conventions of ethnology and the natural sciences are Lewis and Clark's securest sources of authority. The rhetorics of legal and of scientific authority were both powerful tools for objectifying inhabitants of the West and controlling, indeed minimizing, their status in the land. Writing in these rhetorics alone, the traveler could present the peoples as well as the places and resources of the West as the subject matter of a report, rather than as participants in a dialogue (or even a dispute).

Lewis and Clark's portrait of their interaction with western peoples is, however, much more complex than these two rhetorics alone would allow. They recorded much more about their relations with western inhabitants than they were able to categorize legally or scientifically, for a great deal of their time was spent on the day-to-day business of feeding, moving, and directing their party, in all of which they relied heavily on local peoples for advice and material assistance. Their expedition's success owed much to their ability to drop their diplomatic and ethnological tools and communicate in local terms about matters that were, first of all, local. We can isolate a third rhetoric for the recording of practical interactions with local peoples. It is characterized by a sense of time and a set of goals that are comprehensible to native inhabitants. The categories of this rhetoric derive from the local context, in contrast to the Washington-centered views that subordinate the Mandans in the binational agreement negotiated between Washington and Madrid or group them ethnologically with other peoples, perhaps unknown to them, who shared similar religious ideas. This rhetoric of the local context engages the inhabitants in the next step of the expedition and thereby shows the expedition reconciling its goals to indigenous logic and experience, recording progress more in terms of movement from village to village than in terms of natural landmarks. It is in this local mode that we see Lewis and Clark getting where they want to go, especially after they leave behind the navigable waters of the Missouri that allowed them to carry provisions and equipment in boats and begin the journey on foot and horseback during which they were almost entirely dependent on local supplies.[38]

Once Lewis and Clark reach the village of the Shoshones, cross the divide, and enter the Columbia River valley, the terrain becomes difficult and unfamiliar and the food scarce, causing the travelers to enter into close relations with many groups. Whereas their relation to the tribes of the Missouri suggested a stable hierarchy, their interactions with the peoples of the Columbia were much more volatile and, at times, dangerous. As a small isolated party, Lewis and Clark were dependent on the Columbians as trading partners. They had to adapt themselves to the local customs and economy, making the most of whatever advantage their weapons and trade goods offered in order to gain a passage through the western countries. They describe the lives and culture of the Columbia Indians largely in terms of their commerce. Game from the mountains, fish from the rivers, roots and vegetables from the meadows, European manufactures from the ships at the river mouth, all circulated in a system of exchange that both linked and distinguished the dozens of villages along the river valley. The explorers express surprise at the ubiquity and complexity of Indian commerce, and they complain several times that they "are never freed from the visits of the natives" (935). Nonetheless, they render a very thorough account of the commerce's workings, and they habitually include trading patterns in their accounts of particular groups of residents.[39]

Their gratitude for such welcome as they receive is now directed more toward people than toward an abstract sense of nature's bounty, as it had been in the lush foothills east of the mountains. In numerous instances, Lewis and Clark express gratitude and affection toward their Indian hosts. They say that the Wallawallas, for example, "of all the Indians whom we have met since leaving the United States, . . . are the most hospitable, honest, and sincere" (980). They are an "honest, worthy people" (978), who graciously render the travelers many services. It seems that Lewis and Clark appreciate these kindnesses the more because they are aware of the fragility of these peoples' limited prosperity. Their relationships develop local contexts and histories.

They observe, for example, upon returning through their lands, that the Wallawallas "seem to have been successful in their hunting during the past winter," for they "are much better clad" than when they saw them previously "(977). The Multnomah women of the Willamette Valley also elicit their sympathy for having in winter to stand chest deep in water in order to gather with their feet the wappatoo root, a valuable staple and the basis of their commerce (929). The leaders of the expedition take pride in always paying in some way for what they receive from local peoples. This insistence, together with their recognition of gifts freely given, is consistent with the spirit of their careful and detailed observations of the way the western peoples lived.

Lewis and Clark's account of the differences among Columbian peoples displays a remarkably sympathetic understanding of their day-to-day life. They never doubt the superiority of their own civilization, but they are long enough in the Indians' worlds and dependent enough on their knowledge and good will to extend credit for many virtues that transcend cultural peculiarities. It is also clear that they appreciated that the arrival of Americans in the West would be a momentous event in the history of each of the region's societies. Few observers since Lewis and Clark have understood to a comparable degree the complexity of human life in this theoretically empty land, and yet these sophisticated interpreters of its native peoples were simultaneously committed prophets of the American destiny in the West. We see both aspects of Lewis and Clark's achievement in the following passage, in which they describe a complex meeting during their return journey:

> We . . . collected the chiefs and warriors and having drawn a map of the relative situation of our country on a mat with a piece of coal, detailed the nature and power of the American nation, its desire to preserve harmony between all its red brethren, and its intention of establishing trading houses for their relief and support. It was not without difficulty, and not till nearly half the day was spent, that we were able to convey all this information to the Chopunnish, much of which might have been lost or distorted in its circuitous route through a variety of languages; for in the first place, we spoke in English to one of our men, who translated it into French to Chaboneau; he interpreted it to his wife in the Minnetaree language; she then put it into Shoshonee, and the young Shoshonee prisoner explained it to the Chopunnish in their

own dialect. At last we succeeded in communicating the impression we wished, and then adjourned the council. (1004–1005)

As the committed envoys of their own society, they deliver the "message," the imperial motive of their journey. In order to carry out their errand, however, they have had to become initiates of the complex world of the western Indians, arranging simultaneous translation through three intermediate languages, and, as initiates, they perhaps understand more of the eventual impact of their message than is comfortable for them.

This third rhetoric implicitly acknowledges what the legal and scientific deny, that the western continent is a mosaic of inhabited lands whose peoples have their own senses of history and destiny independent of that of the United States. Whereas the legal and scientific modes are intended to subordinate western lands and peoples to the United States's vision of itself as a continental nation, the mode of practical exchange portrays a quotidian reality of shared space in which the explorers' actions stem not exclusively from imperial intentions predating their arrival in the west but in part from their exchanges with local peoples. There is no authority for this mode beyond the travelers' presence in the West, and it has the potential to contradict the subordination that is asserted or implied by the other rhetorics. If the legal and scientific modes are intended to extend themselves over the land by means of their authorized spokesmen, the local mode shows these agents developing themselves as alternative authorities and their errand as a thing in itself, taking its definition from its enactment rather than from its design.

The challenge that this local mode offers the official and the scientific is not simply that of new data requiring the alteration of the categories in which they were collected; it implies another basis altogether for imagining the Euro-American relationship with the western continent. The fundamental assumption of the official and scientific modes is that the inherent superiority of Euro-American institutions is to be made manifest through their imposition on the lands and peoples of the western continent. The local mode, however, recognizes the otherness of the western peoples and portrays, if only as a transient thing, Americans in a relationship of near equality with them. This contradiction is not resolved in the narrative. Lewis and Clark do not end by reflecting on how their initial sense of their authority to discover and announce an immanent America to both East and West has been undermined by their two-year relationship with western countries. They do not retreat from the teleology of their original errand. The official, scientific, and local modes of relating to the western continent assert their respective authorities simultaneously, and no synthesis is really possible.

This contradiction, and the political choices it demanded, are to a large extent evaded by another authority for the Euro-American's presence in the West. This fourth mode was independent of both the imperial and the local contexts, and it proposed to transcend the knowledge that two societies could not occupy that same space simultaneously and that the displacement of one by the other involved a denial of one aspect of the Euro-American's experience of his world. This fourth mode of authority places the explorer in direct contact with the land itself. There are no local peoples to direct him through it, and there are no eastern sponsors to tell him what to see in it.

The rhetoric of this mode of authority makes personal testimony to the beauty and grandeur of the land itself into a transcendent authority for the viewer's presence. It has much in common with what Wayne Franklin calls the "discovery account" of the early voyagers, and perhaps, as he suggests, this rhetoric and its attendant pose survive in later narratives as one of the basic tropes of New World writing. Franklin's discoverer stands "before a purely present landscape," that is, one whose history is unknown or suppressed and whose future is therefore available. His discoverer "achieves through perception alone a communion" with an America seen as "a vast emblem of rejuvenation."[40] Such discoveries, of course, acquire new political implications as Europeans begin to settle the land, and in writings of American-born Europeans, this communion comes to denote entitlement, a transcendent authority for claims to the land. Emerson makes such a claim in his notion of "Commodity" as developed in the essay "Nature." Here the "green ball" of the earth is made not only for our "delight" but our "support," and the natural world is a "divine charity" to "nourish man" (83). "Man" here, of course, means Emerson's new man, the person (probably male) capable of experiencing the kind of fundamental delight in himself and in nature that makes him truly at home in America.

This rhetoric develops most clearly in the *History* after Lewis and Clark recommence their journey in the spring of 1805, after the winter spent with the Mandans on the upper Missouri. Whereas the Mandans inhabited a country with a visible history, where there were remains of previous villages and where the current inhabitants were able to recount their past to the visitors who passed the long winter with them, the foothills to the west were only seasonal hunting grounds through which the expedition happened to pass without meeting any hunting parties. "Beyond this," they say shortly after leaving the Mandans, "no white man had ever been except two Frenchmen," setting up their own fitness to see and discover definitively.[41]

Part of this vision of the high prairies of the upper Missouri is in the pastoral mode: "The country," they say, "is beautiful in the extreme" (296). It "presented the usual variety of highlands interspersed with rich plains," that were "level and fertile" (276). Suggestions of an easy grazing life abound. The travelers are surrounded by buffalo "so gentle that the [men] were obliged to drive them out of the way with sticks and stones" (303), elk, and deer, which provide them with plenty of food. They believe that the coat of the buffalo "resembled that of the sheep, except that it was much finer and more soft and silky," and they have no doubt that an "excellent cloth may be made" from it (276). They say that usually "the game . . . is so abundant that we can get without difficulty all that is necessary" (300, 303, 308). Overall it is a country that yields its abundance to the travelers without much struggle, and they seem to relax and expand with the plentiful food, the relatively easy traveling on the river, and the absence of serious resistance to their presence. This is also country that yields itself easily to the travelers' imaginations. The river, in a typical calm stretch above the great falls, seems to offer the abundance of nature to those who follow it: "The Missouri itself stretches to the south in one unruffled stream of water . . . and bearing on its bosom vast flocks of geese; while numerous herds of buffalo are feeding on the plains which surround it" (370). There are no competing siblings at this bountiful "bosom." What they see is all for them.[42]

As they proceed, however, and the river becomes more broken by rapids and the banks steeper and more treacherous, their response to the landscape changes. Pastoral images give way to visions of the sublime; gentle plenty yields to awesome, frightening beauty, and the travelers catch their first view of the "Rock mountains—the object of all [their] hopes, and the reward of all [their] ambition" (328). As rendered in the Biddle text, Lewis's response to the grandeur of the Missouri Breaks, a portion of the river that frequently required the men to tow the canoes while wading up to their armpits in the cold water, is conspicuously aesthetic, in spite of the hardships they suffered there:

> These hills and river-cliffs exhibit a most extraordinary and romantic appearance. They rise in most places nearly perpendicular from the water, to the height of between 200 and 300 feet. . . . In trickling down the cliffs, . . . water has worn the soft sandstone into a thousand grotesque figures, among which, with a little fancy, may be discerned elegant ranges of freestone buildings, with columns variously sculptured, and supporting long and elegant galleries, while the parapets are adorned with statuary. On a nearer approach they represent every form of elegant ruins—columns, some with pedestals and capitals entire, others mutilated and prostrate, and some rising pyramidally over each other till they terminate in a sharp point. These are varied by niches, alcoves, and the customary appearances of desolated magnificence. (338–339)

The self-conscious resort to the vocabulary of art—a terminology rarely used in the narrative—suggests Lewis's powerful personal response and his desire to convey the scene's effects on a civilized observer. This aesthetic response to a natural scene is even more strictly a response of the non-Indian than the pastoral imagery invoked in the foothills. One presumes that Indians, too, could appreciate the fertility and abundance of the land and make use of it in their way. Here, however, the language of artifice, the references to "elegant galleries," "parapets adorned with statuary," to "columns," "pedestals," and "capitals," denotes a perception that only the heirs to Mediterranean civilization could bring to bear on rocks.

In another passage describing the Great Falls of the Missouri, Biddle's version of Lewis's journals suggests the ideological context of his aesthetic: "Seating himself on some rocks under the center of the falls, Lewis enjoyed the sublime spectacle of this stupendous object, which since the creation had been lavishing its magnificence on the desert, unknown to civilization" (365).[43] The word "desert" is a value term, not to be taken literally, for Lewis knows that other people have often seen this same sight. Indeed, this passage highlights the particular meaning of his viewing by positioning Lewis for the sole purpose of taking in the sight; he has detached himself from the party and is exploring the falls alone. Such a moment had not occurred since "the creation," and he seems to feel that his presence begins a new era. That "Indians" and a few "Frenchmen" have seen these falls before only serves to emphasize the significance of Lewis's arrival.

Perhaps the most intense and personal of his encounters with the land, this passage continues as he proceeds upstream past the several cataracts that make up the Great Falls. Conventional references to the beautiful and the sublime continue to mark each encounter with a new sight as a special act of appreciation. The upper cataract, he says, "was indeed beautiful, since, without any of the wild, irregular sublimity of the lower falls, it combined all the regular elegances which the fancy of a painter would select to form a beautiful waterfall" (368–369). Finally, at the head of the falls, Lewis notes what can hardly be an accidental detail: "Here on a cottonwood tree an eagle had fixed her nest, and seemed undisputed mistress of a spot, to contest whose dominion neither man nor beast would venture across the gulfs that surround it, and which is further secured by the mist rising from the falls" (369). The eagle—adopted in 1786 as the central motif of the United States seal—here calls attention to the fullest meaning of Lewis's encounter with the land. It suggests that it is not just a civilized man who has come to fulfill the destiny of the place, but a civilized American, whose totem, the eagle, is also the presiding spirit of the place. The eagle presides like a nurturing goddess over the mutual recognition of man and nature, of American and America.[44]

Lewis later describes the sources of the Missouri as "chaste" and "hidden" because they had "never yet been seen by civilized man."[45] When the travelers drank from it, "they felt themselves rewarded for all their labors and all their difficulties" (484). Here the river is a synecdoche for a land innocent of human associations, even though Lewis knows that it is known to the local inhabitants. The narrative itself offers copious evidence of native peoples' incorporating the land as a part of their culture; Lewis and Clark relied on these peoples for food, information, and transportation, and in other modes of discourse they did not overlook them. Dealing with dozens of Indian groups along their way and documenting their daily exchanges with them, Lewis and Clark required a special rhetoric so that they could also respond to the land as essentially empty, waiting to be discovered.

General and scholarly treatments of the Lewis and Clark narrative have sometimes effaced this conflict over the land when they assess Lewis and Clark's achievement. They see the subsequent course of the western empire in this mode of merely visual contact with the land. Elliott Coues, one of the most important of the narrative's editors and commentators, says in his "Preface to the New Edition" (1893) that when Lewis and Clark made their journey, "none but Indians had navigated the Missouri river to the Yellowstone, and none had navigated the Columbia to the head of the tide-water" (v). That Coues does not equate the Indians' knowledge of these lands with his explorers' vision is made clear when he dedicates his edition to "the people of the Great West" and exhorts them: "Honor the statesmen who foresaw your West. Honor the brave men who first saw your West." For Coues, this first sight is not only a step toward actual possession but a figuration of the whole history of European expansion. "Seeing" the land in his sense obviates the conflict in the historical process through which it came to be part of the United States, even though the conflicting claims of Euro-Americans and Indians are clearly represented in the contradictory modes of the Lewis and Clark *History*. In Coues's preface, we see an excellent example of what Sacvan Bercovitch describes as a trope using a historian to enforce a certain view of the past.[46] What one might call the "first white man to see" trope encapsulates the key ideological features of the teleology. The figure insists on sight as the signifier for imperial possession, in a metaphor that masks the fact that one people's possession is another's dispossession. Yet the color white signals that this sight is laden with significance for subsequent generations. Those who identify themselves as white are meant to see their present dominance on the continent in the succession of white sightings that until fairly recently have constituted our histories of the earlier stages of European expansion into the Americas. Historian John Bakeless, for example, describes his book *The Eyes of Discovery* as "an effort to describe North America as the first white men in each area saw it."[47] This trope is so crucial that Bakeless explains in his preface how even though "the first explorer in each part of the United States often took but a brief glimpse and then departed before putting on record any detailed account of what he saw," one can "fill in a description of what the first arrival must have seen from accounts given by much later and more leisurely travelers." Not knowing what "the first white man" saw, we are required to construct it. Coues's and Bakeless's sense of what Lewis and Clark saw is not unusual in western historiography, but it is a simplification of the view offered in the original sources. Lewis and Clark see "America," and thus themselves, in the western lands, but in their writing this vision is side by side with the other modes of discourse we have discussed above, in which something of the actual processes and costs of taking over is recorded.

In Lewis and Clark, we find writers whose breadth and scope are such that they cannot manage to attain a unified tone regarding the lands they are seeking to encompass. They teach us immeasurably more about the West than Frémont would later because they were not as confident about their roles there. Their uncertainty is a virtue in that it is an accurate reflection of the relationship of the eastern imperialist ideology to the western territories at the time of their writing. The complexities and the contradictions of their report are those of the historical situation of which they were a part. On the one hand, they were committed to the assertion of United States legal authority over these territories and their inhabitants, and they describe their performance of these duties confidently and clearly. They were also well prepared to invoke the authority of the categories of contemporary science as another, if less direct, assertion of their control. The circumstances of their survival and movement in the West, however, demanded close cooperation with local peoples, and as a result of their reporting of these exchanges, Lewis and Clark opened up a mode of relationship with the West that contradicted the authority of the legal and scientific. This local mode created for the traveling Euro-American a western history of shared experience with local peoples, and such a history threatened, or at least complicated, the basis on which the United States's expansion into the West could be imagined. Finally, what distinguishes the fourth, aesthetic mode from the others and is in part responsible for its success in later western writings, is that it obviates the contradictions among the other history-based claims. In this mode, the Euro-American observer in the West is given a clear title to the land, irrespective of legal claims, through the ritual identification of the Euro-American self and the land. That the land has been waiting for the first white man to recognize it is confirmed, apparently, by the emotion of the viewer himself upon seeing it.

Zebulon Pike and John Charles Frémont:
Pioneers of Popular Self-Discovery

Historians Elliott Coues and John Bakeless are among the heirs of generations of writers about the West who isolated the aesthetic and personal mode of authority we have seen in Lewis and Clark as the best way to tell the story of Euro-Americans taking possession of their present territory. Even in the works of Lewis and Clark's immediate successors, the legal, scientific, and local modes recede into the background as the authority of stories of western travel comes more and more from the individual American's recognizing himself in a landscape he has already identified as American and from which local inhabitants have been abstracted.

Lewis and Clark established Louisiana and the Far West as ground where ambitious young officers could make names for themselves by advancing their country's land claims and scientific knowledge. From Jefferson's presidency through the mid-nineteenth century, factions in national politics were interested in keeping the possibilities of new territories in the public eye.[48] When later explorers set out, they had at least as strong a sense of the official nature of their journeys as Lewis and Clark had had, and they maintained even more unequivocally their sense that the territory they were exploring was, in more than a merely legal sense, already American. Zebulon Pike, Stephen Long, and John Frémont all took it for granted that they would consciously promote the United States's authority and influence by signing treaties, making peace among warring nations, rewarding good behavior, and punishing those who had harmed Americans or their property.

Zebulon Pike's father had been a major during the Revolution and later in the United States Army, and Pike was commissioned as a lieutenant at the age of twenty. He served several restless years in the frontier army until, in 1805, he was sent by General James Wilkinson to investigate the sources of the Mississippi. As an aggressive young officer, Pike made showing the flag an almost obsessive concern, claiming in the narrative of his Mississippi expedition that he managed to communicate something of his reverence for his nation's banner to the people he encountered. On one occasion, for example, he claims that a flag that had fallen from his boat floated downstream into the midst of several Sioux who, "seeing a thing so sacred," determined to set aside a quarrel until they could return the flag and avenge the desecration.[49] Pike makes this incident an emblem of the legitimacy of American authority, for even in their own country, the Indians and British fur traders seem to respect the import of Pike's symbol. Similarly, as he is nearing the completion of his return from the headwaters of the Mississippi, he notes with approval the advance of the American trading frontier in the mere six months since he passed the same spot on his upstream journey: "Thus were we the fore runner's of peace and Inhabitants: for where on ascending was nothing but a Wilderness to be seen, was now trading Houses; and the Wilderness, where unmolested (except by the wandering party of Warriors) roamed the wild beast's, now resounded with the busy hum of men" (116).

Lewis and Clark retained a strong sense of the particularity of the peoples they encountered, but the degree of individuation maintained in the narratives of succeeding expeditions falls far short of theirs. When Lewis and Clark treated with western groups, their rhetoric and ceremony suggest that they conceived of them as individual, foreign nations, however primitive and uncivilized. In later narratives, relations with Indian groups cease to be matters of diplomatic negotiation with autonomous peoples. Some of the rhetoric of international diplomacy remains in Pike, Long, and Frémont, but mostly their attitudes seem proprietary, reflecting their concern to arrange inhabitants' behavior to suit their Euro-American vision of the land. The amenability of peoples to this vision becomes the principal criterion for distinguishing them. Details of culture or nationality fade as western peoples increasingly are perceived merely as either "good" or "bad" Indians.

On Pike's second journey, in 1806, to the headwaters of the Arkansas and Red rivers of Louisiana Territory, his responsibilities included escorting back to their villages a party of Osages and Pawnees who had been redeemed from captivity by the United States government. Pike reports that the reunion of his charges with their friends was a scene of "wives throwing themselves into the arms of their husbands, parents embracing their children and children their parents, brothers and sisters meeting, one from captivity, the others from the towns—they, at the same time, returning thanks to the Good God for having brought them once more together" (304). Pike remarks that the *"toute ensemble* was such as to make polished society blush, when compared with those savages, in whom the passions of the mind, either joy, grief, fear, anger, or revenge, have their full scope: why can we not correct the baneful passions, without weakening the good?" (304). The opposition of savage and civilized is absolute, not qualified or complicated by references to particular European or Indian cultures.

Pike relates these Osages' emotions to a generalized notion of Indian character that has both good and bad aspects. "Savage" expressions of joy are very gratifying to Pike, the arranger of the reunion, and his "good Indian" is a welcome feature of the land, even one that might be retained as a beneficial influence on future civilized inhabitants. The problem, as Pike says, is that the "savage's" feelings are all part of a complex that includes not only admirably candid grief and joy, but also ungovernable anger and lust for revenge. Upon hearing a report that certain "Savages" had vowed to take revenge upon him for his part in arranging a peace between the Sioux and the "Sauteurs," Pike reflects:

> I appeal to my god and my Country, if the laws of self-preservation, would not have justified me, in cutting those scoundrels to pieces wherever I found them. . . . I dreaded the consequences of the meeting with the scoundrels—not for the present danger; but for fear the impetuosity of my conduct might not be approved of by my Government, who did not so intimately know the nature of those savages. (117)

Pike's acquaintance with the savage nature convinces him that, while savage expressions of joy and grief are worthy of emulation, the savage's code of vengeance places him beyond the pale of American civilization. For Pike and many of those who came after him who envisioned the new lands as part of America, the threatening, savage behavior of the Indian was something from which the land had to be protected and liberated. According to this view, aggressive Indian responses to the Euro-American presence are not understandable as resistance to the presence of foreigners but are, rather, the perverse responses of those who cannot recognize the true nature of the land and its destiny.

Add to this sense of the inappropriateness of hostile Indian responses the belief that this hostility was inevitable, and one arrives at something like Francis Parkman's formulation of "the Indian" as a "problem":

> The Indian is hewn out of a rock. You can rarely change the form without the destruction of the substance. . . . He will not learn the arts of civilization, and he and his forest must perish together.

The stern, unchanging features of his mind excite our admiration from their very immutability; and we look with deep interest on the fate of this unreclaimable son of the wilderness, the child who will not be weaned from the breast of his rugged mother.[50]

Parkman illustrates the nineteenth-century historian's tendency to make increasingly general statements about "the Indian."[51] As the western lands came more and more to be recognized as immanently part of America, resistance to Euro-American presence came to be seen as atavistic and, in a sense, un-American. As travelers in the West depended more on information from previous European explorers and less on intimate contact with local peoples, their narratives suggest that their ability to distinguish one people from another rapidly diminished. Increased confidence in their mission made resistance seem all the more shocking.

Lewis and Clark rarely used general terms such as "Indian" or "savage." To a remarkable extent they distinguished the culture and behavior of one group from that of another. They recognized and resented hostility when it appeared, but they did not think in terms of a generalized Other who was globally hostile or friendly to American intentions. Instead of an abstract Indian, their narrative details a complex array of variously cooperative and intractable peoples. They do denounce particular groups, such as the "Eneeshurs" of the Columbia Valley, who are "inhospitable and parsimonious, faithless to their engagements, and in the midst of poverty and filth retain a degree of pride and arrogance which renders our numbers our only protection against insult, pillage, and even murder."[52] While they rail against one people, however, they leave open the possibility of better treatment elsewhere: "We are assured, however, by our Chopunnish guide, . . . that the nations above will treat us with more hospitality" (961).

Pike, by contrast, exhibits the general tendency of later writers to attribute particular misdeeds to the abstract savage. In Colorado, for example, Pike finds himself defending his group "against the insolence, cupidity and barbarity of the savages" in general.[53] Insolence and cupidity were probably characteristic of some of the people he met, but Pike has here ceased distinguishing agents among the local inhabitants.

Similarly, although the Edwin James account of the Stephen Long expedition includes detailed, sympathetic descriptions of many Indian peoples, it often generalizes about "savages" when the party meets with resistance. As they prepare, in June 1820, to proceed west from their winter camp at Council Bluffs, they imagine they are entering a realm of generalized hostility:

> We were well-armed and equipped, each man carrying a yauger or rifle gun, with the exception of two or three who had muskets; most of us had pistols, all tomahawks and long knives, which we carried suspended at our belts. We believed ourselves about to enter a district of country inhabited by lawless and predatory bands of savages, where we should have occasion to make use, not only of our arms, but of whatever share of courage and hardihood we might chance to possess.[54]

With little information about the country they were about to enter and having heard numerous reports about the hostility of the people, they focus their anxiety on a vague "lawless and predatory" savage.

The inhabitants thus abstracted, either as harmless examples of natural goodness or as dangerous (destroyable) embodiments of primitive rage, explorers are free to document, in conscious, utilitarian terms, the potential for pasture and agriculture, sometimes in technical discussions of the soil, other times more directly and personally in such remarks as: "Nature scarcely ever formed a more beautiful place for a farm."[55] But the most powerful assertion of authority in these later writers is the trope of aesthetic appropriation that we have already seen asserting a transcendent claim in the Lewis and Clark *History*. These later explorers often placed themselves on the tops of hills or mountains in order to obtain a sweeping view of the surrounding country.[56] Zebulon Pike, for example, surveys the Mississippi valley from a hill near present-day Winona, Minnesota:

> When we arrived at the Hills we ascended them, from which we had one of the most beautiful and sublime prospects. On the right we saw the mountains which we passed in the morning, and the Prairie in their rear. . . . On our left and under our feet, the Valley between the two barren hills, through which the Mississippi wound itself, as far as the eye could embrace the scene, by numerous channels forming many beautiful Islands. Our four boats under full Sail, with their flags displayed before the Wind, was altogether a prospect so variegated and romantic, that a man may scarcely expect to enjoy such a one more than once or twice in his life.[57]

As in Lewis's reactions to the landscape, references to the sublime and the beautiful signal the "civilized" personal response to the land, but it is a moment when personal experience takes on historic significance, for the individual traveler's response brings his society's values to bear on the new country, and the land itself seems to acquiesce. Pike's eye "embrace[s] the scene," which in turn seems to open itself to the "four boats under full Sail, with their flags displayed before the Wind."

In a similar situation, Pike renders the view from the top of a hill in Colorado, which is again "one of the most sublime and beautiful inland prospects ever presented to the eyes of man":

> The main river bursting out of the western mountain, and meeting from the north-east, a large branch, which divides the chain of mountains, proceeds down the prairie, making many large and beautiful islands, one of which I judge contains 100,000 acres of land, all meadow ground, covered with innumerable herds of deer; . . . this view combined the sublime and the beautiful; the great and lofty mountains covered with eternal snows, seemed to surround the luxuriant vale, crowned with perennial flowers, like a terrestrial paradise, shut out from the view of man. (375–376)

The sweeping vision suggests control of what is seen, and, as is often the case, the passage includes a temporal dimension in which the explorer provides for the future implications of the present scene. The "terrestrial paradise, shut out from the view of man" has, of course, only been unseen by Europeans, as Pike himself, on some level, knows. Pike's first "white sight" is that Adamic moment when the creation is turned over to its intended master, the moment of recognition when "the 100,000 acres of land, all meadow ground," the "innumerable herds of deer," the "luxuriant" state of the valley are all appropriated for the fruitful agricultural society that is Pike's ideal union of people and place. The isolation and sublimity of the scene do not bespeak a land that has to be subdued or wrested from its present owners. Instead, they suggest Pike's "belief in a destiny inherent in the land itself," a vision of a land that "in its material form embodied its own historical destiny."[58]

The related tendencies to generalize about "the Indian," to abstract Indian peoples from their lands, and to envision the land as empty, welcoming the Euro-American advent, are perhaps most clearly evident in the exploration narratives of John Charles Frémont. Frémont's narrative of his journey in 1842 through the South Pass to the Wind River Mountains exceeds all the other accounts discussed so far as a record of the explorer's confident recognition of the supposedly new territory. There is something of recreation, of our sense of camping, in Frémont's detailed accounts of the joys and pains of exploratory travel in the West. His coffee tastes better on the trail, especially when there is cream from their cow to put in it. He chooses campsites because of their beauty. Hunting is no longer talked of as a necessity for obtaining food—it has become sport as well. Frémont renders not only the soldier's and scientist's accounts of the territory; his are also the responses of a young, adventurous, well-read American to what is now manifestly part of his national, natural heritage. Not only the land itself but the experience of exploring it has become such a recognizable part of the American identity that Frémont brings along his wife's twelve-year-old brother "for the development of mind and body which such an expedition would give."[59] His expedition covered no new ground until he climbed one of the Wind River peaks, but his narrative provides a fuller personal experience of the land, and it establishes the idea of "discovering America" as a characteristic source of national identity.

As Frémont's point of view seems more secure, so the native inhabitants' place in the landscape has become rhetorically more clear-cut, even if politically and practically it was still a complicated problem. On the one hand, the generalized "good Indian" has become a matter of local color: "Indians and buffalo make the poetry and life of the prairie, and our camp was full of their exhilaration" (185). "Stories of desperate and bloody Indian fights" have become campfire lore, and the expedition's first "alarm"—when a scout mistakes some distant elk for warriors on horseback—is cause for an "excitement which broke agreeably on the monotony of the day" (179–180). The cry of "Indians, Indians!" occurs frequently in the narrative as the standard reaction to the actual or suspected presence of any of the area's inhabitants.

On the other hand, uncooperative groups or individuals are referred to as though they did not belong to the land at all. Frémont describes a region of fertile grazing land that would seem to be the natural home of such a hunting culture as the Pawnees who, in fact, inhabit it:

Our route . . . lay up the valley, which, bordered by hills with graceful slopes, looked uncommonly green and beautiful. The stream was about fifty feet wide and three or four deep, fringed by cottonwood and willow, with frequent groves of oak tenanted by flocks of turkeys. Game here, too, makes its appearance in great plenty. Elk were frequently seen on the hills, and now and then an antelope bounded across our path, or a deer broke from the groves. (179)

This landscape seems welcoming to Frémont and his men, except for the Pawnees, who "infest this part of the country," "infest," of course, suggesting that they are unwarranted and damaging pests in country intended for some other purpose than their support. In another instance, the expedition meets two Sioux, who "belonged to [a] party that had advocated an attack on [some white] emigrants." Several of Frémont's men suggest "shooting them on the spot," but Frémont "promptly discountenanced any such proceeding." Despite his forbearance here, Frémont generally thinks that good behavior is the Indian inhabitant's obligation, and he clearly disapproves of this pair of Sioux, who "looked sulky" and supplied only "confused information" when questioned within the "little ring of rifles which surrounded them" (236–237). There is really no indication in Frémont's narrative that he retained any sense that the by-then-substantial Euro-American migration was an intrusion into foreign countries. The land has been imaginatively wrested from its inhabitants, who remain only as part of its ephemeral "poetry" or as noisome pests.

Like Lewis and Pike, Frémont also isolated the unique moment when the land, through its beauty, seemed to make a special revelation to him. Frémont's *Report* is rhetorically more unified than most earlier accounts. His tone is simultaneously the most confident, personal, and self-consciously representative of the American exploration writers up to his time. He writes as an American speaking to other Americans about something that concerns them all. He renders his landscape with an enthusiastic, painterly eye, describing not only the elements of the scene but his own avid involvement with them: "Viewed in the sunshine of a pleasant morning, the scenery was of a most striking and romantic beauty, which arose from the picturesque disposition of the objects and the vivid contrast of colors. I thought with much pleasure

of our approaching descent in the canoe through such interesting places"
(232).

The political implications of these aesthetic perceptions are often
evident in the text. Leading up to his climactic description of the view
from the top of a peak near the summit of the South Pass, Frémont
describes the approach as more a beckoning gateway than the "winding"
and "gorgelike" ascents that Americans had encountered in crossing the
Alleghenies. It is like the "ascent of the Capitol hill from the avenue, at
Washington" (253). Frémont makes his achieving the top of the peak,
the westernmost and highest point on his journey, as well as the
rhetorical climax of his narrative, the moment of his clearest assertion
of the connection between his personal experiences and his nation's
future in the West:

> I sprang upon the summit, and another step would have precipi-
> tated me into an immense snow field five hundred feet below. To
> the edge of this field was sheer icy precipice; and then, with a
> gradual fall, the field sloped off for about a mile, until it struck
> the foot of another lower ridge. . . . We mounted the barometer
> in the snow of the summit, and fixing a ramrod in a crevice,
> unfurled the national flag to wave in the breeze where never flag
> waved before. . . . A stillness the most profound and a terrible
> solitude forced themselves constantly on the mind as the great
> features of the place. Here, on the summit, where the stillness
> was absolute, unbroken by any sound, and the solitude complete,
> we thought ourselves beyond the region of animated life; but
> while we were sitting on the rock, a solitary bee (*bromus, the
> bumblebee*) came winging his flight from the eastern valley, and
> lit on the knee of one of my men.
>
> It was a strange place, the icy rock and the highest peak of the
> Rocky Mountains, for a lover of warm sunshine and flowers, and
> we pleased ourselves with the idea that he was the first of his
> species to cross the mountain barrier, a solitary pioneer to foretell
> the advance of civilization. (269–270)

Initially alone on the summit, Frémont experiences a moment of communion with the "terrible solitude" that "forced itself constantly on
the mind." Loneliness, here, is not threatening, however. It is the state
that prepares him for a transforming experience. His solitude and ver-
tigo are given national historic significance as he plants the flag "where

never flag waved before," and then he fancies that the bee, also solitary, is like himself a "pioneer to foretell the advance of civilization." Frémont understands his experience as both unique and typical. He is "the first white man" to set foot on this peak and to envision this landscape, but he understands the significance of this moment as his being the first of many. His solitary identification with the land is a model for every westering American who discovers himself as he discovers the "solitude" of the West.

Writing almost forty years after Lewis and Clark, Frémont relies much more than they on the authority of his personal response to natural beauty. Although Stephen Fender argues that ultimately Frémont felt more secure in the scientific descriptive mode, turning to it much more in his second *Report*,[60] I think that—in the first *Report*, at least—his most overt and vigorous assertions of an American's right to these western lands rely on the authority of what I have called the aesthetic mode. In conjunction with this mode of authority, Frémont demonizes and trivializes the Indian inhabitants, and his narrative offers nothing like Lewis and Clark's mode of intimate contact and shared experience. Reading Frémont after Lewis and Clark, we sense an American who is much more confident about his and his country's western presence, and the popularity of Frémont's narrative among overland travelers, despite its relative lack of new or practical information, suggests that his pose of confident personal possession of the landscape was by this time familiar, reassuring, and easy to imitate.[61]

CHAPTER THREE

Washington Irving: Historian of American Discovery

Dilettantism and commitment have been crucial concepts in the biography and criticism of Washington Irving, the touristic travel of the early sketches serving as the correlative of the former and his return to the United States and his switch to books of travel in the West indicating at least his desire to appear to be an example of the latter. This polarity within the genres of travel writing should not surprise us at this point, since we have already seen how traders and military explorers invoked it as part of their own sense of mission. The sense of these two different kinds of travel was a part of the culture.

The books Irving wrote in the early 1820s concern the travels of Geoffrey Crayon, their narrator/persona, and as Wayne Franklin has noted, they "take as their primary concern the interplay between a limited narrator and his various 'fields' of experience."[1] They focus on "the art of perception, and on the emotions and thoughts which that act calls into being" (122–123). Presenting themselves as the products of leisurely travel and thought, they address the recreational reader in tones that avoid most allusions to matters of state or serious affairs. But beginning with *The Life and Voyages of Christopher Columbus* (1828), Irving occupied a decade of his career with third-person accounts of the historical journeys of exploration and discovery of sixteenth-century

Spaniards and nineteenth-century Americans, with only the narrative of his own western excursion, *A Tour on the Prairies* (1835), serving as a reminder of how he had earlier been the central presence in his own writing. This later decade of work includes accounts of Columbus's four voyages, of the voyages of his less famous contemporaries, of Astor's fur-trading venture in the Far West, and of Benjamin Bonneville's expedition to the Rocky Mountains. The subject matter of all these works connects them with contemporary government policy and with topical ideologies. Indeed, one line of the commentary on Irving's two final western books has to do with his supposed service as a propagandist for the interests of American business and government in the West and his desire to ingratiate himself with his American public through the choice of a popular American subject.[2] Rees and Sandy suggest that Irving's later style "shows him trading the potentially decadent skepticism of the frivolous stylist in himself for the realism of the propagandist of power and order."[3]

If the expatriate somehow divorced himself from the shaping forces of his native culture, the repatriated writer was the conscious servant of business, government, and uncritical popular mythology. What these two poles have in common with respect to Irving's use of travel genres is that in both instances the traveler is seen as traveling in the service of merely personal, or at least clearly limited, goals, and this is felt to be a fault; Geoffrey Crayon's sensibility is not seen as representing anything crucial in American society, and Irving the historian of western expansion is seen as too directly articulating the interests of Astor, the fur trade, and the American government. Mere tourism, according to this view, has no grasp on national issues that would afford Irving a claim as a serious American writer; interested reportage, on the other hand, is somehow *too* interested, too tied to the economic, political, and popular institutions that structured Euro-American expansion into the West. We have noted that the tourist/hireling dichotomy is one that the British traders invoked in their own defense as travelers and writers: that they represented particular interests was both explanation and justification of their travels; what they emphatically were not was idle curiosity seekers. We should recall as well that Euro-American military travelers were not at ease with this distinction. Instead, they tended to call attention to their own feelings and experiences as indexes of the "Americanness" of the new landscapes they surveyed; they were not tourists, but neither did they wish to appear merely to serve the interests of definable governmental institutions. Irving's western travel writing inevitably shares this discourse of Euro-American expansion with the earlier and contemporary exploratory travelers, and his work embodies the kinds of tensions and contradictions we discussed with respect to the American military travelers, contradictions between institutions that were designed to foster American expansion into the western continent and the desire to see the whole continent as already "American."

This critical polarization of Irving's career is related to the view that, in Irving, romantic "influences" did not result in full-blown romantic form. William Spengemann, for example, outlining how Irving's approach to travel narrative differs from that of his romantic successors, argues that Irving failed to seize upon the artistic implications of the journey narrative: "Irving's *A Tour* employs the accidental mannerisms and sensibilities of Romantic literature without ever quite grasping one of the essential elements of Romantic narrative: the original form which arises from the unique experiences of a particular person in a specific environment."[4] Romantic narrative as defined here is the solution to the perceived weaknesses in both phases of Irving's career insofar as the experiences of the narrator become the focus for the events of the narrative and the narrator's personality becomes the touchstone for the values shaping the story. Had this transition to full-fledged romanticism been effected by Irving, Geoffrey Crayon's "sketches" would represent stages in the development of his sense of self, not mere reactions to people and places that remain distinctly alien; Irving on the prairies, or Bonneville in the Rocky Mountains, would render the West as it affected the "whole man," not merely the fur trader, the capitalist, the army captain, and the story would be about the growth of this man through his identification with the West. But falling short of this romanticism, Irving is seen as anticipating, but not seeing his way through to, the narrative achievements of later romantic American writers such as Poe and Melville. Arguing along this line, William Hedges speaks of "the difficulty of creating techniques appropriate to the newness of American experience. Ultimately," he says, "the problem was how to perceive significant form in the experience itself." "Synthesis" of "experience in bulk" was needed; but "the synthesis was not to come until the period now known as the American Renaissance, beginning in the 1830's. The transition to this period must be a central concern in any detailed examination of Irving's career, and that transition was toward a full-fledged romantic subjectivism."[5] While I think it reasonable to contrast Irving's romanticism and narrative practice with that of later American writers, I am uncomfortable with this comparison's implicit valuation of both poles. Both types of Irving's travel narrative, that of the *Sketch Book* and that of his later western writing, tended to emphasize the differences between the narrating character and the worlds he traveled through, and his travel plots did not result in the unification of the traveling consciousness and the foreign world. "Experience" did not transcend history; Irving never achieved the later "synthesis" of the American Renaissance.

My main concern in this chapter is with how Irving's travel narratives register the issues dealt with by the other discovery writers we have discussed so far, for the fundamental political conflicts at the root of these issues did not change in any essential way up to the middle of the century, and the discourse of national expansion was a crucial aspect of the American Renaissance. Part of what has dissatisfied Irving's critics is that, in comparison with the achievements of the later American Renaissance canon, the conflicts inherent in national expansion seem, in Irving, too overt, rendered too much in terms of institutions whose existence is independent of the narrating consciousness; in other words, Irving's narrators remain too much strangers in strange lands. But since the western continent was, in the most obvious sense, a patchwork of strange lands, Irving's approach to it is by no means entirely a bad thing. As Peter Antelyes points out with respect to *A Tour on the Prairies*, the "tour by which Irving hoped to reacquaint himself with his 'native land' is characterized as a journey through Indian territory, a 'native' land in itself as yet 'uncharted' (if not unclaimed) by the 'white man' (here meaning Americans). Irving's pun on 'native' quickly brings into question the basic premise of that designation, that the true natives in and of this land are the white Americans."[6]

Jeffrey Rubin-Dorsky's recent study of Irving's European years convincingly counters one pole of the view of Irving that I have been discussing here, that which sees him in his European works as ineffectual tourist. For Rubin-Dorsky, Irving is "an acute register of the anxieties of his age," whose *Sketch Book* "touched . . . American readers on a deep, subconscious level."[7] The period 1815 to 1832, upon which Rubin-Dorsky focuses, Irving spent entirely in Europe, and so Rubin-Dorsky's study necessarily mainly concerns Irving's relations with the "Old World." But Irving's interest in Europe is read in relation to the "identity crisis" (xv, 68) that Americans were experiencing in the first half of the nineteenth century, when the generation of the founders had passed away and their vision of the nation was both idealized and challenged, the latter by the sheer momentum of expansion and industrialization. Boundlessness, in the positive sense of unlimited possibility, was accompanied by homelessness, a sense of loss as old familial, communal, and institutional bases of identity were left behind. The crucial achievement of Geoffrey Crayon and *The Sketch Book* is that Irving managed to indulge a view of English order and stability without adopting it as a model for Americans. He succeeds in making England both inspiring and Other as far as contemporary Americans were concerned: "Crayon urges his countrymen *not* to imitate England, but to emulate her" (95). Through the self-mockery that is essential to the Crayon persona, Irving allowed his American readers to indulge their desire for an idealized, Old-World past without betraying their necessarily distinct New-World identity: "Laughing at Geoffrey, whose obsessions blind him to critical truths, Americans were in effect making fun of their own desires to experience the moral order of the European social system" (94). Despite the bumbling and sentimentality of his persona, in other words, Irving, as European traveler, is vitally engaged with the contemporary discourse of Americanism. Despite his attraction to the order and stability of the Old World, he does not mistake it for a model his countrymen should seek to reproduce.

Like Hedges, Rubin-Dorsky sees Irving as having "moved American writing in a direction that would culminate with the great Romantics" (254), but he observes that Irving stopped short of the total commitment to the individual vision that characterizes that romanticism, their sense that "only language can create the liberated place," "as if history can give no life to 'freedom' " (253).[8] Prior to the romantic invention of a "New World of timeless interior space, there were those literary sojourners like Irving who sought in the Old World of historically shaped exterior landscapes something nurturing both to themselves and their art."[9] Irving's creativity in the "European" phase of his career springs from his engagement with the monuments of a past from which Americans had in part distinguished themselves. This past was something real, but something Other; its value lay in its stability, which was independent of American change. Geoffrey Crayon could travel among these monuments and achieve self-definition through their resistance to his imagination.

Irving would preserve his sense of "historically shaped exterior landscapes" when he turned his attention from fiction to history and from Europe to the other geographic pole of American consciousness, the West. This shift began with Irving's *Life and Voyages of Christopher Columbus* (1828). Irving's narrators react in personal ways to these landscapes, but the lands and peoples of the American West are not subsumed into the personal story of Irving's personae; his western writings retain some of the overtly "imaginative" passages that characterize his earlier work, but, like England, the American West has an independent existence and history. In Irving's narratives of discovery, unlike those of the later American romantics, discovering America is not equated with self-discovery. His romanticism is evident in the moments of sensibility his heroes exhibit in response to the beauty and sublimity of the land or to the melancholy sufferings of its inhabitants. But the rhetoric of his histories, emerging from a global ("European") perspective, does not allow individuals and moments to be identified with the stories of peoples essentially at war over territory. If anything, his applying "European" terms like "banditti" or "gypsies" to Indian groups grants them more consideration as opponents to the prevailing order than did the timeless and habitual "savages" or "Indians." Was it really a sign of Irving's being out of touch with American "reality" that he should see American native peoples as resembling marginalized groups in Europe? And is it really a sign of Irving's artistic old-fashionedness that whereas he notes his "sanguinary propensities daily growing stronger on the prairies," these feelings do not "influence his subsequent behavior"?[10] I suggest that it is neither sensible nor desirable for us to believe that the fundamental outlook of a middle-aged man, an important writer, could be transformed by a month-long camping trip, even in the American West. Irving's point of view in his histories is sophisticated in the best sense. He does not surrender the wide experience of a lifetime to the effects of a few moments, however exciting they may have been. Nor does he grant the local mythology a monopoly on the way that part of the world should be portrayed in literature.

Like Cooper and every major writer up to the Civil War, Irving, too, was moved to take up the unresolved questions of a recently constituted, territorially unstable society through a rehearsal of what were thought of as founding events taking place on the fringes of the territory that society controlled. And like Cooper's, Irving's writings embody a conflict between institutional, legal modes of conceiving the nation's history and development and a more romantic personal response to American nature. Whereas Irving's earlier Crayon persona questions his relation, as an American, to the culture of the Old World as he travels through it, the personae of Irving's historical works confront the records of European incursion into the Americas, identifying themselves by this choice of subject with the results of discoveries that were motivated by and achieved more tangible results than Crayon's excursions did. For Irving, the tradition of exploration and discovery narratives proved to be an effective means of confronting contemporary American issues and in that sense of intellectually repatriating himself.

Astoria and *Bonneville* are overtly topical, in a way that has sometimes provoked critics to treat them as hack work.[11] Both works deal with Euro-Americans' ongoing competition with British subjects over control of western lands, with the European's and Euro-American's supplanting of Indian peoples, with the role of governments, private capital, and individual ambition in an expansionist society, and with the relationship between events on and beyond the frontiers and the established culture of the East. And these works also represent an important development in the rhetoric for handling these perennial conflicts in the culture. Both works broach these national issues mainly through an accounting of the actions of privately motivated fur traders. Written in the third person from the notes and diaries of others, their fundamental claim on the reader's interest, like that of the earlier British trappers, derives from the journeys that these men have taken in the pursuit of their private interests. It is not what they accomplished of their own goals—in both cases almost nothing—but that they traveled through and reported on "unknown territory" that entitled these accounts to a place in contemporary letters.

Most scholars have discussed Irving's work during this period in terms of its shifting toward history writing, but few have specifically identified the historical genre to which it owes the most—that is, the exploration or discovery narrative. This association may be taken for granted in many cases, but it is important nonetheless to make the link specific in order to understand how far the discovery narrative had come to serve an ideological purpose in Irving's work and in contemporary American culture. In his defense of *Companions of Columbus*, Irving's extension of his work on Spanish exploration, for example, Tuttleton says that this account of the achievements of Columbus's contemporaries is "a fusion of multiple genres—the romance, the epic, the tragic, the biography, and history."[12] The absence of the discovery narrative in this list is puzzling, considering that the central concern in *Companions of Columbus* is the extent to which these men were able to make journeys beyond where "white men had gone before" and that its narrative high points are such famous "discovery" moments as Balboa's first sighting of the Pacific. Most critics agree that Irving's works of this period are properly regarded as history, and more recent commentators have mounted convincing defenses of the comprehensiveness of Irving's research and the accuracy of his accounts.[13] Many refer to evidence in Irving's correspondence that he read extensively in the literature of travel and discovery,[14] and they quote his own claims to a long-standing interest in such matters, including the fur trade, in his introduction to *Astoria*. But until Peter Antelyes's recent *Tales of Adventurous Enterprise*, no one had taken up the specifics of Irving's relation to the tradition of discovery narratives or acknowledged the discovery story that forms the narrative backbone of this body of work.

Even in *Columbus*, which is ostensibly a biography, the fundamental action of the subject's life is exploratory travel. Irving deals with the protracted efforts to initiate the first voyage, the conflict and frustration that attended each subsequent journey, and the ultimate disappointment of his hero's pretensions to consolidate his control over his discoveries, all of which have much to do with court politics, military arrangements, and other stuff of traditional history. It is the history of Columbus's life and of Spanish establishment in the Caribbean. But it is essential to note that Irving isolates Columbus's commitment to his "grand idea"[15] of sailing west to the orient as the key to his worth, and that Irving consistently tries to maintain his subject's "genuine ambition" to seek "a strait which, however it might produce vast benefit to mankind, could yield little else to himself than the glory of the discovery" (471). Whatever complications are involved in the realization of this ambition, this journey of discovery is the fundamental theme of the work and, I shall argue, the basis of its ideological appeal to Irving and his contemporaries.[16] Irving frequently invokes the journey of discovery as a way of distinguishing Columbus from the greed, ambition, and wanton destructiveness of his contemporaries. Similarly, however *Astoria* and *Bonneville* relate to Astor's fur business and to the continental power struggle between the United States and Britain, they capture the reader's attention primarily because they are modeled as much as possible after the conventional narrative of exploratory travel, the Ur-plot that by this time had become a structuring principle of Americans' view of their own history, in which successive generations of Europeans, along with their American-born descendants, had "discovered" more and more parts of the continent. In this context, Astor becomes a kind of enlightened King Ferdinand, whose vision in this case is ill served by his adventurers.

Apart from his own *Tour on the Prairies*, Irving's accounts are not, of course, first-person narratives. *Columbus* and *Astoria* are assembled from a multitude of documents, *Bonneville* from the hero's own manuscript account and several other sources; only *Tour* is based on the author's own travel journal. All but the last are thus, in a sense, "metahistories" of the expeditions that constitute their main action, in which, as one reviewer put it, Irving is "a looker-on who sees more of the game than the players."[17] From his perspective three centuries after Columbus, with better social and political connections than Bonneville (and perhaps even Astor), and a completer command of relevant documents, Irving is able to place the actions of the individuals concerned in their political and economic contexts. He is able to isolate the "story" of each undertaking as a significant, complete entity and to comment on it in relation to its results. He can link the "character" of his actors to the fruits of their efforts. All this is obvious enough in a way, but it should be noted that Irving's use of the discovery tradition is different from that of his immediate successors. Poe opts to imitate in fiction the account of an actual traveler, writing in the first person, depriving us of a fully understood conclusion, much as a found journal might not contain a complete account of a journey. Thoreau eschews fiction but opts to fulfill the demands of the discovery narrative by undertaking to do his own exploring, albeit often in a metaphorical sense, which he can report on in the first person.

Irving, from his vantage point as recounter of what are acknowledged to be the exploits of others, is required by the historiographical conventions of his day to moralize his story, linking character with destiny. Despite this, however, Irving's figures remain in the realm of the actual, and his commentary is what is conventionally required in response to real events in significant lives. Again, this contrasts with Poe's technique of commenting on American society through fictional analogy and Thoreau's appropriation of trappings of the discovery narrative to link his purposive "traveling" in Concord metaphorically with the actions of those he says have "run away" to the actual Far West. Because he is writing history, Irving must confront directly the questions raised by the relationship of his subjects to his American audience. Although Irving has often been accused of easternizing, Europeanizing, and romanticizing the West, I would argue that in fact he addressed the West as history, and this required him to present conflict over possession of the land more directly than his American Renaissance successors, who tended to portray the expansion of American society in terms of merely personal experience. Irving, on the other hand, tells the story of a contest in which the successes of the discoverers are at the expense of defeated opponents, European or aboriginal, as well as of nature.

Irving's *Columbus*

Irving's biography of Columbus was made possible by the publication of Martín Leodoro Fernández de Navarrete's *Colección* (1825–1837) of documents relevant to the voyages of Columbus, as well as by Irving's gaining access to the library of Obadiah Rich, the American consul in Madrid and an avid collector of fifteenth- and sixteenth-century materials on Spain and America. With these remarkable new resources at hand, Irving had an extensive basis for a detailed account of Columbus's experiences.[18] Seeing Columbus's achievements as the beginning of Andrew Jackson's America must have been a difficult undertaking for Irving. What could he isolate in the ideas and experiences of this man of the Renaissance that nineteenth-century Americans could see as bearing on their own situation and ideals?

Irving's Columbus does not recognize the lands he explores and colonizes as a completely unknown place. Irving states relatively early in *Columbus* that Columbus believed "to his last hour, that Cuba was the extremity of the Asiatic continent" (257), and he concludes with the observation that Columbus "died in ignorance of the real grandeur of his discovery. Until his last breath, he entertained the idea that he had merely opened a new way to the old resorts of opulent commerce, and had discovered some of the wild regions of the east" (569). Irving's Columbus does not formulate the idea of a "new world" but wrestles instead with ways of reconciling his first-hand knowledge with what he knows of the geography of eastern Asia. *Columbus*, as a result, is permeated by dramatic irony: Irving assumes that he and his readers know more about what Columbus is doing than did Columbus himself. And given the nearly overwhelming array of natural and political impediments with which Columbus had to deal, Irving's Columbus often comes perilously close to earning our pity rather than our admiration. It was clearly a problem for the author of an admiring biography of the man generally held to have "discovered America" that the subject planned his expeditions and understood his own achievements in terms very different from those of the culture that claims him as a founder.

To some extent Irving's biography rescues Columbus from himself and from his age. In effect, Irving claims that in another, more enlightened age (nineteenth-century America), Columbus would have been free of the weaknesses that he exhibited in his own times, that his faults were cultural rather than personal. Irving makes a virtue, for example, of Columbus's devout piety, arguing that "religion mingled with the whole course of his thoughts and actions, and shone forth in his most private and unstudied writings" (567). He goes on, however, to admit that "his piety was mingled with superstition, and darkened by the bigotry of the age" (567), in that Columbus did not extend "natural rights" to non-Christians. "In this spirit of bigotry he considered himself justified in making captives of the Indians, and transporting them to Spain to have them taught the doctrines of Christianity, and in selling them for slaves, if they pretended to resist his invasions" (567). Irving quotes in Columbus's defense the letter he wrote to King Ferdinand complaining of Ovando's treatment of the inhabitants of Hispaniola while Columbus was away. Columbus argues that "although he [Columbus] had sent many Indians to Spain to be sold, it was always with a view to their being instructed in the Christian faith, and in civilized acts and usages, and afterwards sent back to their native island to assist in civilizing their countrymen" (543). Irving adds that Columbus's actions regarding Caribbean natives should not be "measured by the standard of right and wrong established in the present more enlightened age" but "in connexion with the era in which he lived" (543), prompting one to wonder whether Irving expected his posterity to judge the deportations and massacres of his own era from an analogous vantage point of improved standards. Irving argues, moreover, that given his authorities for his opinions ("St. Augustine, St. Isidor, St. Ambrosius") and the wondrous sights he saw on his voyages, it should not be surprising that Columbus could conceive such ideas as that the Orinoco "was supplied by the fountain mentioned in *Genesis*, as springing from the tree of life in the Garden of Eden" (345). Irving argues, in fact, that Columbus's imagination is part of his greatness: "Had not Columbus been capable of these enthusiastic soarings of the imagination, he might . . . never have had the daring enterprise to adventure in search of it [a continent existing in the west] into the unknown realms of ocean" (346).

In many similar instances, Irving uses this strategy of acknowledging Columbus's participation in the crimes and delusions of his age while isolating the personal attributes that nineteenth-century readers could admire without reservation. Columbus's faults are historical, signs that he was a man of an earlier time, but his virtues are transcendent, qualities that link his enterprise to what America had become. Such a strategy is necessary, given that the bulk of Irving's *Columbus* openly chronicles the violent unleashing of European greed upon what he often describes as a "virgin world" and innocent, hospitable peoples. The feature of Columbus's character that is most important to his role in the discovery mythology of the nineteenth century is his devotion to the idea of discovery itself, as distinct from all the opportunities for power and profit that attended his discoveries and preoccupied his companions. Thus, Irving describes Columbus's exploration of the coast of Veragua, where, he was told, "were the richest mines, and [where] most of the plates of gold were fabricated" (470), but where he did not stop long, in order that he might arrive at the strait through which he would reach the Ganges:

With these ideas Columbus determined to press forward, leaving the rich country of Veragua unexplored. Nothing could evince more clearly his generous ambition, than hurrying in this brief manner along a coast, where wealth was to be gathered at every step, for the purpose of seeking a strait which, however it might produce vast benefit to mankind, could yield little else to himself than the glory of discovery. (471)

This is a prime example of the motivation that Irving establishes early in the biography: that it was Columbus's commitment to his "grand idea," "the conception of his genius," that he could reach Asia by sailing west, which sent him on his journey (31). This theory "became fixed in his mind . . . and influenced his entire character and conduct" (30). It is through the vision and conduct of this figure, that "the ends of the earth were brought into communication with each other," and for Irving it is the "narrative of [Columbus's] troubled life . . . which connects the history of the old world with that of the new" (10).

To make the life of Columbus connect the old world and the new, Irving had to distinguish between the character of the subject and the events of his life, for after his initial landfall, the remainder of Columbus's actions in the Caribbean produced no major advances in his power or understanding. Although it is certainly conventional for a biography to recount the subject's entire life, Columbus's life is of interest because of an event that occurred fairly early in his known career, an event, moreover, in which he did not recognize what later generations isolate as its enduring meaning. Prescott calls this problem that of a "premature *dénouement*" that impairs the interest of the piece, and he says that "it is a defect that necessarily attaches . . . to the history of Columbus, in which petty adventures among a group of islands make up the sequel of a life that opened with the magnificent discovery of a World."[19] In his own *Conquest of Mexico*, which he extends to include the life of Cortez after the fall of the Aztec capital, Prescott grapples with this same problem, struggling to overcome the generic disjunction he sees between the "historical" and "biographical" parts of the work, believing that "the great public events narrated in [the history] will, without violence, open the way to the remaining personal history of the hero who is the soul of it" (xii–xiii). Adopting Prescott's terms, one might say that the problem in Irving's *Columbus* is that the "great public event" that renders the personal "historic" did not occur until after Columbus's death, when the discovery of America was conceived of as a turning point in history. Then, newly independent American nationals turned to him as a founder whose "soul" transcended his and their European origins and whose voyages suggested an innocent contact with America, the place with which they now identified themselves. On the one hand, Irving asks his readers to recall the historical situation of the voyaging Columbus, one in which inconsequential encounters with insignificant islands appeared marvelous: "in order to feel these voyages properly, we must in a manner, divest ourselves occasionally of the information we possess relative to the countries visited," especially when they lead to "no grand discovery," and when we are apt to "feel impatient at the development of opinions and conjectures which have long since been proved to be fallacious."[20] "In this way we may enjoy in imagination the delight of exploring unknown lands, where new wonders and beauties break upon us at every step" (239). But at the same time it is essential to the fundamental rationale of *Columbus* that the voyager's actions be understood as being "the soul" of the "history" that follows them.

As I have said, it is Columbus's "character" that removes him from the confusing events of Spain's first actions in the Caribbean:

> His conduct as a discoverer was characterized by the grandeur of his views, and the magnanimity of his spirit. Instead of scouring the newly found countries, like a grasping adventurer eager only for immediate gain, as was too generally the case with the contemporary discoverers, he sought to ascertain their soil and productions, their rivers and harbours. . . . In this glorious plan he was constantly defeated by the dissolute rabble which he was doomed to command; with whom all law was tyranny, and order restraint. They interrupted all useful works by their seditions; provoked the peaceful Indians to hostility; and after they had thus drawn down misery and warfare upon their own heads, and overwhelmed Columbus with the ruins of the edifice he was building, they charged him with being the cause of the confusion. (565–566)

And like many nineteenth-century American discoverers, the essential being of the man makes contact with the essential America, referred to as "a virgin world" (104), even though the historical man must in some sense be complicit with these spoliations and betrayals.

Irving makes much of Columbus's glowing accounts of the beauty of the climate and natural life, opining that "he appears to have been extremely open to those happy influences, exercised over some spirits, by the graces and wonders of nature" (104):

> His natural benignity made him accessible to all kinds of pleasurable influences from external objects. In his letters and journals, instead of detailing the circumstances with the technical precision of a mere navigator, he notices the beauties of nature with the enthusiasm of a poet or a painter. As he coasts the shores of the new world, it is delightful to notice the enjoyment with which he describes, in his rude but picturesque Spanish, the varied objects around him: the blandness of the air, temperature, the purity of the atmosphere, the fragrance of the air, "full of dew and sweetness," the verdure of the forests, the magnificence of the trees, the grandeur of the mountains, and the limpidity and freshness of the running streams. New delight springs up for him in every scene. He extols each new discovery as more beautiful that the last, and each as the most beautiful in the world; until, with his simple earnestness, he tells the sovereigns, that having spoken so highly of the preceding islands, he fears they will not credit him when he declares that the one he is actually describing surpasses them all in excellence. (566–567)

Like many subsequent readers of Columbus's first letter to Ferdinand and Isabella, Irving makes much of the voyager's infatuation with climate, flora, and fauna, taking Columbus's reactions as evidence of his fitness to be the prime discoverer of "nature's nation."

In the end, however, the character and actions of Irving's Columbus are overwhelmed by the historical epiphenomena that sprang from his voyages. In a positive sense, of course, the reader is always aware that "America" is waiting in the wings, unbeknownst to Columbus. But the events of the European conquest of America, which constitute the known history of America during Columbus's time, are largely matters for regret and apology. Like his literary contemporary, Natty Bumppo, Irving's Columbus is dogged by white men who are capable neither of a full response to the beauty and wealth of the land nor of a just treatment of its inhabitants.

Beginning with Columbus's return to Hispaniola on his second voyage, Irving prepares the reader for the catastrophic effects of Spanish colonization on the populations of this and other islands. His descriptions of local customs and events are colored by ominous references to the future known to the author and the reader: Irving's ethnography presents "a few of the characteristics remaining on record of these simple people, who perished from the face of the earth before their customs and creeds were thought of sufficient importance to be investigated" (229). Returning from his visit to the people here referred to, Columbus is imagined by Irving as surveying their beautiful country, where they live in happy ease "free from most of those wants which doom mankind in civilized life . . . to incessant labour" (230):

> As we accompany him in imagination over the rocky height . . .
> we cannot help pausing to cast back a look of mingled pity and
> admiration over this beautiful but devoted region. The dream of
> natural liberty, of ignorant content, and loitering idleness, was as
> yet unbroken; but the fiat had gone forth; the white man had
> penetrated into the land; avarice, and pride, and ambition, and
> pining care, and sordid labour, and withering poverty, were soon
> to follow, and the indolent paradise of the Indian was about to
> disappear for ever. (231)

Irving reverses the point of view when, after rendering Columbus's account of a part of the southern coast of Cuba "studded with villages" from which the evening breeze from the shore brought "the distant songs of the natives" (250), he quotes one of his contemporaries, von Humboldt, traveling the same coast: " 'What deserted coasts! not a light to announce the cabin of the fisherman. From Batabano to Trinidad, a distance of fifty leagues, there does not exist a village. Yet in the time of Columbus this land was inhabited even along the margin of the sea' " (250).[21]

These laments, and the many others like them throughout *Columbus*, are very categorical in their assertion that "where the civilized man once plants his foot, the power of the savage is gone for ever" (278). So rendered, the yielding of the Caribbean population to the invaders appears as a law of nature, or perhaps of history. One can regret its effects but hardly interfere with its operation. Of course, such melancholy moments are a trope in New World literature, but Irving's *Columbus* insists on them to such an extent that overall they constitute a theme complementary to his development of the exceptional character of the hero. In the end, however, so that his subject may transcend these catastrophes and provide for the future, Irving must in some way separate Columbus from contemporary events, even while making us see how in actuality they overwhelmed him. He mainly achieves this end by showing how the immediate causes of the distress of Europeans and natives stemmed from the misbehavior of a number of the former. Thus he shows us Columbus arriving at San Domingo, exhausted from his third voyage:

> The island of Hispaniola, the favourite child, as it were, of his hopes, was destined to involve him in perpetual troubles, to fetter his fortunes, impede his enterprizes, and fill his latter days with sorrow and repining. What a scene of poverty and suffering had this opulent and lovely island been rendered by the bad passions of a few despicable men! . . . That beautiful region, which the Spaniards but four years before had found so populous and happy, seeming to inclose in its luxuriant bosom all the sweets of nature, and to exclude all the cares and sorrows of the world, was now a scene of wretchedness and repining. (379)

For Irving, it is "incredible that so small a number of men . . . could in so short a space of time have produced such wide spreading miseries. . . . It seems in the power of the most contemptible individual to do incalculable mischief. . . . The fairest elysium fancy ever devised, would be turned into a purgatory by the passions of a few bad men" (380).

By implication throughout his account and overtly at its end, Irving offers us the thought that American history would have been different had Columbus's qualities been shared by others: "Well it would have been for Spain had her discoverers who followed in the track of Columbus possessed his sound policy and liberal views. . . . The new world, in such case, would have been settled by peaceful colonists, and civilized by enlightened legislators, instead of being overrun by desperate adventurers, and desolated by avaricious conquerors" (566). The structuring narrative of *Columbus* is one of historical struggle, albeit one-sided, between European invaders and American natives, and the "soarings" (346) of Columbus's imagination are powerless to direct or curb the forces that his discovery sets loose. Columbus's qualities of mind are portrayed as responding to the natural and historical context in which he finds himself, but Irving does not equate his consciousness with the reality of America in either Columbus's or Irving's own day. Columbus's life ends with his personal frustration and the onset of a hemispheric catastrophe, and Irving's subsequent western narratives would reiterate versions of Columbus's story. The idealizing of Columbus's character offers the possibility of an ideal discovery yet to be made, and in this sense readers of Irving's biography are offered Columbus as a symbol of America's ultimate potential and a focus for renewed hope and effort. But the narrative structure of *Columbus*, as well as that of the western works, remains distinct from the discoverer's personal vision. "America" and history are ontologically distinct in Irving's discovery narratives.

Irving on the Prairies

Irving's *A Tour on the Prairies* recounts "but a small portion of an extensive tour" he made during the seven months after he arrived in New York in May of 1832. It is notable that of his travels through New York, Pennsylvania, New England, Ohio, along the Ohio and Mississippi rivers to New Orleans, through Alabama, the Carolinas, Virginia, Washington, and back to New York City, he only reports on one month's journey "beyond the outposts of human habitation, into the wilderness of the Far West."[22] Most scholars have agreed that with "the strong interest in the West in 1832 it seemed inevitable that America's most popular author should associate himself with that interest" (xx). Irving himself complains in his introduction to *Tour* that even before he had started writing it was "intimated in the papers . . . that a work was actually in the press, containing scenes and sketches of the Far West" (8). He was aware, he says, that he was "expected to write about a region fruitful of wonders and adventures, and which has already been made the theme of spirit-stirring narratives" (8). Stanley Williams ascribes the popular success of *Tour*, as well as of *Astoria* and *Bonneville*, to "the interest of the average citizen of the 'thirties in the conquest of the West."[23] Williams further noted "that in the 'thirties almost any volume on the trans-Mississippi frontier, on the Indians, or on the new lands would command attention" (79).[24]

Irving's choice of subject and the popular success of his volume are understandable in this context. How Irving orients himself with regard to this popular preoccupation, however, as well as to his preceding and forthcoming works on American discoveries, is a more complex question. With respect to *Tour*, coming a few years after *Columbus* and as he prepared the documents that would form the basis of *Astoria,* one sees Irving situating his own little excursion in relation to the grand discovery story of American mythology and to the reports of commercial and government-sponsored exploratory expeditions that began with Lewis and Clark's in 1804. Irving adopts an extremely diffident tone regarding his ability to meet the expectations of a public he imagines as well versed in such accounts of the West. In his introduction to *Tour,* he laments that he "had nothing wonderful or adventurous to offer."[25] In effect, Irving's apology acknowledges that the westering narrative is the genre in terms of which his own account will be understood, while also alerting his readers to his intention to depart from what he imagines are their expectations.

Irving had also undertaken this rhetorical positioning with respect to the discovery tradition when he introduced himself at the outset of *The Sketch Book,* and he would do it again in introducing *Astoria;* moreover, similar issues underlay his handling of his *Life and Voyages of Columbus.* "The Author's Account of Himself" in *The Sketch Book* begins with Irving recalling his childhood "travels" in the city and neighboring villages as "tours of discovery into foreign parts."[26] His "rambling propensity" developed, he says, into a passion for "books of voyages and travels" and an imagination with which he would "waft" himself "to the ends of the earth" (8). The irony with which these early interests are viewed by the adult narrator/author is analogous to the way he later characterizes his adult travel writing in comparison to that of the "philosopher" and "regular traveller who would make a book" (9). These latter are, again, the people Irving has read, who he assumes will have shaped his readers' expectations as well and in comparison to whom his own efforts will appear inconsequential. Though Irving is ostentatiously self-effacing in linking his own travels with the tradition of voyages and discoveries, he is nonetheless serious about placing himself within what was an important category of popular reading matter. The third paragraph of the piece is a paean to American nature, beyond which, he says, no American need look "for the sublime and beautiful" (9), and the fifth is an ironic explanation of how he wished to see the "great men of Europe," reasoning, via Buffon, that they must be superior to those of America and confirming this idea through his own waggish observation of "the compelling importance and swelling magnitude of many English travellers among us; who, I was assured, were very little people in their own country" (9). In effect, Irving validates his own travels through his unironic assertion of the superiority of American nature and his indirectly expressed mission to vindicate the stature of American "great men" through going to see the European ones for himself. Having ironically summoned the traditions of the discovery narrative, Irving establishes his own seriousness through his sincere reference to American nature and then launches himself in the role of an American discoverer returning to the Old World to compare nature with merely human greatness.

In the introduction to *Astoria*, on the other hand, Irving's tone seems sincere as he recounts his early visits to Canada, his acquaintance with the partners, clerks, and traders of the North-West Company, whom he heard recount their "wide and wild peregrinations," and his own desires to make a "visit to the remote posts of the company in the boats which annually ascended the lakes and rivers."[27] These "early impressions," he says, "have always been themes of charmed interest," and he has "always felt anxious to get at the details of their adventurous expeditions among the savage tribes that peopled the depths of the wilderness" (3). Irving cites these early interests and experiences, as well as his own recent "return from a tour upon the prairies of the far west," by way of explaining why the idea of writing the history of Astor's American Fur Company expedition to the Columbia was of interest to him. In this instance, the narrative persona links the writer and his story directly to the tradition of accounts that "throw light upon the portions of our country quite out of the track of ordinary travel, and as yet but little known" (4).

In *Tour* the positioning of the narrator in relation to the discovery tradition within which he writes falls somewhere between the extremes of the ironic distancing of *The Sketch Book* and the complete identification of *Astoria*. Irving wrote *Tour* just as travel into the Far West was becoming a possibility for the average citizen, and his approach seems to be concerned with exploring the basis upon which the individual American could assert a claim to these lands. Could Irving himself, in the role of private citizen, venture forth into the prairies and adopt the poses and rhetoric so familiar from centuries of discovery narratives, in which to see, to set foot, to recite a prayer, to plant a flag, or to fire a gun was to take possession in the name of an authority higher than any native claims?

The answer in *Tour* is formulated in terms very similar to those through which Irving found it possible to treat Columbus as the true discoverer of America. On the one hand, as in *Columbus*, the institutions through which one group imposes itself on another appear clumsy, selfish, destructive, even ineffective at times. They do not really take into account what the more alert and sensitive "hero" sees and records. In *Columbus* there are gaps between the understandings of Columbus and those of his contemporaries and a more profound gap between the narrator's view of events and Columbus's. But this second gap is the product of passing time, and it is implicit in Irving's approach that Columbus's limitations are those of his era, not of his character. In *Tour*, Irving is in the position of having to write in the first person and be his own Columbus, and although he protests initially that he feels like a "poor actor, who finds himself announced for a part he had no thought of playing,"[28] he does manage to find an indirect way to perform a role on the stage of western discovery. Even so, he appears disengaged from the ethos and institutions of American westering, as his Columbus was at odds with the contemporary developments in the Caribbean.[29]

The narrator of *Tour* sustains uneasy relationships with three constituencies: his official American traveling companions, the lands and peoples of the area he travels through, and the readers familiar with the conventions of the discovery narrative or myth. One of the pleasures of *Tour* is the variety of tones as Irving tries to cope with the often contradictory demands of these constituencies. Although he is consistently aloof from, and critical of, the attitudes and actions of the Indian Commissioner and the majority of the Arkansas Rangers, he is not therefore at ease with the western environment (as so many of Irving's critics have enjoyed pointing out). And Irving's obvious diffidence regarding his personal claim on the West leads to many difficulties when he assumes the role of discoverer thrust upon him by the genre within which he writes.

Irving's tone when dealing with his American escorts on the trail, a company of Arkansas militia or "Rangers," and with Indian Commissioner Henry Ellsworth, is quite consistent throughout *Tour*. No one in this group of individuals officially charged with helping to take control of the western lands appears at all effective; Irving's tone ranges from the amused, through the mildly scornful, to the fairly somberly critical, especially as he reflects on the behavior of the young rangers. William Bedford Clark calls our attention to elements of the "mock-heroic" in *Tour* and to the narrative voice's "tone of comic detachment."[30] These seem most in evidence as Irving recounts the actions of these official agents of the U.S. government.

Irving is surprisingly overt in his mockery of the commissioner's ineffectual efforts to impose a *Pax Americana* on the western peoples. Entering an Osage village from which, we are informed, all the young men are absent on a hunting expedition, the commissioner "made a speech from horseback; informing his hearers of the purport of his mission to promote a general peace among the tribes of the West, and urging them to lay aside all warlike and bloodthirsty notions."[31] Irving relates that the "multitude . . . promised faithfully that as far as in them lay, the peace would not be disturbed," but he immediately adds the deflating observation that "their age and sex gave some reason to hope that they would keep their word" (26). Irving adopts an almost identical strategy of mockery late in the account, when "the worthy Commissioner [again] remembered his mission as Pacificator and made a speech" to seven Osage warriors on their way to harass a nearby Pawnee camp. The commissioner assures them that "he was sent to the frontier to establish a universal peace." Irving, however, recounts that as soon as the Osages had left, the interpreter informed him that their leader "had observed to his companions, that, as their great Father intended so soon to put an end to all warfare, it behooved them to make the most of the little time that was left them" (88). These observations are shared with the reader, while the "worthy Commissioner" is allowed to blunder on in his role of "Pacificator" uncorrected by what the narrator knows. The reader sees Irving deliberately distancing himself from the man who invited him on the tour in the first place and who is the highest-ranking representative of United States authority.

Irving betrays even less regard for the Arkansas Rangers who provide the commissioner's party with protection, and although he uses their youth and enthusiasm to suggest some of what was appealing in his tour, he establishes a distinction between their responses to the prairies and his own. The troop was, he says, "a raw undisciplined band; levied among the wild youngsters of the frontier. . . . None of them had any idea of the restraint and decorum of a camp, or ambition to acquire a name for exactness" (34). Although Irving is hardly about to assume the duty of policing the frontier himself, it seems implicit throughout his narrative that he is uncomfortable with the thought that such a responsibility is in these hands. Describing their movement through the country, he says that the scene reminded him of "descriptions given of bands of buccaneers penetrating the wilds of South America on their plundering expeditions" (36). He is worried by their ignorance of the land and its inhabitants, and also by their wastefulness and destructiveness. He repeatedly shows them roused to ineffectual alarm by the rumor that "Indians" are about: "The rangers were scampering about . . . in pursuit of their horses. One might be seen tugging his steed along by a halter, another, without a hat, riding barebacked; another driving a hobbled horse before him that made awkward leaps like a kangaroo" (74). Irving develops the scene along such lines for three more pages before revealing that the panic has been precipitated by members of their own company observing each other on distant hills and mistakenly seeing "Indians!" Irving also describes some young men hanging on the stories of the "vaporing" Tonish, the cook who nowhere receives anything better than contempt from Irving. "His representations . . . were calculated to inspire his hearers with an awful idea of the foe into whose lands they were intruding" (53). It is not the rangers' alarm that is the object of Irving's satire, but their ignorance of the people whose country they are blundering through, and their susceptibility to conventional western stories. As Peter Antelyes points out, Irving is not saying that the West is not dangerous but "suggesting that one should learn to match that fear to the reality of the danger, and not indiscriminately project it onto Indians in general."[32] The rangers are not knowledgeable enough to resist reacting to even the grossest of "Indian" stories.

The wastefulness of the rangers' behavior is the other target of criticism that comes up frequently throughout the narrative. That these young men can kill so much testifies to the wonderful abundance of the land. Nevertheless, their behavior undermines any claim to the territory that they might be inclined to make and is another index of their ignorance as far as Irving is concerned. At one point he notes how he stayed behind in a camp until everyone had left, in order to "behold the wilderness relapsing into silence and solitude."[33] In the present instance, however, the deserted scene of our late bustling encampment had a forlorn and desolate appearance. The surrounding forest had been in many places trampled into a quagmire. Trees felled and partly hewn to pieces and scattered in huge fragments; tent poles stripped of their covering; smouldering fires, with great morsels of roasted venison and Buffalo meat, standing on wooden spits before them, hacked and slashed by the knives of hungry hunters; while around were strewn the hides, the horns, the antlers and bones of buffalos and deer, with uncooked joints and unplucked turkeys, left behind with that reckless improvidence and wastefulness which young hunters are apt to indulge when in a neighbourhood where game abounds. (97)

Irving portrays these men charging off after almost any animal that appears, leaving smaller game to rot when larger interrupts its preparation, riding their horses almost to death (so that many rangers apparently returned on foot). In the end, it seems, they decide to return home when they are tired and bored, rather than when some object had been achieved: "The want of bread had been felt severely, and they were wearied with constant travel. In fact the novelty and excitement of the expedition were at an end. They had hunted the deer, the bear, the elk, the buffalo and the wild horse, and had no further object of leading interest to look forward to" (110).

Such passages are indicative of the distance that Irving keeps between his narrative persona and his American traveling companions. There are scenes of pleasant camp life that balance them to some extent, but no instances in which this distance is bridged and the narrator identified with the values of this group. Although Irving never explicitly links the rangers and the commissioner's inadequacies to their official roles as representatives of United States authority, he does introduce the narrative as reporting on an "excursion . . . through a tract of country which had not, as yet, been explored by white men" (10), and it is certainly a problem that these "white men" do not rise to the role of discoverer as it is conceived by Irving.

Given the failure of the official representatives to effect a "discovery" of the West, one might turn to the author of the narrative, a member of the expedition, as the next candidate for the role. Here we find Irving in a sense caught between the demands of the discourse he has undertaken—that the narrator of a discovery narrative make discoveries—and his own denial that anything of significance occurred. Given this rhetorical dilemma the narrative persona of *Tour* is necessarily ironic about his own role. His irony, moreover, is essential to understanding his situation, signaling that it is not normal that he "had nothing wonderful or adventurous to offer" (9) and thus perhaps prompting the reader to look beyond his expectations of the contemporary narrative of western travel.

In keeping with the denials of his introduction, Irving seems during the first half or so of *Tour* to make something of a show of his personal detachment from the places and people he encounters. His use of literary, historical, and legendary figures and places in comparisons with objects and persons has been roundly criticized, as has his habit of comparing scenes or persons to paintings or works of statuary.[34] The approach, it seems, indicates his unwillingness or inability to describe what is "really there." Whether Irving's manner does justice to what he encountered is a matter to which I shall return, but here I would note that it does make us aware of Irving's own past, both as a traveler and a writer, and that his trip through the prairies is a distinct departure for him in either of these roles. Irving is too sophisticated a writer, and he uses too many such comparisons, not to be invoking deliberately his readers' knowledge of his past. The effect of such comparisons is to distance Irving from most of his companions and from the western inhabitants. It is important to note that after his initial portraits of the romantic young Count de Pourtalés and Englishman Charles Latrobe, Irving virtually ignores the two men on the trip who do happen to share the point of view espoused in his prose.

This distance is also suggested by the class-tinged commentary that sets the scene of the expedition. Tonish, the meddlesome cook, in addition to being placed literarily as a "marplot" and "a kind of Gil Blas of the frontiers," is introduced most generally as a "personage of inferior rank."[35] The Osage Agency near Fort Gibson is peopled by "a sprinkling of trappers, hunters, half breeds, creoles, negroes of every hue; and all the other rabble rout of non-descript beings that keep about the frontiers" (15). Irving's first impression of their guide, Pierre Beatte, is not favorable; he notes that he "had been taught to look upon all half breeds with distrust, as an uncertain and faithless race" (16). Irving's view of the white frontiersman who raises a charge of horse thievery against a handsome young Osage who returns his horse is that he "felt little doubt on whose back a lash would be more meritoriously bestowed" (21). He notes as a generality the "capricious and overbearing conduct of the white men; who, as I have witnessed in my own short experience, are prone to treat the poor Indians as little better than brute animals" (27). Irving appears increasingly alienated as his account proceeds; the focus of *Tour* sharpens, however, and comes to rest on the question of how a man of Irving's demonstrated sensibility is going to come to terms with the western wilderness, given his refusal to identify himself with either his traveling companions or the classes and groups he finds there.

The hero's isolation from his companions in the enterprise, stemming mainly from their inadequate responses to the new territory, puts him in a position similar to that of Irving's Columbus: both heroes retain at least the potential for a superior imaginative relationship with the lands and peoples they encounter, but this potential remains largely unrealized because of the overwhelming crassness of the majority. Irving's Columbus ends his days in Spain, far from the world he has opened to view, fruitlessly pursuing his "rights" to the vice-regal title from an unresponsive Ferdinand. Columbus gains little from his voyages, but because of the potential scope revealed by later generations, he comes to be seen as the discoverer of the New World, and his ineffectuality takes on a tragic air, that of a fate imposed by the great forces of history or destiny. The narrator/hero of *Tour*, too, ends his story with an undignified return to "civilization," struggling along with little to eat and with horses that were literally dropping from fatigue.

Unlike Columbus, however, who is unwillingly detained in Spain by the perfidious Spanish monarch's refusal to honor the terms of his original bargain, Irving makes a show of his eagerness to return to the "old" world and its civilized comforts. His first meal in a wayside farm house—boiled beef and turnips, bread and butter—is a "banquet!" (121). Wayne Kime argues that as Irving returns eastward, he "instinctively affirms his identity as a city-boy."[36] Arriving at the first farm house, Kime says, "the Eastern gentleman is clearly ecstatic" (65). Most of Irving's critics have coupled this comic retreat with Irving's earlier "literary" rhetoric to make the argument that Irving was incapable of rendering an authentic response to the West. According to this view, the reality of the West was too much for Irving's Europeanized sensibility and conventional romantic rhetoric, and as a result he made no real discovery of the West (55–56). Such critical opinion seems to confirm Irving's initial apprehensions that he would be judged in comparison to "spirit-stirring narratives" and found wanting as far as he did not sustain the conventions of the contemporary discovery narrative.[37]

Wayne Kime argues that Irving's returning to the East as if to where he belongs is an indication of the understanding that the narrator of *Tour* has achieved. He treats *Tour* as a "carefully articulated narrative of a single initiatory action" in which the narrator confronts an alienating environment that is both appealing and threatening, from which he returns with an enhanced sense of the particularities of both self and other.[38] For Kime, thus, Irving demonstrates his growing understanding of the West through his awareness of the ways he does not belong there. Discovery in Irving's case consists primarily of a recognition of difference and of a conscious renunciation of behavior that destroys the Other as it attempts to mitigate that difference.

The portrayal of such a recognition seems to be the point of the sequence in which Irving kills a buffalo, an episode that comes at the end of a carefully controlled development of the hunting theme, in which animals get bigger and Irving gets closer to direct involvement. Irving renders a full account of the chase, with much attention to the horse's speed, the natural obstacles, the evasions and threats of the buffalo, the near accidents befalling the rider. It is an exciting passage in which the narrator seems to lose himself in an action that he has hitherto described only from the point of view of a bystander. At the end of the chase, however, his own success seems to prompt an abrupt realization of some strongly held views that have been obscured in the excitement:

> Dismounting I now fettered my horse to prevent his straying and advanced to contemplate my victim. I am nothing of a sportsman: I had been prompted to this unwonted exploit by the magnitude of the game and the excitement of an adventurous chase. Now that the excitement was over I could not but look with commiseration upon the poor animal that lay struggling and bleeding at my feet. His very size and importance, which had before inspired me with eagerness, now increased my compunction. It seemed as if I had inflicted pain in proportion to the bulk of my victim, and as if

there were a hundred fold greater waste of life than there would have been in the destruction of an animal of inferior size. . . .

While I stood meditating and moralizing over the wreck I had so wantonly produced, with my horse grazing near me I was rejoined by my fellow sportsman the Virtuoso, who, being a man of Universal adroitness and withal more experienced and hardened in the gentle art of "venerie," soon managed to carve out the tongue of the buffalo, and delivered it to me to bear back to the camp as a trophy.[39]

The narrator suggests that his truest feelings lie with the living animal, rather than with the dead result of his "adventure," and as on many occasions in *Tour*, the affirmation of his own views distinguishes him from his companions, in this case from Latrobe. Usually, as in this case, these companions are superficially more knowledgeable and adept, but, as here, the tone of the passage asserts the deeper feelings of the narrator as the ultimate value reference.

There are numerous similar moments throughout *Tour*, in which the values and perceptions of the narrator are distinguished from the practices and attitudes of those who "know" the West. A typical description of activity around the camp, a favorite theme of *Tour*, includes many qualifiers indicating the narrator's attitude to what he realizes is normal activity for his companions: "The axe was continually at work and wearied the forest with its echoes. Crash! some mighty tree would come down; in a few minutes its limbs would be blazing and crackling on the huge camp fires, with some luckless deer roasting before it, that had once sported beneath its shade" (89). The narrator is clearly more interested in the "mighty tree" and the "luckless deer" than in the assertions of power of the men who destroy them. Similarly, in a more extended passage about sleeping under the stars (the like of which Emerson and Twain would put to similar transcendental purposes), Irving makes clear that his responses to the world he is exploring are of an order other than those of his companions:

It is delightful, in thus bivouacking on the prairies, to lie awake and gaze at the stars; it is like watching them from the deck of a ship at sea, when at one view we have the whole cope of heaven. One realizes, in such lonely scenes, that companionship with these beautiful luminaries which made astronomers of the eastern shepherds, as they watched their flocks by night. . . . I do not know why it was, but I felt this night unusually affected by the solemn magnificence of the firmament, and seemed, as I lay thus under the open vault of heaven, to inhale with the pure untainted air, an exhilarating buoyancy of spirit, and as it were, an ecstasy of mind. I slept and waked alternately, and when I slept my dreams partook of the happy tone of my waking reveries. (114–115)

For the nearby sentinel, the stars merely indicate the time until the morning that will release him from his duty, whereas for Irving they are symbols of an ultimate spiritual reference. Irving confirms the centrality of his feelings in this instance by ending *Tour* with the confession that, sleeping in comfortable quarters at the Osage Agency, "when I woke in the night and gazed about me in complete darkness, I missed the glorious companionship of the stars" (122).

Irving also clearly has a much more generous curiosity about the Indian inhabitants of the prairies than is exhibited by the bigoted frontier whites, the pompous commissioner, or the semihysterical, basically ignorant rangers. Irving's extended descriptions of Indians are not idealizations but attempts to complicate and normalize both the frontier whites' demonized "brute animal" and the easterners' Indian as "described in poetry" (26). Although still highly general, Irving's Indians are credited with a full range of emotions and behaviors and are capable of "the full scope of criticism, satire, mimicry and mirth" (27). More dramatically, Irving eventually breaks through what he clearly recognizes as his own prejudice regarding Beatte, the "half breed" guide. Eventually the two men have a conversation in which Beatte talks openly about his life. As rendered by Irving, the exchange has the effect of making very clear the gulf between the two men, but it also punctures the barrier of mere ignorance and suspicion that Irving has shown himself maintaining. Beatte comes around to describing the experiences of the Osages, his mother's people, for whom he feels a close kinship:

When he talked to me of the wrongs and insults which the poor Indians suffered in their intercourse with the rough settlers on the frontiers; when he described the precarious and degraded state of the Osage tribe, diminished in numbers, broken in spirit, and almost living on sufferance in the land where they once figured so heroically, I could see the veins swell and his nostrils distend with indignation: but he would check the feeling with a strong exertion

141

of Indian self command, and, in a manner, drive it back into his
bosom. He did not hesitate to relate an instance wherein he had
joined his kindred Osages, in pursuing and avenging themselves
on a party of white men who had committed a flagrant outrage
upon them; and I found, in the encounter that took place, Beatte
had shown himself the complete Indian. (92)

Irving does not approve of the revenge Beatte describes, and he catego-
rizes the behavior as "Indian," but it is clear that he understands the
context in which it occurred, and his going on immediately to relate
Beatte's outrage at being asked by an army surgeon to procure him a
Pawnee skull as a specimen clearly indicates that he understands how
outrage is justifiable among both Indians and whites. Irving does not
identify himself with Pierre Beatte or his people, nor does he take sides
with them. He does, however, rhetorically withdraw to a distance from
which he can see a life such as Beatte's in relation to the historical
conditions that shape it, thus asserting implicitly that discovering the
West must include understanding those conditions.

Irving's refusal of the role of adventurer as it was understood by his
companions and his ironic rendering of his own participation in the
expedition do not mean, then, that he had no serious responses to the
lands and peoples he encountered, nor do they mean that he ultimately
departs from the conventions and ideology of the discovery narrative.[40]
Keeping in mind his account of his early life in terms of voyages of
discovery in his introduction to *The Sketch Book*, his description in
Astoria of his contacts with the fur traders in Montreal, his portrait of
Columbus as the martyred saint of American discovery, and the favorable accounts of the Astor and Bonneville expeditions that he would
soon write, it should not surprise us that the fundamental values of
Tour are those of the most serious efforts to come to terms with the
New World and its history. Of course, the frequenter of European
salons and libraries could not portray himself as suddenly transformed
into a great outdoorsman and explorer. But the very distance that his
diction and imagery place between the scenes of his former experiences
and the American prairies enabled him to view the local events of his
month-long journey in relation to three centuries of European action in
the New World.[41] The Arkansas Rangers, in Irving's eyes, seem to be
repeating the depredations witnessed by Columbus in Hispaniola, the
Osages to be another overpowered people in the process of being forced

to the margins. This history is the site of Irving's excursion, and his narrative is a response to this play of events, as well as to the landscape of the West. His tone suggests that his understanding of the history and geography of the West is superior to that of his companions, and even to that of the western natives, but, as was the case with Columbus, this understanding does not prevent him from being shunted to the sidelines as events unfold. Like Columbus's, Irving's imaginative response to the western lands and peoples does not shape events there, and neither does it shape the events of his narrative. Irving is carried along by the commissioner and the rangers; his own sense of his unfolding experience does not guide his journey.

I would argue, however, that despite the basically comic mode of *Tour*,[42] Irving ultimately reserves for himself something of the role he conceived for his tragic Columbus, that of a man whose personal qualities allow for a relationship with America that transcends the limitations of history. Obviously, in donning the mantle he cut for Columbus, Irving had to be overtly ironic and self-deprecating. Nonetheless, there is finally a serious claim made by the narrator of *Tour* to have seen the "real West" and in that sense to have discovered America and fulfilled the purposes of the discovery narrative. As he does for his Columbus, Irving distinguishes himself from his contemporaries through his confessed alienation from the lands and peoples he encountered. But whereas Irving's Columbus, a great visionary, is prevented from realizing his plans by the incapacity of his fellow travelers, as well as by the very magnitude of the historical events he is seen as initiating, the narrator of *Tour* renounces all direct claims on the West more or less voluntarily, and his very modesty ends up enabling him to present the West as something genuinely beyond the world he has come from and therefore new and deserving of circumspect treatment. As Irving portrays his Columbus as spiritually worthy of more than he was personally able to achieve in his own lifetime, of more than he was able to understand even intellectually, so Irving portrays himself as recognizing, but then renouncing out of respect, what he knows he is personally incapable of possessing; he makes an ideal discovery, like the one with which he credits Columbus, and one that will be imitable at all times in the future, but not one that would influence the course of events.[43] The ideality of Irving's claim suggests subsequent romantic travel rhetoric in America, but its clear position on the margins of American history distinguishes Irving's mode of narrative from that which would equate the discoverer's experience with America's.

Irving's Discovery of the Far West

In the succession of works from *Columbus* to *Bonneville*, as well as within individual works, Irving on the one hand asserts the grandeur of the great projectors of European corporate possibility only to recount the defeats that they suffered. On the other hand, he elevates the role of the mere individual wandering in the wilderness who nonetheless achieves a fundamental, if symbolic, contact with the new world. Thus viewed, Columbus is the greatest visionary of corporate possibility in the West. His defeat as a colonizer, however, is quite complete, and thus it is upon his personal qualities of imagination, sensitivity to beauty, openness to what is different, that Irving founds Columbus's legacy to nineteenth-century Americans. In *Tour*, by contrast, the western work that follows *Columbus*, Irving openly eschews any claims to great wilderness entrepreneurship, conspicuously adopting the pose of one who is out of place beyond the western frontier and who is contemptuous of the bungled efforts of official American representatives. Even so, the perceptions of the narrator of *Tour* do finally constitute a kind of discovery of the new territories and a claim on them. Taken together, *Columbus* and *Tour* constitute Irving's complete statement of the nineteenth-century American discovery myth: a vision of virtually limitless possibilities, which is betrayed in its corporate form almost from the first attempt at realization but kept alive through the individual's response to unpeopled American nature and to native peoples themselves, as symbols of original American potential.[44]

Astoria and *Bonneville* ought to be viewed together as a restatement of this myth in terms of contemporary events. The two works together are analogous to the sequence of *Columbus* and *Tour*, in both their perspectives on events and the contrasting scales of the events themselves. *Astoria*, like *Columbus*, is told from an historian's point of view, one who has access to all the data and can span the years and continents in order to link individual experiences into a single story of national significance. That story is the attempt to realize John Jacob Astor's "Columbian" vision of a western trade depot on the Columbia River, one that would link Europe, America, and Asia through the fur trade.

Astor's (and the narrator's) perspective is global, and he is presented as thinking for the ages, not merely in terms of personal gain. *Bonneville*, on the other hand, is, like *Tour*, told from the point of view of the single traveler (with a few exceptions when Irving quotes other written accounts of the region), a traveler in this case whose motives for undertaking the journey are presented as primarily personal and whose achievements rest almost entirely in the quality of his moral and aesthetic responses to the land and its peoples, he having apparently achieved no financial success as a fur trader nor any geographical firsts as an explorer.

Astor's plan to corner the trade of the Far West is presented as a "great enterprize, which for years had been . . . contemplated by powerful associations and national governments."[45] Astor, we are told, "was not actuated by mere motives of individual profit" (23). His vision is of "a colony which would, in fact, carry the American population across the Rocky Mountains and spread it along the shores of the Pacific, as it already animated the shores of the Atlantic" (23). The main concern of *Astoria* is the viability of this project as Astor attempted to realize it, and the individual experiences of those who went west are presented as determinants of the corporate fate. *Bonneville*, by contrast, is the story of a "rambling kind of enterprise" undertaken by a man who "strangely engrafted the trapper and the hunter upon the soldier."[46] Although Bonneville had military training and experience, he is presented as having the *"bonhommie"* and "excitable imagination" (3) of his father, who we are told loved reading and who regularly "forgot the world and its concerns . . . seated under the trees of the battery, . . . his eyes riveted to the page of his book" (3). Bonneville's immediate inspiration to undertake a trip to the Far West is expressed in quasi-literary terms: "intercourse with Indian traders, mountain trappers, and other pioneers of the wilderness," whose "tales of wild scenes and wild adventures, and . . . accounts of vast and magnificent regions as yet unexplored" were such that "an expedition to the Rocky Mountains became the ardent desire of his heart, and an enterprise to explore untrodden tracts, the leading object of his ambition" (4). Bonneville must obtain leave from the army, which ostensibly offers no support for his expedition, and although his letter granting leave asks him to record the military strength and practices of Indian groups, Bonneville's report is not presented as bearing on any particular corporate errand.[47] Irving says that he found Bonneville's manuscript, from which he mainly worked, "full of interesting details of life among the mountains," but—most significant for what he makes of it in his book—Irving notes that "it bore . . . throughout the impress of his character, his *bonhommie*, his kindliness of spirit, and his susceptibility to the grand and the beautiful" (6).

In *Astoria*, human effort and suffering contribute to a grand project (which fails); in *Bonneville*, the individual experiences in the wilderness appear as ends in themselves. They are not therefore trivial or insignificant. On the contrary, as in *Tour*, Irving implies that the sensitive, intelligent individual's response to unknown territories is an authentic claim upon them. The failure of the Astor project does not, of course, imply the end of United States possibility in the Far West, but even more than in *Columbus*, the historian's rhetorical distance from events inhibits recourse to personal experience as an authority for the project. Such a personal rhetoric is obviously much easier to achieve when the point of view, as in *Tour* and *Bonneville*, is that of the actual traveler.

The popularity of a discovery narrative usually depends less upon the achievement of the expedition's nominal goal than upon the recounting of what happens along the way, and in *Astoria* Irving goes about as far as the popular form of the genre will allow in the direction of subordinating the events of the expeditions to their role in the projector's guiding plan. Then, as now, most readers were interested in the particulars of western life and travel, which make up the bulk of the book, and rather less in Mr. Astor's business plans. Nonetheless, Irving frames his account in terms of the history of the fur trade and of Astor's plan to corner the market in the Pacific Northwest. *Astoria* overtly links knowledge of territories and their inhabitants to economic interest and political power. "Discovery" in *Astoria* implies the ability to profit from knowledge, and eventually political control, of lands and peoples beyond the frontier. *Astoria* is the least "personal" of Irving's discovery accounts, rarely invoking the individual responses of expedition members to what they encounter, relying instead on the commercial and political good sense of the projector as its ultimate claim on the West.

Because it is conceived in terms of economic and political interests of nations, *Astoria* suggests the scale and nature of the enterprise in *Columbus*. Irving's Columbus tries to apply fifteenth-century Spanish ideas of government and social hierarchy to the Caribbean world, whereas Astor's plan follows the business techniques of commodity monopolies funded by private capital, in which legal relationships are first of all matters of business contract and only subsequently brought into the purview of treaties and laws. But in both cases, more or less complete control of lands and peoples is sought, sufficient at least to allow the unimpeded gathering of wealth.

According to Irving, Columbus's enterprise is betrayed by a jealous and inconstant monarch and greedy, competitive colleagues in the New World and then overwhelmed by the very scale of what he finds and its variance from what he expected. Astor encounters similar difficulties. Irving goes to some trouble to show that Astor initially had government interest in and approval for his scheme, quoting a letter from Jefferson in which he recalls having "encouraged it with the assurance of every facility and protection which the Government could properly afford."[48] Given this early interest on the part of the government, Irving regards the ultimate loss of Astoria to British interests as partly the result of the "supineness" (354) of the American government, for not having "properly protected" (355) Astor's undertaking and for suffering "the moment to pass when full possession of this region might have been taken quietly as a matter of course" (356). More immediately, some of Astor's active partners, many of them former North-West Company employees and British subjects, are more or less accused of double dealing, of too easily and cheaply giving up Astor's assets to the North-West Company. Not unlike Columbus returning to Hispaniola to find his authority usurped by a subordinate, Astor's primary agent, the loyal Wilson Price Hunt, is appalled upon his return to Astoria to view "the precipitate and summary manner in which the property had been bargained away by Mr. M'Dougall" and to learn that the latter had secretly and for some time been a partner of the North-West Company, to which he has been selling the Astoria assets (350).[49] In addition to such overt disloyalty, "it was [Astor's] great misfortune that his agents were not imbued with his own spirit. Some had not capacity sufficient to comprehend the real nature and extent of the scheme."[50] As with Columbus, Astor's breadth of vision left him exposed to the failures of those with more limited imaginations and more selfish interests.

Irving's account of the ocean and overland expeditions is thus framed by the history of the personal and commercial conditions that led Astor to conceive this project and by the circumstances that led to its failure. Throughout the account one is reminded of this context by references to Astor as a kind of presiding spirit back in New York. We see him at the opera the evening he hears of the explosion of the *Tonkin* (78), and waiting "week after week, and month after month . . ., without anything to dispel the painful incertitude that hung over every part of this enterprise" (309). We read his letter to Hunt, after the outbreak of the War of 1812, in which he says, "were I on the spot, and had the management of affairs, I would defy them all [the British, who were threatening Astoria from the sea]" (309). "Our enterprise is grand," he continues, " and deserves success, and I hope in God it will meet it" (309).

But Astor is not "on the spot," and the collapse of his grand project leaves him far from the scenes of the action of *Astoria* with little to show for it personally. Like Columbus stranded in Spain, Irving's Astor is accorded his claim on the basis of his imagination and foresight, Irving having shown how the realization of Astor's plans was frustrated by the inferior hearts and minds of those who were prosecuting it. Astor's achievement is a vision that Irving believes is still valid for American society, and in this sense it constitutes a claim on the West transcending legal realities and the actual presence of the British. As in *Columbus*, one senses at the end of *Astoria* that history will prove Astor right.[51]

In the meantime, however, Irving's ability rhetorically to buttress this claim by the personal trials, achievements, and reactions of those who undertook the expeditions is limited by the projector's and the writer's not having been participants.[52] The Hunt party's arrival at the Continental Divide, for example, is presented as an event in the lives of the travelers, a reward for their toil to that point. The panorama is rendered as an aesthetic experience of "Mr. Hunt" and "the travellers," one that is colored by the events that led up to it. The guide pauses to consider "the vast landscape attentively." His opinion that the three distant peaks are situated above a fork of the Columbia River was "hailed by the travellers with that joy with which a beacon on the sea shore is hailed by mariners after a long and dangerous voyage."[53] Mr. Hunt names the peaks, an action that symbolizes a claim and the achievement of a goal. But there are very few such attributed perceptions in *Astoria*; most presentations of the landscape are impersonal:

"This point is said to present one of the most beautiful scenes on the Columbia: a lovely meadow, with a silver sheet of limpid water in the centre, enlivened by waterfowl; a range of hills crowned by forests" (67), and the like. This manner of presentation reminds us that the writer is working from the oral and written accounts of those who were there; he is not in a position to testify from his own experience. Irving renders his considered judgment of the value of what was discovered, of the performance of the expedition's participants, of the ultimate rightness of the original plan, and his views draw their authority from his sources. But he is unable to invoke his own feelings in response to the land, the way earlier and subsequent explorers did, as an ultimate sign of possession. Thus, while *Astoria* makes the most explicit claims to territory of any of Irving's discovery histories, it is also the most dependent on governmental and commercial rationales and the least inclined to cite the aesthetic responses of the participants as an authority. As Peter Antelyes argues, "*Astoria* is presented simply as an objective history" in which the ambitions of American business and government in the West are identified with American society and presented as being in conflict with other companies and governments.[54] This practice in *Astoria* differs from the mode of *Tour*, where dangerous conflicts are "seen as residing within the very ideals and social construction of American society" (159). And whereas Columbus's vision of western possibility is in a sense confirmed in his letters by the warmth of his feelings for what he encountered, the circumstances of the composition of *Astoria* did not favor this kind of affective claim, either to buttress American claims in opposition to those of other nations or as a way of transcending the conflicts within American society.

As I have suggested, an altogether different strategy prevails in *Bonneville*, even though the first chapter refers directly to *Astoria* as a continuation of the history of the fur trade in the Northwest and the last entertains the presentiment of its ultimate passing away. Reflecting the devolution of the American western trade into smaller groups of trappers and traders operating independently in the mountains, Irving's focus shifts from a continental and historical perspective to one mostly centered on the activities of a single traveler in the Far West, one who, as already stated, is explicitly detached from governmental and corporate strategies and authority. Most of *Bonneville* is presented from the point of view of this traveler, without references to the known outcome of his journey. Bonneville is thus the hero of the action in a way that was impossible for Astor, and Irving is thus able to focus more directly on travel as the experience of an individual rather than as the enactment of a plan. Bonneville's own motives, though rationalized through his proposal to trade and to scout the land and its peoples, are more a matter of his curiosity and love of adventure. These latter qualities are the starting point of a narrative whose meaning is closely related to the deeds and experiences of the main active character.

And, like the hero of *Tour*, Bonneville becomes increasingly differentiated from the other American actors in the West as his story unfolds, and the American point of view on the West is adjusted to exclude and invalidate the Americans with whom Bonneville initially associates. Although Irving initially speaks admiringly of the American trader/trappers who explore the Rocky Mountain territory in the 1820s and 1830s, he comes to deplore the excesses of their competition and its effects upon the trappers themselves, as well as upon the Indian inhabitants of the Far West. If the Rocky Mountains from the Russian possessions to California have been "traversed" by the traders, they have also been "ransacked"[55] by "rival bands . . . [whose] constant study . . . is to forestall and outwit each other; to supplant each other in the good will and custom of the Indian tribes; to cross each other's plans; to mislead each other as to routes" (10–11). As a result of this trade, Indian groups have been opened to "sources of luxury of which they previously had no idea, . . . [and] the introduction of fire-arms had rendered them . . . more formidable foes," some of whom "waylay and harass" bands of trappers "in the rugged defiles of the mountains" (11). The narrator of *Bonneville* condemns these "virulent and sordid competitions" in which the parties are "more intent upon injuring their rivals, than benefiting themselves" (108). Ultimately, he says, "we forebear to detail their pitiful contentions" (108). He also explicitly links this competition with harassment by Indians of small groups of traders and, worse, with the traders' atrocious retaliations, such as the burning alive of two Arickara horse thieves (108–109). As Wayne Franklin argues, this kind of competition underlies the frantic and often violent conviviality of the trappers' annual "rendezvous," events that superficially are scenes of western "romance"; in fact, "no safe middle ground exists between those rivalries and the manic festivities of the winter camp."[56]

In *Bonneville*, this competition among the independent traders is on another level from that which constitutes the main conflict in *Astoria*. In the earlier work, rivalry in the fur trade is for the most part shown as occurring between corporate and national entities, and the actions of the men in the field are controlled by central authorities. For example, though the young Americans at Astoria are ashamed and infuriated by the arrogant behavior of the North-West Company men who arrive to take over, their sense of honor and their desire to defend the fort are overruled by the senior partners who have arranged the sale of the company assets.[57] Irving's conclusion in *Astoria* is that the failure to defend the achievement of Astor's expeditions leads to the loss to American citizens of a valuable trade and eventually to a potentially dangerous conflict between Britain and the United States over the territory itself. Despite the importance he attaches to these matters, however, Irving's tone is measured; Astor, he concludes, has done all he can to realize his plan, and seeing no further help likely from the American government, "he abandoned all thoughts of regaining Astoria, and made no further attempt to extend his enterprises beyond the Rocky Mountains."[58] The result of such competition as recounted in *Astoria* is a business loss, to which the capitalist responds with a decision to pursue his interests elsewhere. The American people, presumably, wait for another entrepreneur to step into Astor's shoes.

The results of the later stages of the American fur trade recounted in *Bonneville* are catastrophic in comparison, even apocalyptic. The universally destructive behavior that Irving describes and condemns extends to the resource itself, as traders deliberately "trap out" whole areas in order to deny their rivals. The result, Irving suggests in his conclusion, will be the extinction of the whole way of life:

> The fur trade, itself, which has given life to all this portraiture, is essentially evanescent. Rival parties of trappers soon exhaust the streams, especially when competition renders them heedless and wasteful of the beaver. The fur-bearing animals extinct, a complete change will come over the scene. . . . All this . . . savage life, which yet exists among the mountains, will then exist but in frontier story. (269)

The traders gone, Irving speculates that the western Indians will amalgamate into a permanent outlaw group:

> An immense belt of rocky mountains and volcanic plains, several hundred miles in width, must ever remain an irreclaimable wilderness, intervening between the abodes of civilization, and affording a last refuge to the Indian. Here, roving tribes of hunters, living in tents or lodges, and following the migrations of game, may lead a life of savage independence, where there is nothing to tempt the cupidity of the white man. The amalgamation of various tribes, and of white men of every nation, will in time produce hybrid races like the mountain Tartars of the Caucasus. Possessed as they are of immense droves of horses, should they continue their present predatory and warlike habits, they may, in time, become a scourge to the civilized frontiers on either side of the mountains; as they are at present a terror to the traveller and trader. (269–270)

The "cupidity of the white man" is thus seen as causing the more or less permanent alienation of a large territory and its peoples from American life.

Read together, then, *Astoria* and *Bonneville* envision the failure of governmental, corporate, and small-scale commercial efforts to establish a permanent United States presence in the Far West. However, *Bonneville's* emphasis on the unbridled fur trade competition, along with the hero's lack of overt commitment to the institutions of American western expansion, suggests weaknesses that go beyond the tactical defeats of *Astoria* to a betrayal of American values, failings that render the traders positively undeserving of success,and thus call into question American destiny in the West. The framing of *Astoria* within the geopolitical competition between Americans and British for control of the western trade and coast and Irving's identification of Astor's plans with a Columbian vision of western empire suggest a historical meta-narrative within which the failures of the particular Astor expeditions are merely temporary setbacks for Americans; the narrative of American western destiny remains intact.[59] In *Bonneville*, however, there is no figure to whom such a vision can be ascribed, and neither are there figures acting on behalf of institutions that continue to represent social purpose when individual actors fail or become confused; there are no actors or institutions identified with American national purpose in the

West. The institutions that are present—mainly the organizations of the mountain men—are shown to be inadequate and morally suspect.

Peter Antelyes argues that Irving is not just portraying the conflict and disintegration of the fur trade but that *Bonneville* as a book achieves no structuring that would control the meaning of the events in relation to American society and history. "Bonneville moves West, meets Indians and trappers, explores the landscape, and returns, and nothing in these adventures provides them with a context by which the reader can discover a larger meaning" (189). Whereas in *Tour* and *Astoria* Irving had managed to retain and convey his faith in the redemptive role of American expansion into the West through the expansion of the marketplace, despite his critique of the excesses of self-interest and greed, in *Bonneville*, Antelyes argues, this faith "has become tenuous. Business and imagination appear incompatible. . . . The confusions and inconsistencies of *Bonneville* . . . reflect a deeper despair over both the urgencies of the marketplace and the efficacies of literature" (191).

I share Antelyes's sense that in *Bonneville* Irving is for the most part unable to relate his hero's activities to any very positive sense of American expansion into the West. I am not sure, however, that *Bonneville* renounces completely the American vision of western possibility; rather, I think that, to an even greater extent than in *Tour*, the response of the intelligent, sympathetic individual, who is distanced from prevailing commercial greed and brute force, implies an American claim. Whereas *Astoria* invokes the Columbian characteristic of great forward-looking vision, *Bonneville* updates to the nineteenth-century American situation Columbus's love of the beauty of the land and early sympathy with the New World's inhabitants.

To begin with the second issue, we see the mistreatment of native inhabitants by American traders established as an important theme of *Bonneville*, a backdrop against which the behavior of the eponymous hero is contrasted. Irving takes several opportunities to condemn Euro-American behavior in this regard and to demonstrate that conflict with Indian peoples is often the result of white crimes. After his account of a trader burning alive two Arickaras who were accused of stealing horses, Irving asserts that such "savage cruelties" as white men learn to practice "lead to terrible recrimination on the part of the Indians." "Should we hear," he continues, "of any atrocities committed by the Arickaras upon captive white men, let this signal and recent provocation be borne in mind."[60] Earlier in the narrative, Irving remarks that he knows of several battles that "commenced by a hostile act on the part of white men, at the moment when the Indian warrior was extending the hand of amity" (67).

The most developed example of white crime against Indians is the behavior of the party split off from Bonneville's that intended to explore the Great Salt Lake region but ended up in California. This group, harassed by the petty thefts of the "digger" or "poor devil" Indians— whom Irving characterizes as "a simple, timid, inoffensive race, unpractised in warfare, and scarce provided with any weapons" (209)—shoots one and then another twenty-five in cold blood (208–209). Irving has led up to this outrage by describing these Indians on several occasions as generally the least aggressive, the poorest, and most retiring of the mountain peoples (138, 156, 162, 164, 166). This same party of Bonneville's men later includes Mexicans who "hunted the poor Indians like wild beasts, . . . chasing their unfortunate victims at full speed; noosing them round the neck with their lassos, and then dragging them to death!" (216).

Bonneville's separation from such acts is as crucial to Irving's account of this expedition as it had been essential to distinguish Columbus from the cruelest behavior of his contemporaries in the Caribbean. The writer of a popular western discovery narrative, Irving had to consider the relationship implied between his readers and the lands that they saw as, at least immanently, a part of their nation. If the institutions of American business and government were seen to be inadequate, and if individual Americans further disqualified themselves through their immoral behavior, Irving nonetheless needed some way of representing the American imagination in the West. Bonneville, though he does not pretend to represent American institutional power in the West and though he is not even very successful as an independent trader, can nonetheless be presented as having his ethical and aesthetic senses about him; he can still represent moral agency in a theater of chaos and predation. We are told, accordingly, that Bonneville was "so indignant at the atrocities related to him that he turned, with disgust and horror, from the narrators" (216). The narrator goes on to suggest that it would have been "a salutary act of retributive justice" had Bonneville "exerted a little of the Lynch law of the wilderness" (216). A somewhat later reference to this affair, in which one of the murderers is unable to endure the presence of people who remind him of those he has killed, draws the observation from Bonneville that such behavior demonstrates "the effect of self-reproach, even upon the roving trapper in the wilderness, who has little else to fear than the sting of his own conscience" (242).

Although *Bonneville* begins as an account of the fur trade, the focus shifts increasingly to Bonneville's experiences with the various Indian peoples he encounters, and, overall, I think there is at least as much attention devoted to Indians' lives as to the trappers'. Moreover, Bonneville's discussion of Indians shifts from Crow and Blackfoot "banditti" who harass the traders to his own more extended and complex relations with friendly groups. Irving portrays Bonneville as well disposed to Indians before setting out on his expedition (25), and he asserts early on that Bonneville "throughout all his transactions" showed himself "the friend of the poor Indians"; his conduct, according to Irving, was "above all praise" (69). There is a remarkable amount of pleasant interaction recounted, and although some of the commentary is condescending, there is nonetheless an attempt to get beyond facile categories and stereotypes, whether these be the "poetic speculations" (25) to which Bonneville alludes initially or the dehumanizing attitudes of many of the trappers. *Bonneville* ends with Irving's vision of a mountain wilderness populated by "roving tribes," the "essentially evanescent" (269) fur trade and those who pursued it having vanished altogether. And while we may be amused by his notion that there Indians and "white men of every nation, will in time produce hybrid races like the mountain Tartars of the Caucasus" (270), we are nonetheless well prepared for Irving's prophesying by the accounts of the local peoples who have gone before. Irving recovers the fact of a populated and complex land simply through the weight of incident in his narrative. It is the white men of *Bonneville* whose presence is evanescent. Living "in the heart of the wilderness," Bonneville still describes it as a "populous solitude" (69).

Bonneville is interested in trade and is "desirous, through the Indians, of becoming acquainted with the secret places of the land" (74), yet the tone of many of his observations is disinterested. The Nez Perces make him "wonder at such unaffected tenderness and piety" (57), and he passed his time with them "in the continual experience of acts of kindness and generosity" (181). Irving notes that in *Astoria* he had characterized the Nez Perces according to the traders "who had casually been among them, and who represented them as selfish, inhospitable, exorbitant in their dealings, and much addicted to thieving" (180–181). In *Bonneville,* he now exclaims: "How difficult it is to get at the true character of these wandering tribes" (180). While we would quarrel with the idea of a national "true character," it is nonetheless apparent in *Bonneville* that Irving recognizes the complexity of life in the West and is willing to acknowledge his own ignorance. The last quarter of *Bonneville* is typified by a palpable increase in incidents stemming from Bonneville's interactions with local peoples. There are extended, flattering accounts of the "Skynses," "Flatheads," "Eutaws," and "Shoshonies" (257–261), and as a result, when Irving speculates at the end about a "belt of rocky mountains and volcanic plains . . . affording a last refuge to the Indian" (269), one senses that (minimal as this refuge is) these remarks spring from his concern for the continued existence of the peoples who have taken on a certain reality under his pen.

Bonneville's sympathetic relationships with various western peoples is only one way that Irving distinguishes him from the rank and file of the mountain men. Building upon the initial characterization of Bonneville as disinterestedly curious about the West, Irving endows him with a mentality quite distinct from that of any of his companions. In fact, Irving takes pains to show how Bonneville's character is closely allied with the narrator's, saying at the outset that "there was something in the whole appearance of the captain that prepossessed me in his favor" (5). It is important in this regard that Bonneville had not profited from his expedition, that his "wanderings in the wilderness, though they had gratified his curiosity and his love of adventure, had not much benefited his fortunes," that, in fact, "he was too much the frank, freehearted soldier, and had inherited too much of his father's temperament, to make a scheming trapper, or a thrifty bargainer" (5).

Insofar as he is thus ill-suited to compete on the same terms as the other Americans in the West, Bonneville should be seen as a further development of the figure Irving cut for himself in *Tour*, a character whose responses to the West, because they spring from a disinterested imagination, do justice to the beauty of the land, its long-term potential for growth, and the individuality and natural rights of its inhabitants. As in *Tour*, this figure emerges gradually out of the waste and failure around him, but in *Bonneville*, the scale of the failure is much greater, encompassing American possibilities among the lands and peoples of the mountain region. Such is the ultimate result of what at the end of *Bonneville* Irving calls "Mr. Astor's dream" (276).

If Irving's portrait of Bonneville among the western Indian peoples complicates the vision of American possibility in the West, another aspect of Bonneville's personality opens onto the empowering rhetoric of the "discoverer's vision." In this important trope, as we have seen elsewhere, the sensitive individual traveler responds to a panoramic view of the land he has been struggling through or toward. *Bonneville* affords notable examples of the way Irving distinguished his last discoverer from his more limited contemporaries and shaped the rhetoric of Bonneville's account in accordance with his own sense of how Americans could be said to have a claim on lands to the west.

To begin with, Irving is explicit about his hero's susceptibility to inspiration from natural beauty and plainly identifies this quality as fundamental to Bonneville's role as a discoverer. Throughout, Irving both recounts Bonneville's experiences and feelings in the third person and quotes Bonneville directly. Moreover, in several cases Irving merges his narrator's perspective with Bonneville's by ascribing his own reactions to his hero, thus confirming our sense that Bonneville is an exemplary figure as far as Irving is concerned, a kind of armchair explorer's registering consciousness. For example, when Bonneville attains his first view of the Rocky Mountains, "the grand region of his hopes and anticipations" (31) and "a magnificent prospect burst upon his sight," the narrator suggests that "we can imagine the enthusiasm of the worthy captain. . . . We can imagine with what feelings of awe and inspiration he must have contemplated" the panorama of rivers and valleys below him (31). The sensibilities that we see here are confirmed somewhat later in an explicit assurance that "Captain Bonneville had the soul to appreciate " the "glories and beauties" of an immense winter landscape (86). Despite the sufferings of Bonneville and his party in this landscape, "these brilliant scenes . . . stamped pictures on their memory, which have been recalled with delight in more genial situations" (86).

The fundamental link between Bonneville's susceptibility to such impressions and his errand as a discoverer is made overt through Irving's statement of Bonneville's goals, in which the desire to explore "unknown tracts of the Far West" is fulfilled by "the vivid impression on his mind" made by "the grand features of the wilderness about which he was roaming" (114). Immediately after telling us that "the exploring of unknown regions" was "uppermost in [Bonneville's] mind," Irving repeats Bonneville's account of his view of the Great Salt Lake: "As you ascend the mountains about its shores, says he, you behold this immense body of water spreading itself before you, and stretching further and further, in one wide and far reaching expanse, until the eye, wearied with continued and strained attention, rests in the blue dimness of distance, upon the lofty ranges of mountains, confidently asserted to rise from the bosom of the waters" (114). This panorama is the rhetorical fulfillment of the desire to explore "unknown tracts," an instance of the way that aesthetic responses to the West serve as knowledge and as authority for the viewer's presence. As is frequently the case in such passages, the land is here said to be "spreading itself" before the viewer, in this case, a generalized "you."

Perhaps the supreme example of the "discovery vision" trope in *Bonneville* is the account of the captain's ascent of a peak in the Wind River Mountains upon whose summit he achieves an almost mystical state of identity with what he surveys. As in other similar sequences, Irving very skillfully makes this vision the climax and reward of an arduous journey through extremely difficult terrain. In this case, the travelers think each slope they are scaling will be the last, only to see from its summit the "they were on the brink of a deep and precipitous ravine, from the bottom of which, rose a second slope, similar to the one they had just ascended" (134). After two days of "rocks," "precipices," and "rugged defiles," they reach a valley "locked up in this singular bed of mountains. Here were two bright and beautiful little lakes, set like mirrors in the midst of stern and rocky heights, and surrounded by grassy meadows, inexpressibly refreshing to the eye" (135). The imagery of this passage is in high contrast to the rocky steepness of what precedes it. The hitherto threatening mountains now form a boudoir offering "bed," "mirror," and "inexpressible" refreshment. What has been dangerous and exacting now seems to offer safety and repose.

From this resting place, Bonneville and some of his men undertake the ascent of the highest of the surrounding peaks, again occasioning a passage of danger, sweat, and struggle until "they at length attained the summit":

Here a scene burst upon the view of Captain Bonneville, that for a time astonished and overwhelmed him with its immensity. He stood, in fact, upon that dividing ridge which Indians regard as the crest of the world; and on each side of which, the landscape may be said to decline to the two cardinal oceans of the globe. Whichever way he turned his eye, it was confounded by the vastness and variety of objects. Beneath him, the Rocky Mountains seemed to open their secret recesses: deep solemn valleys; treasured lakes; dreary passes; rugged defiles, and foaming torrents; while beyond their savage precincts, the eye was lost in an almost immeasurable landscape; reaching on every side into dim and hazy distance, like the expanse of a summer's sea. Whichever way he looked, he beheld vast plains glimmering with reflected sunshine; mighty streams wandering in their course toward either ocean, and snowy mountains, chain upon chain, and peak upon peak, till they melted like clouds into the horizon. For a time the Indian fable seemed realized: he had attained that height from which the Blackfoot warrior, after death, first catches a view of the land of souls, and beholds the happy hunting grounds spread out below him, brightening with the abodes of the free and generous spirits. The captain stood for a long while gazing upon this scene, lost in a crowd of vague and indefinite ideas and sensations. (135–136)

It is notable that despite the activity required to reach the summit, Bonneville's experience on top is essentially a matter of his receiving impressions from the landscape. Irving begins the description by reminding us of Bonneville's susceptibility to such impressions. It is the scene that "burst upon the view of Captain Bonneville," not he who bursts upon the scene. Bonneville is "astonished and overwhelmed"; his "eye" is "confounded by the vastness and variety." He is ultimately "lost in a crowd of vague and indefinite ideas and sensations." Irving's referring to the "Indian fable" that this spot is where warriors first catch a view of the "land of souls" is a way of further developing the notion that Bonneville is achieving a liminal state. In this case, the man whose "pride" had made him "obstinate" (135) to reach the top is somehow changed by his experience. It is important to Irving's sense of Bonneville's fitness as a discoverer that he be capable of thus relinquishing his ego and ambition to a sense of awe and reverence.

The continuation of this passage, however, shows that it is not

Irving's intention to have his hero renounce all aspirations to control what he discovers: "A long drawn inspiration at length relieved him from this enthralment of the mind, and he began to analyse the parts of this vast panorama" (136). Here follows a paragraph singling out the features visible from this height, and what is important in this inventory is that most of them have names by then familiar, having been visited and named by earlier travelers and by Bonneville himself. As a result, the initial effect of the whole scene upon Bonneville's control of his faculties is quickly regulated by the assertion of what is already known. This movement toward controlling the scene continues as the discussion moves into a fairly technical passage about the height of the mountains, both in absolute terms and in comparison to the great mountain ranges throughout the world (137). What has begun as an overwhelming of the discoverer by what he sees changes into an inventory of the territory that, from the heights, he can visually dominate. Irving's references to the ridge as the place from which the worthy Blackfoot warrior is said to go to his reward is a good analogy for the spiritual qualification that entitles Bonneville to his view of the great land below him. Irving insists on Bonneville's constitutional perceptivity, but here he also makes clear through the long description of Bonneville's struggle through the mountains that he earns his moment of ecstatic vision.

As with his friendly relations with local peoples, this response to a panoramic vision can initially be understood as humility in the face of the grandeur of the landscape and the qualities of its people. But *Bonneville* should be read within the context of Irving's commitment to the myth of western discovery, a commitment that, as we have seen, he himself dates to his earliest awareness of the world around him and that shows up early in his writing and lasts at least through *Bonneville* itself. In this context, wonder at the expanse of land opened to the eyes of the traveler is a trope that connects Bonneville to the tradition of European expansion in the Americas going back to the earliest voyages.[61] The effect, here as elsewhere, is to reconnect the discoverer with the full potential of the "virgin" continent after he has recognized that European "contact" to date has not respected that potential. Astor and Bonneville are, as it were, on opposite sides of the narrative divide in the myth of western discovery. Astor projects eastern institutions into the West with an eye to realizing their economic and political potential.

His plan fails as a result of human weaknesses and historical forces beyond his control. Bonneville arrives in time to witness the effective waste of what Astor wanted to harness, but he nonetheless is able to see past the results of the betrayal to contact perhaps a purer vision of the West, but one that is, at least in the manner of its rendering, now detached from economic and political power.

Irving's individualist discoverers advance their own superior sensibilities, as evidenced in their responses to land and peoples, as their claim to have discovered something of the West. In terms of the nature of the claim they assert on the West, and thus of their relationship to the American myth of discovery, Bonneville and Irving's narrator in *Tour* are very much alike. They articulate Irving's response to the conflict embodied by the myth: between the "unknown" western region as a sign of untapped corporate potential and the evidence of successive frontiers as regions of potential somehow betrayed. Bonneville and the narrator of *Tour* appear increasingly to abandon the corporate errand as they explore the West, making instead their own personal discoveries. With respect to Bonneville, Peter Antelyes argues that because Bonneville "is *only* an appreciator, and because that appreciation is . . . presented as a means of escaping from, rather than entering into, the marketplace, he can succeed neither as a participant nor as an observer."[62] But I would argue that Bonneville's observer status is not ineffectual. As an American registering consciousness in the West, his perceptions, and the values underlying them, serve as an authority for American presence in the West that figuratively transcends the economic and political conflict inherent in American westward expansion.

Despite these heroes of sensibility, however, Irving's accounts of western discovery are firmly situated in the commercial and national institutions through which the forces of the American expansion were marshalled. Irving's western writings are primarily histories, and as such they strive to represent the actual conflicts in the West. *Tour* is based on a sortie of the local militia and an official circuit of an Indian Commissioner. In it we see the cooperation of the national government and the recent settlers along the frontier against the Indian peoples farther to the west. *Astoria* recounts the rivalries of the large trading companies and their relationships to the international competition for control of western lands. It includes many details about how local peoples cooperated with, opposed, or competed with these European and Euro-American interests and how the advent of the fur trade changed the relationships among western peoples themselves. *Bonneville* is more like subsequent narratives of the American frontier in the sense that its plot is more aligned with the actions of an individual hero. Nonetheless, apart from the hero himself, the motive of the Euro-Americans in the West is commerce, and the source of the conflicts among themselves and with the local peoples is the scarcity of resources. Irving accords Indian peoples a presence in this interaction, going beyond idle exoticism and its converse, an apparently unmotivated native opposition to newcomers. He achieves individuation of particular Indian characters and cultures, and his Indians' actions are connected to their needs and interests in relation to the politics of the commercial frontier.

Irving's heroes of sensibility are submerged within the framework of these institutional interactions. In *Tour,* Irving tags along with the commissioner and his ranger escorts and is careful to demonstrate in diverse ways his detachment from the goals and mentality of his party. In *Bonneville,* the hero is given an explicitly literary sensibility, detached from his army identity, and then progressively distanced from the concerns of a fur trader as the narrative advances. These heroes' personal responses are not given any official sanction or authority, and the implication seems to be that frontier relationships of Euro-Americans and Indians will continue to develop according to the patterns of competition for space and resources, regardless of whatever "higher" views of the matter men such as Irving and Bonneville achieve. In this framework, Irving is quite willing to judge the imagination, performance, and morality of the individuals involved and to find fault, as he does for example at the end of *Bonneville,* with the "cupidity of the white man" (269). He does not, however, seem to expect the history of European expansion into America to be altered by his views. Nor does he approach the position that through their misbehavior Europeans and their American descendants have permanently forfeited their claim to their "discovery," even though the behavior chronicled, in *Tour* and *Bonneville* especially, fairly thoroughly discredits the majority of the persons involved. Somehow, in spite of what he shows us in the way of white "cupidity," the momentum of the discovery myth prevails, lifting rare individuals up onto mountains where they can reconnect with the vision of a vast, pristine land. In Irving's works about the West, however, these discoverers and their visions remain rhetorically marginal, even though they are central to Irving's basic values and vision. Succeeding writers would isolate what in Irving is really an exceptional figure, making his arrival on the mountaintop the goal of their narrative strategies and a central emblem of Euro-American empire building.

CHAPTER FOUR

Poe and Thoreau: The Romantic Discovery Narrative

Discovery and Violence: Poe's
Narrative of Arthur Gordon Pym

As with Irving, critics often cite the popularity of voyages and discoveries as a reason Poe took up the genre with *The Narrative of Arthur Gordon Pym*.[1] Some see it is a matter of Poe's (or Irving's) merely wanting to "write a narrative that would sell to a large public."[2] Others contend that, through the discovery narrative, Poe is engaging the central issues of American society. Edwin Fussell's *Frontier* (1965) is perhaps the best example from the latter camp. Arguing that the American West and the frontier experience are the "ultimate source[s] of Poe's ambition," Fussell says that Poe translated "the generic cultural experience of the actual Westward Movement into parallel psychological and individual terms."[3] Fussell convincingly demonstrates that "no important American writer was more realistically concerned with, and more accurately informed about, that literature of the West which in the mid-1830's flooded the country" (132). He discusses in some detail Poe's commentaries on the "Western poems, sketches, and fiction [that] poured over [his] desk" as editor of the *Southern Literary Messenger* in order to make the case that, even when he sent his heroes south and out to sea, Poe was exploring issues arising from Euro-Americans' westward movement in North America. To this end, Poe "exploited the widespread identification (or confusion) of the South and West" (132–147). In a very real sense, however, notwithstanding Fussell's evidence of Poe's western interests, Poe's intentions in this regard are not crucial, for the narrative of discovery was so much a part of the discourse of European colonial expansion that to resort to it was to engage the issues inseparable from that discourse, regardless of whether an author was purporting to write history or fiction or where he or she sited the narrative.

Like Irving's, Poe's handling of the genre entailed his defining a relationship with the genre's main characters and institutions. The primary difference between the ways the two writers handled these matters lies in the relationships they set up with institutional authority. In Irving's works on discovery, whether they concern his own or others' travels, the significance of a traveler's experiences is defined in relation to the institutions fostering European and Euro-American expansion into the New World. In other words, Irving was writing history, in the mainstream of the American historiography of that expansion. Even when, as in *Tour* and *Bonneville* especially, he expressed doubts about the individuals whose actions he was recounting, Irving remained publicly committed to westward expansion as a defining action of Euro-American society. As the writer of *Columbus, Tour, Astoria, and Bonneville*, Irving's public role was as a historian of that action, and he was clear that his intention was to speak directly to his readers about it.

It may hardly seem necessary to point out that *Pym* predicates a very different relationship between its author and readers. Poe prefaces *Pym* in the persona of the hero of the title, who refers to Poe in the third person as the former editor of the *Southern Literary Messenger* who published the first few chapters of the narrative serially, as though they were fiction written by himself. Pym claims that his narrative is in fact a true one and that it is merely so strange that it seems fictitious. The "Note" that ends the account is presented as being written by an anonymous editor or publisher who refers to both Pym and Poe in the third person. Add these obscuring gestures to the fact that many of the events of the tale are incredible and that Poe's name did not appear on the original title page, and it is hardly surprising that all the contemporary reviews cited by Pollin (1974) grapple with the question of whether there is any factual basis for the account. Readers were unsure whether to regard it as an imaginary voyage, a verisimilar voyage narrative (in the manner of *Robinson Crusoe*), or a true voyage narrative, and it is certainly arguable that it was Poe's intention to blur the boundaries between these related genres, but it is clear that readers recognized a host of "discovery" conventions in *Pym* and were prepared to deal with this kind of story and the issues it raised.[4]

That Poe chose to fictionalize the discovery narrative where Irving had undertaken accounts that acknowledged the authority of the public discourse of European colonial expansion is not in itself particularly significant. But Poe's obscuring of the authorship of his narrative is only one aspect of a disruption of the links between individual action and social authority that runs throughout *Pym*. Poe construes exploratory travel as an act of transcendent insubordination in which the voyager sloughs off the ties of family and nation so that travel may signify in relation to the soul. Geographic discovery is virtually equated with self-discovery, and the discovery narrative is reorganized as a quest for self-knowledge. In Irving's western narratives, romantic sensibilities are somewhat at odds with the institutions of American western expansion, but individual perception does not reject or transcend the public, historical discourse of American destiny. In *Pym*, romantic sensibility asserts its own development as a metanarrative superior to that of the institutions of American expansion.

It is crucial to the effect of *Pym*, however, that Poe meticulously evokes the rhetoric of voyage and discovery accounts. As J. V. Ridgely points out, until the Tsalal episode, *Pym* might be called a "verisimilar voyage narrative," and I would further suggest that the account of the events in Tsalal, apart from incredible details like multicolored water and the inhabitants' black teeth, is also very much in the manner of many accounts of encounters with unknown peoples.[5] Poe retains the events and tropes typical of early nineteenth-century voyage and discovery accounts, but he shifts the locus of their significance from the institutions of national expansion to the effects of that expansion on the Euro-American individual. This shift has been noted by other critics,[6] but how Poe's romantic recentering of the discovery narrative ought to be read in relation to the contemporary discourse of discovery in America remains to be determined.

The Narrative of Arthur Gordon Pym incorporates all the major formal and thematic characteristics of the exploration narrative. It is the traveler's own story, told by him in the first person as though it were based on a journal. Reflecting its supposed source, it is strictly chronological, with little foreshadowing of future events. The plot is conceived of as one man's journey, eventually into territory beyond what any "white man" has ever before visited. The narrator's positions in time and space are abstractly rendered, according to conventions of navigation. Paragraphs sometimes begin with dates, as in a journal, and the narrator indicates his position in terms of the coordinates of longitude and latitude. The narrator describes land and seascape as seen for the first time by a white "discoverer."

Poe places his narrator within the tradition of scientific exploration. Pym affects the empirical position that accepts all unusual plant and animal life, geological details, and climatic phenomena as being worthy of notice, however peripheral they were to the action at the time they were observed. Overall, *Pym* is characterized by abrupt shifts between the traveler's recording of external phenomena (in the categories of nineteenth-century natural science) and his hardly less systematic attention to his own reactions to unusual and often threatening experiences. Edwin Fussell suggests that these "shifts from sequence to sequence" resemble similar devices in Washington Irving's *Astoria*, which Poe reviewed and drew upon heavily in *Pym*.[7] However, the pattern is also characteristic of the exploration narrative as a genre, and Poe certainly had read many examples of this form besides Irving's (150).

The rhetorical stance of eighteenth- and nineteenth-century explorers suits Poe's narrator very well. At least during his southern voyage on the *Jane Guy*, he relishes the responsibilities to observe and record, and in anticipation of his adventures, he positively glories in the open-ended journey that promises "incidents . . . beyond the range of human experience."[8] It is in accord with the conventions of exploration narratives for Poe to include long discussions of "proper and regular stowage" of a ship's cargo, of "laying-to" in a gale, of Antarctic bird life, and frequent references to wind, weather, water, direction, speed, course, and the like (98, 105–106, 151–153). Pym's performance of the routine chores of exploratory reportage stems from his espousal of the great ambitions of the self-conscious explorers. He is aware of the record of previous related voyages. He knows when he has "advanced to the southward more than eight degrees farther than any previous navigators," and he asserts that he must "be allowed to feel some degree of gratification at having been instrumental . . . in opening the eye of science to one of the most intensely exciting secrets which has ever engrossed its attention" (166).

Pym undergoes both major types of suffering that constituted another theme of the exploration narrative: the want of food, water, and shelter in an unmediated environment, and the hostility of foreign, little-understood peoples. As far as the basic form and content of his traveling experience are concerned, it makes little difference that Pym's journey was by sea rather than land. Like the explorations of North America, his traveling involves many kinds of hardships, and his contacts with new lands and peoples involve the same basic attractions and risks. Like Hearne, Henry, and the others, he regards the extent and nature of his sufferings as information, part of the standard subject matter of the type of report he was writing.

Sufferings of the first category abound from the outset, when Pym's career is prefigured in the midnight excursion in the *Ariel*. At the mercy of a storm, Pym experiences "an intense agony of terror," which he never forgets but often equals during his succeeding voyages (60). Such extremes are typical of the explorer's account. Samuel Hearne details his many involuntary fasts, noting that "none of our natural wants, if we except thirst, are so distressing, or hard to endure."[9] Hearne also agonizes over the Eskimo massacre he was forced to witness, shedding tears even as he wrote of it (100). Alexander Henry recounts how he suffered agonies while hiding in a French trader's attic, fearing discovery and scalping at the hands of Indians attacking Michilimackinac.[10]

Like these actual explorers, Pym nearly starves and suffocates in the hold of the *Grampus*, only escaping this fate to fall into the hands of the drunken, deranged mutineers who have already dispatched most of the rest of the crew. He suffers through the storm that effectively destroys the ship lashed to the windlass and exposed to the full force of the elements. Surviving the storm, he and his three companions grapple with thirst and hunger until they finally resort to cannibalism, the act that conventionally signaled the ne plus ultra of privation in wilderness accounts. Stories of cannibalism abound in exploration literature, and the possibility lurks as the final horrific choice in most accounts of prolonged shortages of food. Hearne relates how on "pressing occasions," he has frequently seen Indians examine their wardrobe, which consisted chiefly of skin clothing, and consider what part could best be spared . . . to alleviate extreme hunger. . . . Those who are conversant . . . with the distress which the natives of the country . . . frequently endure, may consider [such hardship] as no more than the common occurrences of an Indian life, in which they are frequently driven to the necessity of eating one another.[11]

Like many travelers, Pym also suffers at the hands of foreign peoples, though who ultimately receives the worst treatment is debatable. Like Alexander Henry, Pym sees most of his countrymen murdered by outraged local inhabitants, and, like Henry, he hides in order to avoid the same fate. After the ambush, Pym and Dirk Peters are "the only living white men on the island," and they watch from the hilltop where they are trapped as the *Jane Guy*, at anchor in the harbor, is boarded by the Tsalalians and her remaining crewmen are "borne down at once, overwhelmed, trodden under foot, and absolutely torn to pieces in an instant."[12] Trying to avoid a similar end, Pym and Peters subsist almost solely on wild filberts, "the use of which occasioned . . . the most excruciating torment." Eventually they attempt to escape their hilltop prison by descending a cliff face, from which Pym falls (196, 198).

Poe well understood that the reader's interest in the traveler's suffering depended partly upon the extraordinary circumstances that occasioned it, but he also seemed to realize that, to a perhaps greater extent, interest also sprang from the very extremity of the suffering itself. Like the narratives of Henry, Hearne, Mackenzie, Lewis and Clark, Pike, and Frémont, *Pym* isolates and dwells upon the situations in which the traveler's suffering surpasses in character or severity the bounds of average experience. Hearne admits that his accounts of eating skin clothing and of cannibalism "may perhaps gain little credit in Europe," but his extensive treatment of the subject suggests that he considered it a central part of his experience.[13] Pym, too, proceeds with his story "in utter hopelessness of obtaining credence for all that [he] shall tell."[14] This is standard rhetoric, however, in part an assertion of the uniqueness and interest of the traveler's experiences and thus of the merit of his account.

As in the narratives of North American explorers, the encounter with an unfamiliar society figures prominently in *Pym*. Pym's account of his early meeting with the Tsalalians resembles those of land travelers in North America. Like Lewis and Clark and Mackenzie, Pym and his party meet people who have "never before seen any of the white race," and for this "degree of ignorance [the explorers] were not prepared" (169). Pym describes an initial period of mutual inspection, of which the main concern is determining whether anyone has aggressive intentions. As was usually the case, the visitors are greatly outnumbered and therefore on their guard. Even so, Pym immediately assumes his superiority over the black people of Tsalal, and his tone echoes that in accounts of innumerable such encounters, in which Europeans and Euro-Americans had become accustomed to dominate.

The Tsalalians know nothing of firearms. They are frightened by mirrors. Their dwellings are of the "most miserable description imaginable." They have some domesticated animals—piglike creatures with bushy tails and slim legs—and their women, though naked, are "not altogether wanting in what might be termed personal beauty." In fact, with a conventional leer in the male reader's direction, Pym notes that the women "were most obliging in every respect" (172–174, 180). If Lewis and Clark had to become accustomed to eating dog flesh and Hearne to the contents of caribou stomachs, Pym and his party are treated to a welcoming feast in which the "palpitating entrails of a species of unknown animal" are the main course. Pym declines these "delicacies, . . . having just finished a hearty *déjeuner*" (175–176). His archness here resembles the irony of Lewis and Clark, Frémont, and others who recount similar instances of well-intended but unacceptable hospitality. Poe here shows his understanding of the exploration narrative's need to astonish; he exceeds the repulsiveness of many factual accounts.

After this meal, the conversation typically turns to "the chief productions of the country, and whether any of them might be turned to profit." The explorers determine that a species of mollusk, which Poe calls *biche de mer*, is sufficiently abundant that they could "easily load a dozen vessels," and Pym's party immediately arranges to put the islanders to work gathering and preparing this cargo in exchange for "a stipulated quantity of blue beads, knives, red cloth, and so forth" (176–178). He explains the world market for this commodity, and thus it appears that the trader/explorers have established a friendly and profitable relation with this people. Lewis and Clark, Mackenzie, and Hearne recount many similar encounters, proceeding from initial, delicate contact, through a basic sketch of the people and their material culture, to the transaction in which the explorers exchange their knives, beads, and cloth for food and information. Common to all such accounts is the initial anxiety attendant upon the complete, or nearly complete, mutual ignorance of the two parties.

Poe's narrative even includes the guide figure of many actual expeditions, most of which depended on native information. Henry is adopted, rescued, and initiated into Indian society by Wawatam. Hearne is guided to his destination by Matonabbee. Lewis and Clark have their Canadian interpreter, Toussaint Chaboneau, and his Shoshone Indian wife, Sacajawea. Frémont employed an entire crew of Creole and Canadian voyageurs "who had become familiar with the prairie life in the service of the fur companies in the Indian country."[15] In *Pym*, the guide figure is the mysterious Dirk Peters, whose father was a fur trader and whose mother was "an Indian woman of the tribe of the *Upsarokas*, who live among the fastnesses of the Black Hills, near the source of the Missouri."[16] Peters's mediating role links him to the generic guide figure, and his western history is another link between Poe's story and the American cultural context.

Peters is very much like the guides described by Robert F. Sayre, who "function as interpreters and priests who philosophically *guide* the travelers into secrets of the West, initiate them into mysteries of Indians and wilderness life."[17] Peters does not intercede between Pym's party and the Tsalalians, but he leads the resistance against the deranged mutineers, helps Pym survive the ship-wreck, and catches him as he falls from the cliff face. In his description of this fall, Poe captures something of the ambivalent feeling inspired by such liminal figures, who usually have a foreign and mysterious aspect insofar as they spring from the unfamiliar peoples and country they interpret. Pym is led out onto the ledge by Peters. He becomes dizzy and is overcome by a "longing to fall." He sees a "dusky, fiendish, and filmy figure" beneath him, swoons, and "plunge[s] within its arms." This "filmy figure" is Peters himself serving as both a beckoning fiend from a threatening world and the rescuer who leads the hero to safety. "On recovery," Pym says, ". . . I felt a new being,"[18] prompting one to recall Alexander Henry's sense of relief and well-being once he accepts the help of Wawatam and adoption into his family.

Such are the formal arguments for reading *Pym* as a discovery narrative of the kind discussed in the preceding chapters. In addition to such formal resemblances, *Pym* contains references to published discoverers that further assert its kinship with the narratives of actual expeditions. Pym discusses the careers and achievements of explorers who visited and reported on southern waters. Among these, he cites the narratives of Captain Cook, noting that Cook "reluctantly turned to the northward," whereas Pym continues southward past the same point (150, 158–162). Moreover, Poe wrote other stories about exploration. *The Journal of Julius Rodman, Being an Account of the First Passage Across the Rocky Mountains Ever Achieved by Civilized Man* (1840) was begun for *Burton's Gentleman's Magazine* but never completed. It is a meticulous imitation of narratives such as those of the Lewis and Clark and the Long expeditions, which followed the Missouri River on the way west to the mountains. Poe's introduction to *Rodman* contains a detailed discussion of the accomplishments of other western explorers, including Jonathan Carver, Hearne, Mackenzie, Peter Pond, Lewis and Clark, David Thompson, and Stephen Long.[19] The amount of borrowing in Poe's text indicates his familiarity with the contents as well as the existence of these narratives.[20]

Apart from his artistic interest in this genre, Poe no doubt also recognized a subject with popular appeal. In short stories such as "MS. Found in a Bottle" and "A Descent into the Maelström," Poe focuses on journeys to "the limits of horrified endurance."[21] In the manner of the short story, these recount limited, intense experiences, while in the manner of the exploration narrative, they are told from the point of view of the principal character. Many of Poe's stories having nothing to do with travel to unknown lands concern, even so, the narrator's bafflement and anxiety in confronting something beyond his sense of the normal, a situation at the heart of the exploration narrative.

Poe was clearly sensitive to the conventions of his models, Lewis and Clark's *History*, Alexander Mackenzie's *Voyages*, Zebulon Pike's *Journals*, and dozens of exploration accounts like them. He was aware that they were important sources of knowledge for the corporate and governmental bodies that mainly sponsored them, that they were also popular reading, to some extent substitutes for fiction, and that, like literary fictions, they often dealt with the cultural, as well as the physical, landscape of the New World. Poe portrays the confident explorer's economic and scientific claiming of the lands and peoples he encounters, in what were by Poe's time standard tropes if not outright clichés; however, as if to accommodate his acute sensitivity to clichés, he also explores the new, romantic mode of New World claim staking, which perhaps seemed to dispense with the familiar modes of asserting power but nonetheless entailed its own, perhaps greater, cultural and psychic dangers.

The earliest voyagers grappled with the need to establish a basis upon which the staggering possibilities they envisioned could be seen as legitimately theirs, and I have argued that North American discovery narratives characteristically refer to the authorities that offer the surest legitimation of the traveler's claims. These authorities were seated in the institutions that sponsored exploratory travel: the church, the corporation, the academy, the state. As a Euro-American "man of letters" and as a romantic, Poe is not directly beholden to any such institutions; neither does he rely on them as the ultimate authorities for his hero's initiatives. Poe alters the rhetorical bases of the factual exploration narrative by radically shifting the authority for the traveler's undertaking from sponsoring institutions to the traveler's personal experiences. Whereas actual explorers answered to, and often literally wrote to, the authorities of trading companies, military high commands, scientific academies, and national governments, Poe's narrator systematically rejects the economic, scientific, political, and legal underpinnings of actual exploratory travel and of the rhetoric of exploration accounts. The "discoveries" that Pym conceives of are framed in individualistic terms and are arrived at through increasingly metaphysical, almost mystical, kinds of contact with unfamiliar lands and peoples. As a result, historically complex interactions among Euro-American and native American groups, through trade, treaty making, intermarriage, even warfare, are refocused through the mind of a romantic individualist and projected as vivid images of his struggles on what seem increasingly his own psychic frontiers. Pym's journal is essentially a private record, presented not by its author but by an "editor" who has obtained the manuscript in mysterious circumstances and cannot vouch for its authority or accuracy.

Although Pym's "expedition" is a trading voyage, like most actual explorations, Poe distances his hero from the commercial concerns of the *Grampus* and the *Jane Guy*. The latter is on a "cruise to the South

Seas for any cargo which might come . . . readily to hand," and when Captain Guy learns that Tsalal offers quantities of tortoise and *biche de mer*, he responds to economic motives, planning to look into the country thoroughly "in the hope of making a profitable speculation in his discovery."[22] Pym, on the other hand, is "earnestly bent on prosecuting the voyage to the southward" and cannot "listen with any patience to a proposition of stopping longer than . . . absolutely necessary for the health of the crew" (170). Captain Guy is cautious, whereas Pym feels himself "bursting with indignation at the timid and ill-timed suggestions of [the] commander" that they return northward (166).

This conflict between economic interests and scientific or personal curiosity figures in the narratives of the British fur traders, where narrator and trader are one, and where it is trade that must be seen to take precedence over science. Poe alters the equation by giving his adventurous hero scientific pretensions and having him only accidentally a part of a trading voyage with no commitment to its success. First as a stowaway and then as a shipwrecked sailor, Pym drops in on commercial ventures, but he keeps his own ideals of curiosity and adventurousness distinct from the economic concerns of the ship. Poe's explorer is thus much more free to espouse the pursuit of knowledge and experience for their own sakes than are the captains of the vessels that carry him toward these goals. Moreover, Pym's deception of his father and grandfather and his contempt for the captains he sails under make him very unlike nearly contemporary United States military explorers insofar as these latter took their official roles as authorized envoys of the home society very seriously. Poe detaches Pym from the restraints of trade and hierarchical authority, making the hero's personal experience the locus of discovery and pure (sometimes perverse) curiosity the main motive of his journey.

By rejecting the practical motives of exploratory expeditions, Poe's explorer dismisses material benefits from consideration as measures of his journey's success or failure. Pym initially values his mission in terms of its contribution to empirical science, but his curiosity eventually ends up seeming more metaphysical and psychological than scientific. In fact, Pym ultimately looks for an absolute knowledge that can be obtained only by pressing onward to the very limits of the globe and of human endurance. Pym is not the type of explorer who returns home with a cargo of furs, a few plant specimens, and a tale of his adventures.

Neither will he write merely a meticulous account of each day's observations and events. Like the narrator of Poe's "MS. Found in a Bottle," Pym is "hurrying onwards to some exciting knowledge—some never-to-be-imparted secret, whose attainment is destruction,"[23] by means of which "a new entity is added to [his] soul" (141). He models his behavior after the great texts of geographical discovery but is not interested, finally, in any slow process of assembling information, of matching data to hypothesis, even of making conquests. He wishes, purely on the basis of his own travels to add "a new entity" to the territory of his soul.

Pym's mentality also resembles that of the narrator in "MS. Found in a Bottle." The latter, finding himself on a ship that "thunders on to the southward" (145) daubs unwittingly with a tar brush along the edges of a folded sail. When the sail is hauled aloft, "the thoughtless touches of the brush . . . spread out into the word DISCOVERY" (142). Just as these "thoughtless touches" suddenly take the form of a word that stands for the traveler's most intense desire, the land and people Pym encounters are also utterly baffling until their purposes and meaning appear suddenly and fully articulated. Then, the black people of Tsalal become "the most wicked, hypocritical, bloodthirsty and altogether fiendish race of men upon the face of the globe."[24] Similarly, from out of the "chaos of flitting and indistinct images" that constitute Pym's final observations as he approaches the pole, there emerges another vision of the absolute, a "human figure" the hue of whose skin "was of the perfect whiteness of the snow" (206). Detached from such mediating activities as trade, or even war, through which complex relations with land and people can be developed, Pym's experiences become increasingly polarized and personal as his narrative proceeds. In the end he flees the blacks' absolute wickedness toward a vision that is white, human appearing, and—can we assume?—responsive to the previously unexplored wishes of his soul.

Pym's experience is not ultimately destructive of his person (he survives to tell the tale), but the metaphysical absolutes that constitute the terms of its understanding isolate it from his social identity and from the institutions that allow him to explore. The legacy of those institutions—that is, of the past in America—in fact seems to be a source of anxiety for Pym and, as such, one of his motives for undertaking his revisionist journey. Pym's search for new knowledge is also a flight from what is already known, from the evidences of history in home and family.

As Poe's wholesale adoption of the exploration narrative itself indicates, Pym's identity as a Euro-American is in part founded on the work of earlier explorers and settlers, and the title and early pages of *The Narrative of Arthur Gordon Pym of Nantucket* identify him in terms of his home and family. His inclination is not, however, to accept the fruits of this past; his decision to travel is couched in terms that suggest his reluctance to accept a historically based understanding of his identity and a comfortable, middle-class life. Rather than take up a role in his family's Nantucket home, he seeks self-confirmation in experience, initiating a journey that leads him to repeat the basic pattern of Nantucket's discovery by Europeans. Tsalal, the land he discovers, is an island, too, and it has a population that its discoverers hope either drive off or subdue to the purposes of their seafaring, trading life. Pym encounters new lands and peoples, risking his life and inheritance in order to work through his own version of American discovery-as-self-discovery.

The rejection of home and family for a life "on the road" is, of course, a much discussed pattern in American literature. In the nineteenth century, there are Natty Bumppos, Ishmaels, and Huck Finns enough to suggest the possibility of a whole society of voyaging individuals. Like Cooper, Melville, and Twain, Poe felt the need to detach his Euro-American hero from the institutions that sustained his society's expansion, yet by couching his hero's travels in the rhetoric in which the planning, events, and results of actual expeditions were reported, Poe shows how Pym's explorations depend upon those same institutions. With equal deliberation, however, Poe casts his hero's romantic individualism into high relief by having him renounce all commitment to these institutions. The result is a text in which the values of the individualistic traveler/narrator appear to be at odds with the social consensus of expansionist Euro-America.

One might think Pym's rejection of Nantucket society and its economy part of the rising generation's spurning of a tainted patrimony, a strategy for distancing himself from society's goal of expanding and legitimizing its presence in America. To some extent Pym's rebelliousness does seem to run in this vein. The way he refers to his own "intense hypocrisy" in his relations with his home and family suggests

some serious uneasiness. One might argue, however, that Poe's romantic hero makes an even greater claim than that of his pragmatic ances-
tors; Pym strives for an identity, implicitly that of a Euro-American,
that transcends the conflicts and compromises among the European and
Indian inhabitants of the New World. Instead of a Euro-American
presence legitimated by powerful but finite religious, economic, scientific, and legal authorities, Poe's Pym makes his personal responses to
lands and peoples the ultimate object of his researches, and we are
forced to ask ourselves to what extent Pym's construction of personal
experience comes to serve as a new authority in the culture of his
readers.

William Spengemann has shown how *The Narrative of Arthur Gordon Pym* breaks stylistic ground by developing the implications for a
narrative of romanticism, specifically of the romantics' locating of truth
and their founding of identity in the ongoing processes of individual
experience. He points out that some European romantic poets came to
see New World exploration as "an apt metaphor for their own artistic
quests after revitalizing spiritual truth."[25] For such poets (Spengemann
mentions Coleridge in his *Rime of the Ancient Mariner* as an example),
"the voyage symbolizes a progress from historical guilt to aesthetic
redemption" (138), achieved in the act of traveling rather than upon
arrival or return. In Poe's work, moreover, the notion of identity
through process is pushed to the extreme as the voyage becomes radically open-ended. Poe's hero and his actions are cut loose from the
control of any narrator who knows the conclusion as he recounts the
story; there is no home authority that can reintegrate the aberrant hero
after his journey. His traveling self becomes his identity. Poe achieves
the effect of the tale-teller not knowing the ultimate results of his own
experiences by nesting Pym's abruptly discontinued account within the
commentary of an editor who presents Pym's manuscript to the public
but knows nothing further about its writer. As part of this strategy, Poe
includes within Pym's account passages purporting to be actual journal
entries—that is, accounts of events written soon after their occurrence
with no knowledge of what happened later. The effect of this presentation, Spengemann argues (I think correctly), is to make the hero's
mental landscape the real terrain of Poe's exploration narrative.

Spengemann ends his discussion of *Pym* by suggesting that its radical
open-endedness is a bequest to later American fiction (*Moby Dick*,

Huckleberry Finn, and *The Ambassadors* are his examples) and, somewhat paradoxically, the basis of an American sense of self that is distinct from its roots in European culture: "*Arthur Gordon Pym* suggests that our true being, our home, lies in an undiscovered country which we will create in the act of going there; that the journey necessitates a radical, fatal change in the traveler's mind or soul" (150). While Spengemann here suggests how the act of rejecting "home" can in itself be the basis of a claim to a new identity, he is not concerned with the implications of this attitude in the discourse of Euro-American expansion; for him, it seems unproblematic to found the rock of national identity on the fairy wings of the hero's flight. Spengemann regards Poe's privileging of the truth of individual experience as an artistic advance and as a critique of Euro-American complacency. Undoubtedly, as we shall see in Thoreau's work, authorizing geographical exploration as a mode of self-discovery did turn out to be a highly successful strategy for nineteenth-century Euro-American culture, but it ought also to be recognized that this empowering rhetoric did not lessen the conflicts over land and cultural survival that were ongoing on the actual frontiers.

It seems to me that Poe himself was on some level alert to the dangers of his hero's individualist explorations, as well as to their potential to serve as the basis of a claim on exotic territory. Unlike Thoreau's exploring self in "Ktaadn," which we shall discuss in the next section, Pym does not self-consciously evaluate and then challenge the legitimacy of Euro-American institutions; Pym's word for his relationship with his family is "hypocrisy," and this word accurately denotes his duplicitous relation to the institutions of his society in general. Poe's explorer/narrator is more impulsive than Thoreau's, and his romantic urge for "DISCOVERY" remains in obvious conflict with his relationships with the institutions that sustain his travels, as well as with the people he encounters along the way. Pym is like a punk Natty Bumppo, overtly flouting the conventions that the elder scout quietly resented. Even though Poe moves his hero closer to the center of the plot than Cooper did his, Poe, like Cooper, does not envision his hero as founding a model of relationship for American society. Pym's explorations are so destructive that they may be construed as something of a cautionary tale for anyone who would take up the romantic mode of discovery.

Poe was not an Emersonian transcendentalist, confident in the fundamental correspondence between natural and spiritual facts. Although Poe may be thought of as participating in Emerson's and Thoreau's strategy of individualizing the Euro-American's relationship with the continent, his work does not place ultimate confidence in a style devoted to the individual's relationship with the world he is exploring. In contrast to Thoreau, who shows himself becoming more "at home" away from Concord, Poe's Pym discovers a country "differing essentially from any hitherto visited by civilized men." Although Poe, like other American romantics, explores the ultimate possibilities and dangers of an individualist mode of New World identity, Poe's explorer happens upon a land that is profoundly alienating. Tsalal's rivers contain water "made up of a number of distinct veins, each of a distinct hue,"[26] "like the hues of changeable silk" (171–172), and "the trees resembled no growth of either the torrid, the temperate, or the northern frigid zones. . . . The very rocks were novel in their mass, their color, and their stratification" (171). Tsalal resists any transcendental correspondence with the discoverer's sense of self. In this respect Poe's new land also differs in emphasis from the images of the American West published by contemporary American explorers, who by the early nineteenth century were using moments of personal aesthetic vision as bases for a territorial claim.

Pym's doubts and fears in Tsalal seem to provoke him to strive all the more for a definitive discovery, "the negation of transcendence" serving paradoxically to figure the *"possibility* of transcendence."[27] One such figuration, before Pym leaves Tsalal for the absolute South, suggests a definitive connection with the land by having his hero describe forms of the land that resemble writing. Pym reproduces the figures of the deep chasms that he and Peters explore in their attempt to find a way out of their hilltop prison. He also renders the indentations they find in one of the chasm walls, which bore "some little resemblance to alphabetical characters." In spite of the crafted appearances of the chasms and indentations, however, Pym adduces reasons why all are "the work of nature."[28] Pym's "editor," however, will not let the matter rest there. He takes up the question in his concluding note, suggesting that the chasms, considered as characters, "constitute an Ethiopian verbal root—the root . . . 'To be shady.' " Similarly, the

indentations in the side of the chasm resemble an "Arabic verbal root
. . . 'To be white,' " and "the full Egyptian word . . . 'The region of
the south' " (207–208). Having his hero argue the natural origin of
these figures while the "editor" shows their suggestive meanings as
words, Poe hints at the kind of transcendent relation to the land that
Thoreau develops when he "reads" the shapes of the thawing railway
cut in *Walden*. In *Pym*, however, although such a reading is suggested
by the "editor," it is contradicted by the traveler who is on site. As on
other occasions when Pym approaches the limits of his perception,
understanding, or endurance, he again stops short of an ultimate discovery. He does not achieve a definitive connection between his desires and
the land he explores.

In *Pym*, the question of the explorer/writer's relationship with the
inhabitants of the unknown land is framed in similarly absolute terms.
Pym does not depict any personal interactions beyond the initial exchanges, when Pym's party are enlisting the Tsalalians as processors of
biche de mer. After the initial contacts, Pym's interest in these people
centers almost exclusively on the nagging doubt as to whether they are
indeed friendly and docile—in other words, insignificant. The appearance of the Tsalal people—black skin, curly hair—along with their fifty-
foot war canoes and primitive weapons, suggests a sort of composite
primitive people, with allusions to Africans and Polynesians. Euro-
Americans were of course familiar with the fear of slave uprisings, and
South Sea islanders had been infamous since the later eighteenth-
century voyages in which several Europeans—most notably Cook—had
been attacked. Poe is adept at tapping an anxiety that probably had
figured in the lives of every generation of Euro-American up to his own
time. He does not include any motives for the Tsalalians' murderous
attack, no suggestion, for example, that it might be a logical response to
the visitors' encroachments. It simply turns out that "the islanders for
whom [Pym] entertained such inordinate feelings of esteem were among
the most barbarous, subtle and blood thirsty wretches that ever contam-
inated the face of the globe" (180).

With the matter set forth this way, the vulnerable Euro-American's
reaction is predictably extreme. His profoundest wish is simply to be
free of the problem. It is hard not to sense satisfaction and relief in
Pym's description of the aftermath of the explosion that takes place

when the Tsalalians set the *Jane Guy* aflame. This catastrophe fulfills the desire simply to annihilate. Having killed the last six crewmen, the Tsalalians themselves are devastated:

> The whole atmosphere was magically crowded, in a single instant, with a wild chaos of wood and metal and human limbs . . . and a dense shower of the minutest fragments of the limbs tumbled headlong in every direction around us.
>   The havoc among the savages far exceeded our utmost expectation, and they had now indeed reaped the full and perfect fruits of their treachery. (190)

Poe grants Pym the relief that Zebulon Pike had to deny himself when he wanted to cut "those scoundrels to pieces" but had to refrain "for fear," as he says, "the impetuosity of my conduct might not be approved by my Government."[29] Poe's explosion is the Tsalalians' own doing, but it is apparent that it suggests, at least to Pym, a simple solution for a very complex and difficult problem.[30]

Poe's *Pym* relies on the established imaginative appeal of the venturing, individualist traveler and his experiences in unknown places. But by freeing the traveler from the economic and political constraints that governed the goals and rhetoric of actual explorers, Poe emphasizes the growing tendency to conceive of exploration in increasingly personal and individualist terms and to cite personal experience as the absolute authority for exploration and adventure. Poe seems aware, however, of the dangers attending the personal errand as it ultimately, and perhaps inevitably, becomes metaphysical and mystical, detached from the mediations of a social identity or mission. He dramatizes how the original inhabitants are viewed as "contaminants" of the land and obstacles to explorers who are seeking some sign that the land is intended for their particular destiny. He demonstrates the way romantic individualism could intensify rather than mediate the conflict over territory, portraying a land more starkly polarized than any historical one along the lines of skin color (even the Tsalalians' teeth are black). He identifies and pushes to the extreme the tendency of American explorers, actual and literary, to see a reflection of their own desires in the land and to make personal experience the basis of a New World identity.

Thoreau's Discovery of America:
A Nineteenth-Century First Contact

> In what school was this fur-trader educated? He seems to travel the immense snowy country with such purpose only as the reader who accompanies him, and to the latter's imagination, it is, as it were, momentarily created to be the scene of his adventures.
>
> Thoreau, *A Week on the Concord and Merrimack Rivers*

Compared with Poe's, Emerson's was a much more optimistic idealism, and it is not surprising that Emerson conceived of discovery as a repeatable epiphany that would liberate Americans from their past and connect them with a new world of possibilities. "I think we must regard the *land,*" he says in "The Fortune of the Republic," "as a commanding and increasing power on the citizen, the sanative influence, which promises to disclose new virtues for ages to come."[31] Everyone has access to this land; anyone can make the discovery of its potential, for according to Emerson's *Nature* (1836), it is the eye that gives us title to "the best part of . . . men's farms." No one, he says, "owns the landscape." In *Nature,* when he describes becoming "a transparent eyeball," which *is* nothing and *sees* all, Emerson perhaps renders the definitive statement of that process of identification of self and land that was also apparent in American explorers both before and after him. "In the . . . landscape, . . . man beholds somewhat as beautiful as his own nature." At this moment of discovery, "the name of the nearest friend sounds foreign and accidental: to be brothers, to be acquaintances, master and servant is then a trifle and a disturbance." The positive effects of such a vision are not merely personal or mystical; they shall gradually—as more and more people make the discovery—make themselves felt: "a correspondent revolution in things will attend the influx of the spirit."[32] Though each person is required to teach himself to read his own potential in the land, this larger revolution through self-discovery is still possible. Emerson conceives of the original discovery of America as something that happens again and again as part of a gradual ameliorative process in which each person learns to transcend all that is "foreign and accidental" to the place.

In *Nature,* Emerson undertakes to alert Americans to the way in which, viewed aright, their surroundings may be the basis of their identity. The sloughing off of historical, genealogical, religious—in short, of institutional—identifiers opens the way for the recognition of how "the landscape" informs one's "own nature." Emerson's prose announces an insight that leads from old ways to new, but Emerson himself, by the time of "The Transcendentalist" (1841), seems to have recognized that what he and the so-called transcendentalists he is defending have to say is not easily translatable into reformist action. A good deal of "The Transcendentalist," in fact, is devoted to the defense of the idealist's right to resist demands for action in the present, in the interest of truth and the future:

"What will you do, then?" cries the world.
"We will wait."
"How long?"
"Until the Universe rises up and calls us to work."
"But whilst you wait, you grow old and useless."
"Be it so: I can sit in a corner and *perish*, (as you call it,) but I will not move until I have the highest command. If no call should come for years, for centuries, then I know that the want of the Universe is the attestation of faith by this my abstinence."[33]

In accordance with this commitment to idealism, it seems, Emerson "confesses" that "our American literature and spiritual history are . . . in the optative mood" (207), and in this confession one can observe a fact about Emerson's own writing: that the lecture/essay that became his characteristic mode is not well suited actually to narrate the events of the transformation he envisions. The reader of *Nature,* and of such essays as "The American Scholar" and "Self Reliance," is enjoined to see what is there to be seen, to become, as a result, the American he *can* become, but Emerson is by no means telling the story of a series of actions or events. He leaves events to take care of themselves, as he believes they will if individuals learn to "attend the influx of the spirit." Emerson's essays expand the moment of insight and explore its implications, while retaining its essential atemporality. Can "America," he seems to ask, be seen in its entirety in a forest clearing, from beside the falls of a great river, or from atop a mountain? It is to be desired. It is to be asserted. But it may not, strictly speaking, be told.[34]

In a sense, one may regard the careers of the romantic American writers who took up Emerson's challenge as evolving from their struggle with what Emerson seemed to know instinctively: that his vision was incompatible 'with narrative. I have argued that in American exploration writing, moments of transcendent vision are privileged because they remove the hero from the irresolvable conflicts in the story he is trying to tell. But in factual narratives, transcendent moments are still just moments, isolated from the main course of events. Undertaking to enact the prophetic implications of such moments, however, to tell the story of their unfolding in individual lives and the nation's history, American writers had to narrate in the indicative mood what hitherto had been mere subjunctive intervals in accounts of institutional and international conflict.[35]

Allowing the hero to act toward the realization of his newfound identity and to narrate the story of his actions seems to go hand in hand with a denial of the institutional basis of Euro-American expansion across the continent. Sensing his true identity incarnate in the land itself, the romantic American hero casts aside previous identifying associations in order to begin a journey of national self-discovery.[36] The plot of his narrative consists in his working *against* rather than for the institutions that materially support his travels. Arthur Gordon Pym exhibits what he calls his "intense hypocrisy," disguising himself as an old seaman in order to escape his comfortable family and begin his travels. Poe's writer/explorer repeatedly severs his connections with the official authority of fathers and sea captains as he plunges forward into the unknown. Thoreau, in his accounts of his sojourn in the Concord woods and of his journeys through Maine, glories in his independence from the larger community and seeks a new "economy" for himself and the American landscape. He is not at Walden Pond to scout the way for the unregenerate merchants of Concord but to forge an alternative link with the land, bypassing the power of money, guns, and railroads by means of an intimate recognition of the self in the land. Melville's Ahab and Ishmael both knowingly exploit the whaling industry in order to further their own explorations. Each in his own way claims his independence from the institution that makes his explorations possible, looking instead to nature (as symbolized by the whale and the sea) for an alternative to the authority of the Bildads and Pelegs of venturing capitalism.

None of these literary explorers returns home with information that can be thought of as directly advancing his position in society or as consolidating or extending his family's, employer's, or government's claim to new territory. Indeed, none of these protagonists owns anything, and more than one makes a point of rejecting his inheritance (as Pym does) or of disdaining to consider the value of mere property (like Ahab). Melville is famous for having thought *Moby Dick* a "wicked book," and Poe's mockery of countinghouse values could hardly be more overt and gleeful than it is in *Pym*. Thus it is a tradition among the authors themselves, as among many of their commentators, to consider these protagonists as essentially subversive figures and therefore to read such works as doubting rather than affirming the American errand.

It is certainly true that they question some of the values and institutions entailed in the actual exploration of the continent, and it is clear that these American authors perceived the dilemma of Hearne, Henry, and Lewis and Clark when faced with the violence of the European entry into an existing American world. There seems little question that profound doubt figured in their attempts to define American identity, given the continuing presence of an American Other. However, the responses of such writers to doubts about American society as then constituted were not so much efforts to reform the economic and political institutions that most affected Euro-American interaction with the land and its peoples as they were attempts to adapt literary narrative to the transcendental formula for American self-realization that Emerson had articulated. They are attempts to describe *as events* the processes of transcending the whole history of conflict and exploitation that figured as part of the discovery of the Americas and that now loomed as an obstacle to a secure American identity. If they deplored the effect of American institutions on "America" and rejected the limited and selfish motives of progressive commerce and politics, it did not follow that they identified with Indian peoples in their defeat. Rather, they claimed an alternate authority for an American identity in their own experiences as nineteenth-century "discoverers" of the land. But unlike Emerson, they asserted this claim in narratives imitating the conventions of North American discovery writing.

As I have said, however, American narrative artists confronted the fundamental incompatibility of Emerson's symbolic nature and narrative itself. The symbol, apprehended in the moment, refused to unfold in history. The story of the Euro-American's realization of his relationship with the symbolic land refused to be told, and the farther the hero traveled, the more maddeningly enigmatic his goal became. The plot of the romantic discovery narrative required, in fact, that the hero systematically leave behind what was actually known. Melville, for example, begins *Moby Dick* with a catalog of the past researches on the whale, but it is clear that what both the bookish Ishmael and the aggressive Ahab desire is not an understanding of the history of the element they explore but unmediated contact with it. Historical records must be cleared away before the narrator can approach the discovery of the thing itself. Melville's whale is a romantic symbol of America; Ishmael describes the whale's skin as being covered with crossed and recrossed lines that remind him of "the famous hieroglyphic palisades on the banks of the Upper Mississippi," adding that "like those mystic rocks, too, the mystic-marked whale remains undecipherable."[37] Melville demonstrates that the discovery Ishmael seeks is one of which no previous account is adequate. Melville's explorer/writers exhibit an epistemological fundamentalism, a desire to read for themselves the text as it comes from the hand of the Author, and Melville's narrative art embodies the glorious and baneful results of this urge to confront and decipher the "mystic marks" of nature. While it is true that *Moby Dick* is an exhaustive collation of "what has been promiscuously said, thought, fancied and sung of Leviathan, by many nations and generations" (2), the driving impulse of the book is toward an original, complete discovery in which the fullest potential of author and subject are revealed once and for all, and all previous statements are left behind. The discovery of the *narrative* of *Moby Dick* is, however, that such a fundamental first contact is untellable. The plot goes down with the ship.

Melville is like Poe in dramatizing the romantic discovery impulse in an extreme form and in showing how the violence of its curiosity wreaks destruction on the object of its interest. For Melville and Poe, it seems impossible to separate the desire for knowledge from the desire to profit from and dominate the exotic world. Because of this linkage, there is an important element of the cautionary tale in even their most energetic narratives of travel and adventure. It is to Thoreau that one can turn for the most seductive narrating of the romantic discovery impulse, in which the clash over possession of the land is obviated. Thoreau's journey narrative in "Ktaadn" recounts the spatial and temporal leaving behind of all previous interactions of the Euro-American and the original American worlds. Battlegrounds, logged hillsides, and abandoned farms recede as Thoreau's plot prepares us for the moment of recognition between the Euro-American and the landscape that Thoreau makes serve as the very sponsor of his presence in it. Thoreau asks one to imagine abjuring the proceeds of participation in the Euro-American economy in order to imagine Euro-American society without its history. Part of Thoreau's genius is his insight that readers identify themselves with the hero/narrators of discovery narratives. In "Ktaadn," the narrative I shall discuss in detail, Thoreau journeys toward the most elevated kind of mystical encounter with "America," but the actual traveling he does is of a type that can be repeated by almost any reader. In Thoreau, as in Frémont, the fruits of exotic travel are hung within reach of all, as though their enjoyment were merely a matter of opening our eyes to what the continent has had to offer all along.

"Ktaadn" recounts Thoreau's 1846 trip to the mountain of that name in Maine, a journey he made during the second summer of his stay at Walden Pond. The first of Thoreau's narratives of his three trips to Maine, it and "Chesuncook" were published in magazines during his lifetime and then, after his death, collected along with the third account, "The Allegash and the East Branch" and published as *The Maine Woods*. "Ktaadn" takes the form of an expanded and reworked journal in which Thoreau records the way he traveled, what he saw, what he ate, whom he met and talked with, in short, the actual processes by which he achieved his goal of learning about the back country of Maine.

At the end of his journey, however, Thoreau sees himself not as a nineteenth-century tourist but as one of the earliest discoverers of America. Having recorded how the contemporary Maine lumbermen, settlers, and Indians lived, he yet says, "You have only to travel for a few days into the interior and back parts even of the old states, to come to that very America which the Northmen, and Cabot, and Gosnold, and Smith and Raleigh visited."[38] Traveling into the interior, Thoreau says he saw what the earliest Europeans in North America saw, notwithstanding the two centuries separating him from the voyagers he names. The criterion by which Thoreau identifies his land as the "very America" visited by the early discoverers is that there "still waves the virgin forest of the New World." He distinguishes what he calls "the republic," which "has acquired a history," from "America," which he describes as still "unpeopled and unexplored" (81, 83). The relative emptiness of the interior serves Thoreau's rhetorical purposes. Because it is "unpeopled," it can image both the America he discovers and that discovered by the earliest voyagers and settlers.

Thoreau's use of this image of an empty America was part of a developing convention that we have traced beginning with Lewis and Clark, and we have seen in American accounts of exploration in the Far West an increasing tendency to focus on emptiness as the essential quality of the land. The instructions given such nineteenth-century explorers as Lewis and Clark, Zebulon Pike, and John Charles Frémont directed them to observe and record the inhabitants of the West as well as the character of the land, and they all dutifully noted much about the many peoples they encountered.[39] Side by side with dramatic accounts of their exchanges with North American peoples, however, there also appear rhetorical set pieces in which the solitary explorer confronts an empty land. Poised at the brink of a waterfall, straddling the crest of a ridge, or perched on a mountaintop, the man who has just obtained directions, guides, horses, and food from the local inhabitants will expand, as Lewis does, for example, on "the sublime spectacle of this stupendous object [the Great Falls of the Missouri], which since the creation has been lavishing its magnificence on the desert."[40] Such contradictions abound in nineteenth-century accounts of exploratory travel. The tendency in such writers as Lewis, Pike, and Frémont was to regard the landscape itself as an image of the America they represented, an image waiting to be recognized and properly interpreted.

Thoreau confronts essentially the same rhetorical problem in *Walden* and in his travel pieces when he adopts the personae of settler and explorer. The "old states" in which he makes his discoveries are already settled and explored, and Thoreau reports prodigious amounts about the Indian and European peoples in the land before him. Because his journals are a virtually complete record of what he read from his college days until his death, we know that he was as well acquainted as anyone of his time with accounts of settlement and exploration from the earliest European contacts to the contemporary expeditions in the West, and he clearly gleaned much that was useful to his thinking from earlier writing about America.[41] But his vision of American discovery in "Ktaadn" is often at odds with the earlier accounts he knew, and his seeming dismissal of what in "Ktaadn" he calls "mere history" belies his lifelong interest in what was written about the past.[42] Sixteenth-century accounts such as Bartholomew Gosnold's and John Smith's, which Thoreau mentions in "Ktaadn," record early contacts chiefly in terms of exchanges of goods and information between Europeans and Indians. Eighteenth-century travelers like Alexander Henry and Samuel Hearne, whose narratives Thoreau also knew and admired, are similarly occupied with trade and human relations.[43] And nineteenth-century explorers of the West, by that time directly involved in the westward expansion of the United States's settlements, could not avoid dealing with the inhabitants already there, even if they viewed Indians more as problems than as sources of information or assistance.

Thoreau's rhetoric in "Ktaadn" advances the possibility of a fundamental contact with America that makes many of the intercultural events recorded in his written sources seem accidental and even irrelevant. The empty land he finds in the Maine interior is his image of the "very America" he wants to establish as essential for Americans of any age. The individual's contact with this empty land becomes a paradigm of a fundamental New World experience, an imagining of American discovery that tends to replace what Thoreau himself knows from earlier sources and that has affected thinking about discovery in subsequent generations. Thoreau's "Ktaadn" achieves (and records the steps of) the transformation of the discovery narrative from its basis in international conflict and its reliance on institutional authority to its new role as the expression of personal identity with the continent as a symbol of American potential.

Thoreau's revisions contributed to the creation in the mid-nineteenth century of what we might think of as a lens through which we still look at earlier events in New World history.[44] Indeed, later readers of Thoreau sometimes lose sight of the difference between his idealist discovery of the self in the land and the history of Europe's complex interaction with the Americas. More generally, scholars of the nineteenth century have often taken that century's images of "free" or "virgin" land too much at face value, in effect accepting them as geographical determinants of American cultural development. It is not that critics of Thoreau overlook the metaphoric nature of his concept of discovery. In fact, there are several major studies of how Thoreau makes historical sources into the signifiers of metaphors. Sherman Paul, for example, says that Thoreau chose images of exploration "because they were the symbolic equivalents of his determination to adventure spiritually."[45] John Aldrich Christie says that Thoreau's "geographical knowledge contributed appropriate means for symbolizing the qualities of mind and spirit which were his ultimate subject matter."[46] However, in their efforts to chart this "ultimate subject matter," it often seems that scholars lose touch with Thoreau's knowledge of his original sources. The material concerns both of early explorers and settlers and of his contemporaries were of interest to Thoreau. In taking Thoreau's idealism seriously, it seems that one can forget the historical conflict over place that is the cultural context of Thoreau's literary expression.

With reference to Thoreau's travel writing, Paul cites Thomas Wentworth Higginson's view that "the domain of external Nature" was Thoreau's "peculiar province." Thus, Paul says, Thoreau "went to Maine to see the wilderness, to Canada to see the Great River, and to Cape Cod to see the ocean."[47] Thoreau's interest in such sights notwithstanding, it is evident in "Ktaadn" that Thoreau must confront all evidence of the history and economy of Maine before he can achieve contact with the "external nature." Paul seems to overlook this effort on Thoreau's part. He immediately goes on to say that "on each excursion . . . [Thoreau] fronted those natural facts that had first been seen by the discoverers . . . of America" (379). This is the identical claim made by Thoreau, but only at the end of his narrative. I would argue that Thoreau's are not at all the same natural facts as those confronted by early discoverers, that they are rather what we can see being created by Thoreau as alternatives to what he knew, from early voyage and settlement accounts, of the seventeenth century's discourse of America. And one finds, in fact, that the idea of a nature stripped of all signs of human presence was not an important object of desire for the earliest travelers; it seems unlikely, in fact, that such a thought would have been comprehensible to them. Thoreau's "natural facts" are, at least in part, the creation of Thoreau's literary art.

Thoreau himself indicates the history he has to overcome in order to achieve his vision of the "very America" of his ideal first discoverers. Reading Thoreau with his extensive knowledge of American exploration writing in mind, one is able to see how a skillful writer could develop such a rhetoric of first contact, one in which absolute emptiness is elevated over other contradictory qualities as the "very America" common to all generations. Signs of the land's history surviving in Thoreau's journey account suggest the conflict to which this rhetoric is a response and remind one that emptiness was not always North America's most significant feature.

Thoreau's method is to "front" the cultural facts before going on to discover nature. Whether in the form of a journey from settlements to the backcountry (as in "Ktaadn") or in the rationale for his experiment at Walden Pond, Thoreau recognizes the labor of dissociation he must undertake in order to confront the naked continent. When, at the end of "Ktaadn," Thoreau cites "the Northmen, Cabot, Gosnold and Smith, and Raleigh" as voyagers who saw "the very America" he saw in "the back parts of . . . the states," we are aware of the journey Thoreau has undertaken to arrive at this supposed meeting ground of American discoverers.[48]

The journey accounts of John Smith and Bartholomew Gosnold in fact present America in terms very different from Thoreau's virgin forest. The attempted colony that John Smith describes in his *History of Virginia* (1624) seems to have survived on Indian foodstuffs. Rather than an empty land, Smith describes towns and villages, such as the one he calls Powhatan after its ruler. This town, he says, consisted "of twelve houses pleasantly seated on a hill, before it three fertile isles, about it many of their cornfields." Later, Smith recounts how, when the colonists' provisions were gone, "the savages . . . brought us such plenty of their fruits and provision that no man wanted."[49] In a later part of his history, Smith describes the coast of New England. Here, again, his subject is an inhabited country, not an unaltered landscape. He characterizes the "country of the Massachusits" as "the Paradice of all these parts, for here are many Iles planted with Corne, Groves, Mulberies, salvage Gardens and good harbours. . . . The Coast as you pass shewes you all along large Corne fields, and great troupes of well proportioned people" (215). Similarly, the 1602 account of Bartholomew Gosnold's landfall on Cape Cod records clear evidence that the coastal Indians had been trading with Europeans before his arrival. John Brereton, who wrote the account, describes how, when they dropped anchor, "eight Indians, in a Barke Shallop with mast and saile, and iron grapple, and a kettle of copper, came boldly aboard us, one of them apparelled with a waistcoat and breeches of black serdge, made after our sea-fashion, hose and shoes on his feet."[50] Of the nine pages that recount Gosnold's stay in and around Cape Cod, roughly five describe communication with the inhabitants, some of it remarkably sociable. Much of the rest concerns arable land and valuable commodities such as the furs, cedar logs, and sassafras that Gosnold took back to England.[51]

That much of the European discovery of North America simply involved Europeans learning from Indians what Indians already knew about their countries, bringing the "so-called unknown territory into the written record of European civilization,"[52] was a view held by certain early colonial writers. Perhaps the best-known example is Roger Williams, who recognized Indian cultures of the Northeast as repositories of knowledge and conceived of the discovery of their lands in terms of verbal and commercial exchange. His *Key into the Language of America* is a vocabulary of the language spoken in the region of the English colonies, and in his introduction he tells his countrymen in Old and New England that this is the key to "the mighty continent of America" and that it consists of the "native language of it, [which] happily may unlock some rarities concerning the natives themselves, not yet discovered." With this key he has himself "entered into the secrets of those countries wherever English dwell."[53] For Williams, the continent, though "mighty," is not a speechless mystery. Nor can its being and meaning be read by the discoverer in the land itself. In Williams's opinion, the English had to learn the languages of the Indians in order to learn about the place they were colonizing.

I have argued that eighteenth-century accounts by traders and travelers among the interior peoples reflect such a multifarious process of adjustment and portray discovery as a series of contacts that are part of a gradual learning process. Narratives by Samuel Hearne and Lewis and Clark, whom Thoreau cites in other contexts, are detailed records of how the explorer/writer's initial goals—the discoveries he hoped to make—were gradually modified by the day-to-day business of traveling and trading. The goals of such men are expressed in economic or geographical terms. Their experiences did not make them "new men," radically altered by their discovery of a new place, but taught them new things, made them competent canoeists, good interpreters of Indian cultures, of new languages, and trade routes. The people they met and the land they traveled over were also changed by the encounter. America was different as a result of the exchanges among Europeans and Indians. The rhetoric of these traders' accounts is not one of unmediated contact with an essentially symbolic landscape but of complex social relations that change according to the dynamics of commerce, war, disease, politics, and love.

In Thoreau's "Ktaadn," however, we find a vision of first contact that is at odds with the contents and import of colonial and contemporary exploration accounts. Like early travelers, Thoreau records the complexities of exploratory travel, but his goal is an ahistorical moment of discovery when prior difficulties and doubts seem to fall into the background and an individual's unqualified wonder emerges as the full expression of future American possibilities. In this respect, "Ktaadn" is within the tradition of the American "discovery" (as opposed to "exploration" or "settlement") narrative defined by Wayne Franklin, at the heart of which Franklin finds "the ravished observer, fixed in awe, scanning the New World scene." His is a "simple timeless stare," which in itself constitutes "a full adventure," "a ritualistic, even eucharistic act."[54] Thoreau's journey is not toward a quantifiable discovery, but rather away from a notion of American life as commerce or ongoing exchange. The climax of "Ktaadn" occurs when Thoreau reaches land where "not even the surface had been scarred by man," where he finds "a specimen of what God saw fit to make this world."[55] At this point, the notion of learning or exchange becomes unthinkable, for his experience no longer lends itself to expression in commercial, or even verbal, terms. In Thoreau's first contact with it, the "virgin forest of the New World" becomes like Captain Ahab's "blank wall." Thoreau says: "Talk of mysteries! Think of our life in nature,—daily to be shown matter, to come in contact with it,—rocks, trees, wind on our cheeks! the *solid* earth! the *actual* world! the *common sense! Contact! Contact! Who* are we? *where* are we?"[56] This emphasis suggests what I think is true of Thoreau's explorer persona throughout the narrative: that he values his encounter with the absolute far more highly than any material or informational gains that could attend his journey. Thoreau manages the "mere history" of his journey so that it leads to "*Contact!*" with the essential place.[57]

"Ktaadn" is, thus, both a typical account of an exploratory journey— one that owes a great deal to Thoreau's reading in this genre—and a revision of the genre such that the plot leads up to Thoreau's attempt at an absolute discovery of a definitive America. The journey account, in fact, tries to disencumber both the traveler and the land from their visible relations with Indian and Euro-American society.[58] The very means of movement suggest such a process. Thoreau records his having traveled by railroad and steamboat, buggy, bateau, and finally on foot. As he moves inland, he drops civilized aids to travel, including boatmen and guides, one by one, until he ascends Mount Katahdin alone, to view land "such as man never inhabits."[59] Thoreau sees his means of travel as detachable from his destination and purposes. He relies on the lumber business for the transportation he employs, saying, "I was glad to avail myself of the circumstance of a gang of men being employed at the foot of Ktaadn" (46), but there is certainly no question of his reporting any fine stand of white pine he happens to come across to his "relative engaged in the lumber trade in Bangor" (3). Thoreau sheds the motives of other travelers even as he employs their means.

In a similar way, he frees the land itself from present and previous inhabitants, in order that it may serve as the visible sign of the "very America" appropriate to his vision of first contact. The lumber industry is one historical mode of discovering the land; harvesting timber is one way of knowing the country. As he passes the log booms and sawmills of Bangor, however, Thoreau imagines "the white-pine tree on the shore of Chesuncook, its branches soughing with the four winds, and every individual needle trembling in the sunlight" and asks himself whether the reality of this tree is recognized by what he calls the lumber company's "steel riddle," through which the tree passes, "till it comes out boards, clapboards, laths, and shingles . . . , slit and slit again, till men get a size that will suit" (5). Something of an organic complexity answering to the inquiring gaze of Thoreau the poet is reduced by lumbermen to "a size that will suit" and sold, "perchance to the New England Friction Match Company" (5). Thoreau must pass beyond the effects of the lumberman's response to his "virgin forest of the New World" if his expedition is to reach its goal.

Thoreau both admires and deplores what he calls the "mission" of the lumbermen with their great energy and appalling greed. Similarly, he exalts isolated settlers who clear themselves a patch of ground and "begin life as Adam did" but is shocked by the waste involved in their burning what he says are trees "enough to keep the poor of Boston and New York amply warm for the winter" in order to clear ground for a farm (17). He distinguishes his own vision from the lumbering and farming of the land, which translate what he calls nature into property.

Typically, he turns economic activities into metaphors for his own imaginative possession. Observing piles of logs bearing the owner's brand that are stranded above the last flood's high-water mark, he thinks, "that must be where all my property lies, cast up on the rocks on some distant and unexplored stream, and waiting for an unheard-of freshet to fetch it down" (53). The freshet that will release this property is "unheard-of," as the land that Thoreau takes as his destination is "unexplored" and "distant." The results to date of the exchange between Europe and America are not what Thoreau seeks. He must go past the loggers' camps and the settlers' clearings until the land is a suitable image of what he wants to discover.

Thoreau also must deal with his Indian contemporaries, whom he knows have inhabited the country up to the time of his journey, though they are now much reduced by centuries of conflict. At the confluence of the Mattawamkeag and the Penobscot, on what Thoreau knew to be the site of a battle between "Eastern Indians and Mohawks," he finds "some flakes of arrow-head stone, some points of arrowheads, one small bullet, and some colored beads" (12). Although he recognizes that Indian wars occurred there, the meanness of the material remains suggests a slightness in the Indians' past hold on the land that seems consonant with Thoreau's view of their contemporary presence. He encounters his first Indian as the ferry passes Indian Island at Old Town:

> I observed a short shabby washer-woman-looking Indian; they commonly have that woe-begone look of the girl that cried for spilt milk—just from "up river,"—land on the Oldtown side near a grocery, and drawing up his canoe, take out a bundle of skins in one hand, and an empty keg or half-barrel in the other, and scramble up the bank with them. This picture will do to put before the Indian's history, that is, the history of his extinction. (6)

These contemporary Indians, though citizens of what Thoreau calls "the republic," are not the inhabitants of the America Thoreau seeks to discover. He says, "even a row of wigwams, with a dance of pow-wows, and a prisoner tortured at the stake, would be more respectable than this" (7).

Thoreau hires Indian guides at the beginning of his journey, hoping to learn from their knowledge of the land, but they are delayed by a drinking spree so that they meet him only as he is returning from the mountain. He describes them coming up the river, seemingly "disguised" in broad-brimmed Quaker hats. Comparing them to "the sinister and slouching fellows whom you meet picking up string and paper in the streets of a city," he concludes that there is "a remarkable and unexpected resemblance between the degraded savage and the lowest classes in a great city. One is no more a child of nature than the other" (78). Like the urban poor, he suggests, the modern Indian has little claim to the territory he inhabits. Not only has he been physically displaced by the European, but he has, in his degradation, forfeited even the moral claim to the land that might hitherto have been based on his "nobility"; "in the progress of degradation the distinction of races is soon lost" (78).

Once he confronts the wilderness of the Maine interior, Thoreau is like the nineteenth-century westering explorers he read in emphasizing the vastness and emptiness of the land. "It is even more grim and wild than you had anticipated" (80), he says, passing beyond the cultivated valleys into the forests. Atop Katahdin, he describes the scenery as "vast, Titanic, and such as man never inhabits" (64). Some commentators have argued that the mountaintop and the endless forest threaten Thoreau's transcendental confidence in the unity of human and material nature and that his experiences there suggested the limits of his hermeneutics. They cite such passages as that recounting his experience on top of Katahdin, when "some part of the beholder, even some vital part, seems to escape through the loose grating of his ribs" (64). The mountaintop, he says, "was no man's garden, but the unhandselled globe. . . . It was the fresh and natural surface of the planet Earth, as it was made forever and ever" (70). Cecelia Tichi posits that his experience of unaltered nature marked a limit to what she calls Thoreau's "paradise of personal vision," that it "threatened both life and self" with "dissolution and derangement." She reads "Ktaadn" as detailing a state of mind in which Thoreau was not able to confirm the "higher laws" that emerged from his encounter with the more domesticated natural environs of Walden Pond.[60]

I would suggest, to the contrary, that although the landscape of "Ktaadn" is not the "middle landscape" of *Walden*, which blends the best of civilization and savagery, Thoreau's response to the wild land is consistent with his relation to nature in *Walden*. He is not rejecting—even if he fears rejection by—its vastness and indifference. Rather, he is securing this land as a guarantee that there is more to man and nature than is easily realized or expressed, a promise that what he calls "mere history" can never triumph.[61] Thus the mountaintop scene reminds him of the gods, fabulous creatures, and heroes of "the old epic and dramatic poets, of Atlas, Vulcan, the Cyclops, and Prometheus."[62] Because "not even the surface had been scarred by man," this terrain is valuable to him as what he later, in an analogous situation, calls "a specimen of what God saw fit to make this world" (70). The lakes, too, "are something which you are unprepared for." "They lie up so high exposed to the light, and the forest is diminished to a fine fringe on their edges, with here and there a blue mountain, like amethyst jewels set around some jewel of the first water,—so anterior, so superior to all the changes that are to take place on their shores, even now civil and refined, and fair, as they can ever be" (80).

Is this not the transcendentalist's fundamental desire—a nature that is "so anterior, so superior" to change that he need never fear meeting its limits?[63] Thoreau, like Fitzgerald's Dutch sailors at the end of *The Great Gatsby*, honors something "commensurate with his capacity for wonder," something that is not subject to so-called Euro-American "progress" or Indian "degradation." He represents this incommensurable state by land "unmediated by the traditions of human inhabitants."[64]

Neither the lumbermen, nor the settlers, nor the contemporary Indians can claim Thoreau's first-contact world. Instead, Thoreau imagines a solitary New World man at one with this otherwise empty landscape. Immediately upon leaving his would-be guides, Thoreau tries to conjure up the man to do justice to the place he has discovered. Like the land he inhabits, this man is an extended metaphor, carefully shaped. The frontier settlers Thoreau admires in the present and the Indian he imagines in the precontact past combine with the observing narrator's ideal American self to stand for what he calls a "primitive man" living in "a new world, far in the dark of a continent," a man who reflects the unlimited potential of the unmediated place. This man "shall live his life away here on the edge of the wilderness . . . , shall live, as it were, in the primitive age of the world. . . . Yet he shall spend a sunny day, and in this century be my contemporary. . . . The ages and the generations are now. . . . [This man] lives three thousand years deep into time, an age not yet described by poets."[65] The verb tenses in this passage suggest this new man's freedom from history. He "shall lead" his life "here," yet his world is "primitive." This man also currently "lives . . . deep into time." He is of the future, the past, and the present. He is the "ancient and primitive man" whom Thoreau next imagines turning up "into the mouth of Millinocket stream":

> In a bark vessel sewn with the roots of the spruce, with horn-beam paddles he dips his way along. He is but dim and misty to me, obscured by the aeons. . . . He builds no house of logs, but a wigwam of skins. He eats no hot-bread and sweet-cake, but mu-squash and moose-meat and the fat of bears. He glides up the Millinocket and is lost to my sight, as a more distant and misty cloud is seen flitting by behind a nearer, and is lost in space. So he goes about his destiny, the red face of man. (79)

This distant and misty time and space, seen as though through a cloud, Thoreau has earlier identified as the realm of "mythology." As I under-stand him, he means a realm contacted only in his art. Yet this man and this myth so pervade Thoreau's rhetoric that they make the historical white and red presences seem like obscuring vapors. Because this man is outside history, he is neither European nor Indian. What Thoreau sees when he looks at the untenanted land is not the face of the existing Red Man, but "the red face of man," the primitive ideal man of his first-contact world.

That the force of Thoreau's rhetoric makes this ideal seem more important than the historical European and Indian presences he simul-taneously documents should not surprise readers of *Walden*, where the replacing of historical event with its personal significance almost be-comes a mannerism. There we are advised to ignore the Northwest Passage and be rather "the Lewis and Clarke [*sic*] and Frobisher" of our own "streams and oceans," to resist the call of patriotism because "only the defeated and deserters go to the wars, cowards that run away and enlist."[66] In "Ktaadn," however, Thoreau's historical concerns are more sharply focused on the particular place through which he is traveling, so the implications of his dismissal of "mere history" are more evident.

Thoreau's "Ktaadn" is a journey through the measurable world of sawn boards and human conflicts to a land "perhaps never seen by the white man before." His exploration separates him from contemporary and recorded experience in the New World, even as he travels through it. He moves beyond the stumps, clearings, and Indian hovels into the realm of wonders that he says is the same one contacted by the earliest voyagers. He makes this connection with the past by proposing a myth that transcends time and historical change. In his account of trout fishing in the Aboljacknagesic, for example, he equates his direct experience of the abundance of nature with the "truth of mythology," which is available to any age. The fish "fell in a perfect shower" around him. They "glistened like fairest flowers . . . ; and the beholder could hardly trust his senses, as he stood over them, that these jewels should have swum away in the . . . water for so long, so many dark ages;—these bright fluviatile flowers, seen by Indians only, made beautiful, the Lord knows why, to swim there."[67] One notes that because the fish, as symbols, are not significant to the uninitiated Indians, the uninitiated themselves are insignificant. The wonder of contact with such "jewels" he calls the stuff of "fable." He says that such experience belongs not to history but to "mythology," the realm of his primitive man. These fish are not resources to be harvested but signs of welcome to one who knows how to see them aright. "I could understand better . . . how all history, indeed, put to a terrestrial use, is mere history; but put to a celestial, is mythology always" (54).

This empty America and the primitive man who inhabits it are both the creations of Thoreau's narration of discovery. Thoreau's metaphorical use of discovery in "Ktaadn" is like his purchase of a farm in *Walden*: "Wherever I sat, there might I live, and the landscape radiated from me accordingly."[68] It is essential to his relation to the land, however, that he "never got [his] fingers burned by actual possession" (81–82). His discovery and his farming are both metaphorical appropriations of the land to his own best use, notwithstanding his awareness of the exchanges and conflicts that constitute the land's history. He proceeds knowingly. "I considered," he says in *Walden*, "that I enhanced the value of the land by squatting on it" (64). Similarly, in "Ktaadn," Thoreau's discovery of America is an event that happens in spite of prior European and Indian interactions with the place and with each other. Thoreau's narrative recounts a real journey, but the discovery it describes is not the product of a historical process; Thoreau's discovery is a personal event, but one that can be repeated in successive generations. In contemporary western narratives, the economic and political reasons for obscuring the Indianness of the land are fairly evident in the official goals of the expeditions. Although Thoreau's intentions seem more complex, the powerful appeal of his rhetoric of first contact suggests that for nineteenth-century Americans—and, I suggest, for later North Americans—his vision of discovery was another energizing simplification of America's history of commerce and conflict.

Conclusion

Borrowing from the conventions of the discovery narrative, Thoreau invented a new way of mediating the conflict between Euro- and Native American claims. Without actually denying the existence of this conflict, his version of the romantic discovery narrative suggested a way to place Euro-Americans in contact with their continent without requiring them to countenance the killing and displacing of its first peoples. Whereas the sensitive heroes and narrators of Cooper and Irving can only look on helplessly in emblematic dismay as their countrymen eradicate Indian inhabitants from their lands, Thoreau offers a narrative of personal contact with the American land that the most conscientious can endorse: Thoreau adapts the conventions of the factual discovery narrative to the optative vision of Emerson in which individual knowledge of the American land transcends historical, political, legal and economic concerns.

We have seen how in his "Ktaadn" narrative Thoreau appropriates the action of the earliest discovery narratives as an image for his individual travels, finally making his personal experience—his transcendental *"Contact!"* with the place—the authority of his claim to it. Thoreau was not ignorant, nor did he suppress mention, of the other kinds of claims to the land; his journey begins with the Old Town

203

Indians and proceeds through the settler's clearing and the lumber camps to the "unhandselled" land, and Thoreau's sympathetic interest in the history of American native peoples is well documented.[1] But the story of "Ktaadn" is Thoreau's journey to a place where these institutional and historical claims seem to have no standing. Thoreau claims that he has found "the very America" of the earliest European voyagers, and his implication seems to be that this America is available to those who are able imaginatively to discover it.

Of course, Thoreau's claim is ostentatiously metaphorical, and one might argue that one ought not to confuse Thoreau's metaphors with the actual claims to territory that serve as their vehicle. In other words, the argument goes, the transcendentalist's self-discovery is not the basis for a claim to the ground on which that discovery occurs. Leo Marx argues this view of how one should read Thoreau's figures of regeneration in *Walden*, referring to the famous description of the thawing bank of the railway cut:

> Thoreau's study of the melting bank is a figurative restoration of the form and unity severed by the mechanized forces of history. Out of the ugly "cut" in the landscape he fashions an image of a new beginning. Order, form, and meaning are restored, but it is a blatantly, unequivocally figurative restoration. The whole force of the passage arises from its extravagantly metaphoric, poetic, literary character. At no point does Thoreau impute material reality to the notion of sand being transformed into, say, leopard's paws. It assumes a form that looks like leopard's paws, but the form exists only so far as it is perceived. The same may be said of his alternative to the Concord way.[2]

According to Marx, Thoreau does not intend this image of organic regeneration and unity actually to heal or even obviate the "cuts" of the "forces of history." Likewise, Thoreau's alternative versions of American discovery and westering are not intended as practical alternatives to the forces of history that have given Euro-Americans possession of the continent. Marx continues:

> The melting of the bank and the coming of spring is only "like" a realization of the golden age. It is a poetic figure. In *Walden* Thoreau is clear, as Emerson never was, about the location of meaning and value. He is saying that it does not reside in the

natural facts or in social institutions or in anything "out there," but in consciousness. It is a product of imaginative perception, of the analogy-perceiving, metaphor-making, mythopoeic power of the human mind. For Thoreau the realization of the golden age is, finally, a matter of private and, in fact, literary experience. (264)

I certainly agree that Thoreau's realizations of America in *Walden* and "Ktaadn" are consciously metaphorical and that Thoreau was well aware of the difference between his mode of metaphor and the narrative history of Euro-American society. Marx hits the crucial point: Thoreau locates "meaning and value . . . not . . . in the natural facts or in social institutions or in anything 'out there,' but in consciousness." The question that concerns me, however, is the effect such a powerfully expressed epistemology has had on not just "literary" but political experience and actions. Insofar as Thoreau clearly values the experiences realized in his writing above those that he finds typically denoted by accounts of American westering, it seems to me that they assert a claim on more than "literary" matters, that they are available as a version of Euro-American experience, that they cannot be isolated from political thought and action, that in fact Thoreau would be a trivial writer if they could be. So to say that Thoreau's vision of American discovery is metaphorical is not to say that this vision is irrelevant to how the politics of Euro-American expansion have been conceived. In the long term, Thoreau may possibly be the most influential of all American Renaissance writers because he appropriated the central paradigm of his country's history, reversed the direction from which it drew its authority—from the legal and institutional to the spiritual and personal—and then returned it to his countrymen as a new basis upon which to understand their presence in America. The discovery of America, the exploration and settlement of the West, do not mean the same thing in Euro-American culture once Thoreau's works begin to be assimilated. The "location of meaning and value," to return to Marx's terms, is shifted to Thoreau's narratives and, eventually, to his readers' analogous versions of their own personal first contacts with "America."

In understanding the impact of Thoreau's revision of American discovery, it is important, as well, to bear in mind that Thoreau's appropriation of the *form* of the discovery narrative was not entirely metaphorical. Thoreau did go on journeys; he did see things that none of his readers had seen. His reports, like all discovery narratives, are accounts of experiences unique to the writer. Thoreau's faithful adherence to the conventions of the discovery narrative are part of his claim that what he reports be taken seriously, as something that will really change one's relation to one's world, since this claim had been fundamental to the discovery narrative as a genre. Implicitly, his narrative of his journey, like all discovery narratives, pretends to offer a new possibility to readers. Thoreau's narratives recount a new way of discovering America, but their claim to having made a real discovery is not fanciful. Imitating as it does the actual discovery narrative, the rhetoric of "Ktaadn" claims for the actions and experiences of its narrator the status of events in the history of its readers. Something has been found on this trip; something has happened; writer and reader are different as a result.

Walden, Thoreau's masterpiece, also addresses its audience very much in the manner of the factual discovery narrative. Even though it ends with the figurative dawning of a new day, it presents itself initially in relation to American history and contemporary society. Thoreau initially announces as the basis of his account that, like any explorer, he has "travelled a good deal" ("in Concord," of course) and that, like anyone who has new discoveries to report, he will write "some such account as he would send to his kindred from a distant land."[3] The rhetorical force of *Walden* derives substantially from Thoreau's adaptation and manipulation of the conventions of the discovery narrative; his metaphorizing of the actions of travel and exploration would be trivial, however, if he did not at the same time take completely seriously the discoverer's mandate systematically to investigate and record the sights and events of his journey, on the assumption that they are radically unfamiliar, and yet important, to himself and his readers. Thoreau's account of the equipping and the physical maintenance of his person is completely typical of the eighteenth- and nineteenth-century exploration narrative. So are his "Reading," his research into what other travels have shown; his interest in wildlife; his mapping; his measuring of depths, heights, temperatures, and distances; his account of climate and his dependence on the seasons; his accounts of the economics and customs of the peoples he encounters along the way, from Irish immigrant, to Quebecois woodcutter, to local ice harvester, to grotesque Concord bourgeois staggering under his load of furniture. And so, as we have seen, is his personal meditation on the meaning of what he sees and experiences.

But are there any historical *events* in "Ktaadn" or *Walden*—that is, *events* that, in Hegel's sense of the term, have to do with the history of a state? Do "Ktaadn" and *Walden* recount stages in the conflict over territory that is unavoidably at the center of American history, and do they assert the legitimacy of the Euro-American state's presence and power in the continent? According to Hegel, "it is the State which first presents the subject-matter that is not only adapted to the prose of History, but involves the production of such History in the very progress of its being"; and, again, "only in a State cognizant of Laws, can distinct transactions take place, accompanied by such a clear consciousness of them as supplies the ability and suggests the necessity of an enduring record."[4] Certainly the United States of Thoreau's day qualified as Hegel's "State," and we have seen how, writing with the consciousness of the authority of the institutions of this state, Lewis and Clark, Pike, Frémont, and Irving wrote accounts of deeds and experiences in the Far West that we generally accept as part of the history of the United States. We recognize that this history is the story of the rise of one nation at the expense of many other peoples, that this history is a story of conflict, of winners and losers. *Walden* attacks the American state's actions on the western frontier through its parodying of the western travel narrative; Thoreau's irony condemns "the defeated and deserters [who] go to the wars, cowards that run away and enlist," rejecting any literal imitation of the actions of actual westering literature.[5] Instead, he urges his readers: "Start now on that farthest western way, which does not pause at the Mississippi or the Pacific" (322). The historical basis of the discovery narrative genre is transformed into metaphor when Thoreau finally counsels: "Explore thyself" (322).

Thoreau is essentially a judge of this history, a particularly stern evaluator of past actions and events in relation to American ideals. He reviews past and contemporary events in American society, but what he proposes further to this review is not a reformed or re-directed continuation of the same story of winners and losers. As we have already determined, the "very America" that Thoreau discovers in "Ktaadn" is not a state in which events occur or about which history of Hegel's sort can be written; Thoreau appropriates the American frontier as a source of metaphors for individual development. But it is essential to recognize that the *form* of Thoreau's "Ktaadn" and *Walden* reasserts those metaphors as reference points for American society. Thoreau managed to construe a literary form in which the transcendentalist analogies between nature and the human mind could be presented as a narrative account of events in American history; Thoreau's story establishes essentially personal consciousness as the authority for true Americanness, and out of the "story" of this event rises implicitly a claim to the land that is the theater of these experiences.

What Thoreau would change from the conventions of the discovery narrative, what he wrestles with, in fact, all the way through, is its economic and political dependence on the society from which he departs and, ultimately, to which he must write. Thoreau's account would have his readers imitate—or at least entertain the implications of—his method for transforming himself into an explorer, having all establish their own "original relations" to the continent while severing the compromised dependence on nineteenth-century institutions. All Americans should be metaphorical explorers, all readers writers of their own narratives; for everyone, "if he has lived sincerely, it must have been in a distant land to me" (3–4).

Despite his frequent hyperbole, Thoreau had his millennial urges in check. *Walden* makes more sense read as a response to the conflicts of the American past, in which Thoreau was steeped, and to those of the American present, which seem only too much like what he knew of the past, than as a reformist prescription for the future. Nonetheless, Thoreau's account of his individual actions as a settler in Emerson's woodlot asserts the possibility that Thoreau's experiences may come to be regarded as a new founding event in American history, in the sense that his narrative represents a mode of action that can serve as a basis of American identity and a source of legitimacy in the continent. Thoreau proposes a history whose events are constituted in relation to an American State of Mind. The individuals who may share this state are his audience, and it is upon the potential authority of their experiences that he claims for his personal experiences the status of historical events in the real America.

Thoreau wrote after the first half-century of the republic, during which time land, according to Malcolm Rohrbough, "was the nation's most sought after commodity," when "the effort of men to acquire [land] was one of the dominant forces."[6] According to Michael Rogin, during this period "land in America was not only a symbol of national identity but also—in a more thoroughgoing sense than anywhere else in the world—a commodity. . . . Land had not only symbolic value and use value, but exchange value as well. It was at once sustainer of American uniqueness and uniquely available to be exploited, bought and sold" (79). In the early 1850s, when Thoreau published *Walden* and "Ktaadn," the United States had just acquired all its present-day contiguous territory, Indian removals east of the Mississippi had been complete for a decade, and Indians west of the Mississippi were beginning to be confined to reservations as settlers poured into Texas, California, and Oregon. Narrative accounts of overland journeys to these parts flourished in the press, and in them were many vivid instances of the energy and conflict that moving from de jure to de facto control of the continent entailed.[7] In the midst of, and directly in response to these events, *Walden* and "Ktaadn" propose a new "economy," a different response to land, a new form of settlement, a noninstitutional basis of American identity. These works are like desert individualist islands in the midst of the national furor over land, transcendentalist versions of Ishmael Bush's bluff fortress in Cooper's prairie sea of territorial strife. It would be twenty years until the establishment of Yellowstone Park in 1872, but already Thoreau had worked out the relation to the land and its corresponding narrative of American experience that would guide the creation of the national parks, those reservations in reverse, where generations of Euro-Americans could reenact Thoreau's narrative of American first contact with "virgin land" and keep alive the appealing version of the founding event that he established as a kind of American history.

The political implications of this rhetoric and its claim to historicity are what concern me here. To what extent does such a patently metaphorical mode of exploration and discovery succeed as an alternative to other contemporary historical accounts of the Euro-American presence in the continent? To what extent does a narrative of personal contact offer itself as an authorization of the actions of the past? The romantic discovery narrative that Thoreau participated in developing became an influential, if ostentatiously figurative, alternative prophecy of Americans' relation to the land of the United States. Although the romantic discovery narrative is often thought of as an artistic advance over the more historicist plots of Cooper and Irving, in many respects its treatment of the conquest of the continent amounts to a silencing of commentary on the historical processes and politics of exploration, conquest, and settlement that continued until nearly the end of the nineteenth century. The political implications of this literary style seem profound: the achievement of a sophisticated native literary idiom, the conscious goal of all those writers inspired by Emerson's "The American Scholar," also tended to displace the discordant voices of historical struggle.

Notes

Introduction

1. Miller, "The Romantic Dilemma," 199, 204.

2. The term *Euro-American* designates citizens of the United States who see themselves as having European roots. Euro-Americans are, on the one hand, distinct from Europeans, who may act a part in the Americas but remain identified with a European nation. On the other hand, they see themselves as distinct from people who trace their roots to any of the pre-Columbian peoples of the New World. For the collective sense of these latter I have chosen to use "Indian" in most cases. In its original, albeit misinformed, sense, "Indian" identifies people in terms of where they live and is normatively neutral, equivalent with "European." The term *Native American* is apt to be confusing in a discussion that often needs to distinguish Europeans from American-born descendants of Europeans; moreover, it is not generally used by or for the Indian peoples outside what is now the United States who are frequently discussed in this study. Whenever possible, I use the specific name of a people. Spellings other than those of the author under discussion are from the *Handbook of North American Indians*.

Collective terms are necessary in this discussion of the late colonial and early national periods of United States history, when their broad usage was being shaped. This study concerns the language of Euro-Americans as they came to identify themselves with the continent, calling themselves Americans and excluding Indian peoples from this category despite their priority as inhabitants. I believe that the term "Euro-American" disrupts to some extent this habitual identity. These terms may not be what one would prefer for discussions of the present situation or other periods of American history.

3. Rogin, *Fathers and Children*, 297.

4. Limerick, *Legacy of Conquest*, 19.

5. Rogin, *Fathers and Children*, 100.

6. Lawrence, *Studies in Classic American Literature*, 35.

7. Lewis, *The American Adam*, 88. Lewis is quoting de Tocqueville here.

8. Rogin, *Fathers and Children*, explores the importance of land acquisition in the early national period.

9. Lewis, *The American Adam*, 9.

10. In *Regeneration Through Violence*, Richard Slotkin addresses this oversight with his emphasis on the violent confrontation between Europeans and Indians in Indian captivity and war narratives.

11. Smith, *Virgin Land*, 4.

12. Smith, "Symbol and Idea," 27.

13. Slotkin, *The Fatal Environment*, 34.

14. Rogin, *Fathers and Children*, 100.

15. Hulme, *Colonial Encounters*, 2.

16. Green, *The Great American Adventure*, viii.

17. O'Gorman, *The Invention of America*, 45.

One
Trading and Telling: Discovery and the British Fur Trade

1. Henry, *Travels and Adventures*. See the preface for Henry's comments on the rashness of this venture. For a discussion of the extent of the French fur-trading network, see Innis, *The Fur Trade in Canada*, 111.

2. Innis, *The Fur Trade in Canada*, 111, 167–169.

3. I am indebted for many of the sources cited in this section to MacLulich, "The Emergence of the Exploration Narrative."

4. Crone and Skelton, "English Collections," 78.

5. MacLulich, "The Emergence of the Exploration Narrative," 10–12. I am indebted here to his discussion of Cook's impact on travel reporting.

6. On the editing of the journals of Mackenzie and Hearne, see MacLaren, "Samuel Hearne's Accounts," 25–51; "Alexander Mackenzie," 141–150; and "Creating Travel Literature," 80–95.

7. MacLaren, "Creating Travel Literature," 81.

8. White, "The Value of Narrativity," 5.

9. Hearne, *Journey*, lvii.

10. Franklin, *Discoverers, Explorers, Settlers*, 23. In Franklin's definition,

the "exploratory narrative" is more focused on the future implications of what the traveler finds. "Exploration is the hunter's art, the locating of a desired commodity" (71). This characterization is closer to the way I see Hearne's *Journey*.

11. Writers also attached noneconomic motives to exploring expeditions. The advancement of science was one motive that was always mentioned, even when the contribution to science was small. The "civilization" of Indian peoples was another goal mentioned occasionally, though often in such a way as to suggest that the thought belonged to the editor and not to the traveler. (The infrequency of such allusions in North American fur trade narratives may be a sign of candor in the writers.) Sheer curiosity was also mentioned from time to time, often on behalf of European culture in general; in reality, however, the expense, danger, and discomfort of the journeys described were sufficient to blunt the touristic impulse. "Curiosity" was gratified only here and there, as security and commercial activity allowed.

12. Long, *Voyages and Travels*, 73–74.

13. Hearne, *Journey*, lvi–lvii.

14. A water route across North America, even one involving portages, would have meant that furs obtained in America could have been shipped directly to the Far East from the Pacific coast, thus linking the independently lucrative American and Far Eastern trades by substituting fur for some of the silver and gold sent to China from Britain. See Mackenzie, *Journals and Letters*, 24 n. 1.

15. Mackenzie, *Journals and Letters*, 417.

16. Hegel, *The Philosophy of History*, 60.

17. In "The Value of Narrativity," Hayden White comments on the same passage from Hegel's *The Philosophy of History* to which I refer. White notes that

> once we have been alerted to the intimate relationship Hegel suggests exists between law, historicality, and narrativity, we cannot but be struck by the frequency with which narrativity, whether of the fictional or factual sort, presupposes the existence of a legal system against which the typical agents of a narrative account militate. And this raises the suspicion that narrative in general, from the folktale to the novel, from annals to the fully realized "history," has to do with topics of law, legality, legitimacy, or more generally, *authority*. (17)

18. White, "The Value of Narrativity," 7. The phrase is from Benveniste, *Problems in General Linguistics*, 208.

19. Brebner, *Explorers of North America*, 326.

20. Hearne, *Journey*, 3–4.

21. Ian MacLaren discusses the substantial differences between the pub-

lished account of the massacre and existing transcriptions of Hearne's earlier journal and field notes ("Samuel Hearne's Accounts," 28–36).

22. Hearne, *Journey*, 104–105.

23. Hearne managed this kind of development very well, stepping with some relish into the role of gatherer of data for the scientific "gentlemen" at home. "Providence," says Hearne, has placed these gentlemen

> too remote from want to be obliged to travel for ocular proofs of what they assert in their publications; they are therefore wisely content to stay at home, and enjoy the blessings with which they are endowed, resting satisfied to collect such information for their own amusement, and the gratification of the public, as those who are necessitated to be travellers are able or willing to give them. It is true, and I am sorry that it is so, that I come under the latter description; but I hope I have not, or shall not, in the course of this Journal, advance any thing that will not stand the test of experiment, and the skill of the most competent judges. (130)

24. See Mackenzie, *Journals and Letters*, 1–4.

25. Mackenzie, *Journals and Letters*, 417.

26. In this regard, it is interesting to compare Hearne's and Mackenzie's rates of travel on their respective journeys to the Arctic Ocean. Mackenzie made the round trip in 102 days, while Hearne took 18 months, 23 days, to go roughly the same distance.

27. MacLaren, "Alexander Mackenzie," 144. MacLaren deals with the changes in landscape rendering effected by Combe's editing. Franz Montgomery, however, identifies Combe as Mackenzie's ghost writer in "Alexander Mackenzie's Literary Assistant," 301—-304.

28. Mackenzie, *Journals and Letters*, 249.

29. "Alexander Mackenzie, from Canada, by land, the twenty-second of July, one thousand seven hundred and ninety-three."

30. *Edinburgh Review*, 142.

31. Mackenzie, *Journals and Letters*, 300.

32. Henry, *Travels and Adventures*, 1.

33. In *The Fur Trade in Canada*, Innis says "the technique of the fur trade built up by the French remained practically intact. Carver noted at Grand Portage in 1767 the effectiveness of the French traders with the Northwest Indians as contrasted with the English traders on Hudson's Bay. . . . Under these conditions recovery of the fur trade was rapid" (168–169). Innis further notes that "although Henry and other traders suffered serious losses because of the Indian wars, they rapidly became acquainted with the methods of the trade as conducted from Michilimackinac and assumed active direction. . . . The success of the partnership of Henry and Cadotte was symbolic of the necessary combination between English capital and French experience" (168).

34. In *Pontiac and the Indian Uprising,* Howard Peckham emphasizes the British handling of trade goods as a major cause of the Indian wars that began in 1763: "The Indians' grievances against the English were solid and numerous. Foremost among them was the English refusal to supply ammunition for hunting. . . . Secondly, the prices of trade goods were not as low as the Indians had been led to anticipate. Thirdly, the English did not make them presents as often or as bountifully as the French had done, either as rent for land, or as gratitude for friendship" (101–102). Peckham quotes Pontiac's reference to the war that developed as "the beaver war," alluding to the importance of trade in the hostilities, but Peckham says that "what it developed into, of course, was a war for Indian independence as modified by French economic penetration" (111). He argues that Pontiac and his warriors did not want total isolation, just independence and access to the goods that they had been accustomed to acquiring through trade (319–320).

35. The authenticity of *Travels and Adventures* has been a matter of dispute, with respect both to its accuracy and to its authorship. The main discussions of these matters are James Bain's introduction to the 1901 edition, Milton Milo Quaife's introduction to the 1921 edition, and Freda F. Waldon's unpublished M.A. thesis, "Alexander Henry, Esq. of Montreal." The last is by far the most comprehensive treatment of these matters, and I am not aware of subsequent work that adds much to Waldon's information or conclusions.

I do not think resolutions of these questions would have much effect upon the approach to the text that I take here. *Travels and Adventures,* regardless of its exact authorship, is a narrative representation of a particular, crucial moment in North American history. As such, it asserts a view of the relationships among the principal actors. It has always been regarded as sufficiently close to other accounts of the same or similar events and to the consensus of the time that its version could not be ignored. If it is a "fiction," it is one that demands to be read in relation to the actual politics of its day, which is what I try to do here.

I wish to thank David McNeil, a colleague in the English Department at Dalhousie University, for allowing me read his unpublished paper "In Search of Alexander Henry" and other notes on Henry.

36. In Henry, "Canadian" denotes the French-speaking inhabitants of the St. Lawrence valley and their many descendants in the West and North.

37. Hulme, *Colonial Encounters,* 2.

38. Describing Cumberland House, Henry notes that the house "had been built the year before, by Mr. Hearne, who was now absent on his well-known journey of discovery" (*Travels and Adventures,* 262). Henry refers readers to Mackenzie's *Voyages* for information on the Montreal-to-Michilimackinac canoe traffic and on the potential for mining along the shores of Lake Superior (14,

226). He cites Carver on the subject of mines (227, 218), on the performances of native shamans (164), and on the subject of Lake Winnipeg (257). There had been twenty editions of Carver's narrative by the time Henry published in 1809, and Henry refers to them often.

39. Henry's book was the least influential of the four; its publication was little noticed, and there were no reprints until 1901 (Waldon, "Alexander Henry," 59–61).

40. Mackenzie, *Journals and Letters*, 58.

41. Hearne's introduction includes his instructions from the Hudson's Bay Company: "It will be very useful to clear up this point [whether there is a passage through the continent] . . . in order to prevent farther doubts from arising hereafter respecting a passage out of Hudson's Bay into the Western Ocean" (*Journey*, lxix–lxx).

42. Carver, *Travels*, xviii.

43. See Pratt, "Conventions of Representation, " 139–155, and "Scratches on the Face," for two interesting discussions of how aesthetic and scientific description of land in travel narratives is implicated in the imperial claims of European powers.

Of related interest are Harley's "Deconstructing the Map," 1–20, and Huggan's "Decolonizing the Map," 115–131, both on the ideological nature of maps, which are often thought of as purely objective representations of physical reality. Harley says: "Cartographers manufacture power: they create a spatial panopticon. It is a power embedded in the map text. We can talk about the power of the map just as we already talk about the power of the word or about the book as a force for change. In this sense maps have a politics. It is a power that intersects and is embedded in knowledge" (13).

44. Mackenzie, *Journals and Letters*, 58–59.

45. See Axtell, *The Invasion Within*, 302–328, for a comprehensive discussion of "white Indians," that is, those Europeans who assimilated to Indian societies after capture. Commenting on the adoption practices of Indian societies in *Red, White, and Black,* Nash notes that

> even before the arrival of Europeans, Indian cultures had customarily adopted into their society as full-fledged members any persons captured in war. On some occasions a captive was even taken into a particular family to replace a lost child or other relative. This integration of newcomers into the kinship system and into the community at large, without judgmental comparisons of the superiority of the captor culture, made it easy for the captured 'outsider' to make a rapid adjustment. (284)

46. See Vaughan and Clark, *Puritans Among the Indians*, 1–28, for a general discussion of the historical significance and literary history of the Puritan captivity narrative.

47. Preface, Henry, *Travels and Adventures.*

48. Henry is Francis Parkman's main source for the account of this massacre in *The Conspiracy of Pontiac*, 1:48, and Thoreau recounts the story of Henry and Wawatam in his *Week on the Concord and Merrimack Rivers*, 274–275, as part of a meditation on friendship. See *Travels and Adventures*, 75–91, for Henry's account of the massacre.

49. Hulme, *Colonial Encounters*, 79.

50. Henry, *Travels and Adventures*, 160.

51. Adapting Victor Turner's theory of the process of initiation from one social identity to another, Vaughan and Clark in *Puritans Among the Indians* treat captivity narratives as primarily recounting the marginal or "liminal" phase between captives' "separation" from their natal environment and their subsequent "reaggregation" into the society from which they had been taken. In Vaughan and Clark's view, the bulk of what is recorded in captivity narratives is experienced during the "liminal" phase of initiation, after a violent separation that caused great physical and psychological stress. In the liminal phase, the captive "was relatively free from the social strictures and cultural values of his previous life. His natal culture's values were called into question. . . . Cut loose from his normal guideposts of language and social relationships, he entertained ideas and values that colonial New England did not allow" (12). Vaughan and Clark point out, however, that the narrative is written in the "postliminal" phase, when reaggregation is supposed to occur. They go on to describe the various barriers to reintegration that redeemed captives experienced, in particular the community's requirement that captives "reaffirm their natal culture's values more fervently than ever and . . . deny the attractions of 'savage' life" (14). Vaughan and Clark imply, but do not quite say, that the writing of the captivity narrative is part of the captive's effort of reaggregation, his or her attempt to return "home."

Two
Early Western Travels and the American Self

1. Juricek, "American Usage, " 21.

2. Turner, *The Frontier*, 3.

3. Juricek, "American Usage," 18.

4. I do not with agree with Lee Clark Mitchell's assertion in *Witnesses to a Vanishing America* that "America had been imagined from the beginning in terms of timeless space, as a vacant land awaiting the starter's gun of history" (6). Mitchell's book is about the nineteenth-century recognition that the "empty" land would be filled and ruined, and he cites much interesting evidence to prove and develop this thesis. I think he overlooks the fact, however, that the sense of

America as empty, timeless space is largely a creation of the nineteenth century. I think, as well, that Mitchell similarly projects nineteenth-century attitudes onto earlier periods when he asserts that it was during the 1870s that "whites for the first time looked closely at native cultures and came to appreciate their extraordinary diversity, intricacy, and autonomy—even their values" (9). Mitchell is thinking in particular of anthropological study and the growth of a discipline within which cultures could be compared, but even so this generalizes too much about the seventeenth and eighteenth centuries, when there was a much clearer and more widespread sense of distinct, aboriginal nations than there was in the nineteenth century. Among those who traveled beyond the settlements, at least, the names of particular peoples were often used rather than the generic "Indian," and anyone involved in trade, treaty negotiation, warfare, or missionary work had to be aware that he was dealing with different peoples with differing ideas on these matters.

5. Bartram, *Observations*, ii.

6. Limerick, *Legacy of Conquest*, 27.

7. Bartram, *Observations*, i.

8. Lewis and Clark, *History of the Expedition*, xxvii.

9. Thwaites, *Early Western Travels*, 14:37. The Thwaites edition, from volumes 14 through 17 of which I cite throughout, is based on "The Preliminary Notice" of the Philadelphia edition (1823) and the text of the London edition (1823) of James's *Account of the Exploring Expedition*.

10. Lewis and Clark, *History of the Expedition*, xxxvi.

11. Thwaites, *Early Western Travels*, 14:35.

12. In fact, the detailed zoological and botanical descriptions included in the account of the Long expedition appear to have inspired James Fenimore Cooper with the idea for Dr. Batius, the obsessive, and sometimes tiresome, naturalist in *The Prairie*, Cooper's novel about the great plains. It is known that Cooper relied heavily on the Long narrative for his information about the western territories; see, for example, Orm Overland, "James Fenimore Cooper's *The Prairie*," 108–116. Cooper develops a ludicrous effect of these accounts, when a traveler otherwise "much engrossed in making arrangements for the subsistance and safety" of the party, takes time "to scrutinize the productions of the country . . . with the eye of a Linnaeus or Buffon" (preface, Pike, *The Journals*, xxiv).

13. Lewis and Clark, *History of the Expedition*, xxi–xxii.

14. "Publisher's Preface," in Frémont, *Narrative*, iii.

15. Mitchell, *Witnesses to a Vanishing America*, 29.

16. *A Journal of the Voyage*, by expedition member Patrick Gass, preceded the authorized history into print by seven years, but it was not an adequate substitute for the records of the two commanders. There were also numerous

apocryphal accounts of the expedition based in part on Jefferson's 1806 message to Congress and material lifted from older western accounts such as those of Jonathan Carver. (See Coues, "Bibliographical Introduction," in Lewis and Clark, *History of the Expedition*, cvii—-cxxxii). Elliot Coues's edition of the *History*, based on the 1814 edition of the *History* compiled by Nicholas Biddle, came out in 1893, and Reuben Gold Thwaites's edition of the *Original Journals* in 1904–1905.

17. Moulton, *The Journals*, 2:37.

18. See Lawson-Peebles, *Landscape and Written Expression*, 227–228, for another view of the Biddle edition.

19. In discussing particular passages from the *History*, I refer where possible to the author of the journal record upon which the passage is based.

20. Jehlen, *American Incarnation*, 9.

21. Letter to Archibald Smith, January 25, 1786, in Jefferson, *The Papers of Thomas Jefferson*, 9:218.

22. Dwight, *Greenfield Hill*, 52–53.

23. In discussing the 1790 debate over the location of the American capital in *Atlantic America*, Meinig comments on the new nation's imperial outlook:

> If there was reason to doubt whether an Atlantic America could extend and sustain itself as a viable geopolitical system across half a continent, there was no doubt at all about Americans themselves spreading across such an expanse, for they were busily doing so. The only uncertainty about that advance was how far they might go, for there was little reason to think that they might halt at the Mississippi or be deterred by the bounds of any other political claims. Fervent spokesmen were already declaring a transcontinental destiny for the American people and asserting that "westward course of empire" must indeed soon take its way. (367–369)

24. See, for example, Elliott Coues's dedication, "To the People of the Great West," at the beginning of his edition of the *History*: "Jefferson gave you the country. Lewis and Clark showed you the way. The rest is your own course of empire. Honor the statesmen who foresaw your West. Honor the brave men who first saw your West. May the memory of their glorious achievement be your precious heritage!"

25. Franklin, *Discoverers, Explorers, Settlers*, 155.

26. Lewis and Clark, *History of the Expedition*, 133.

27. Mackenzie, *Journals and Letters*, 381.

28. As Myra Jehlen argues, "The most interesting aspect of the general belief in the national destiny to expand ever westward is one we tend to overlook, perhaps because we take it for granted: The American teleology cites

the will of heaven and the human spirit, but it rests its case on the integrity of the continent" (*American Incarnation*, 5).

29. Zebulon Pike, for example, upon hearing that certain "savages" had threatened him, asks whether "the laws of self-preservation, would not have justified [his] cutting those scoundrels to pieces"; but he admits that he dreaded meeting those individuals "for fear the impetuosity of my conduct might not be approved of by my government, who did not so intimately know the nature of those savages" (*The Journals*, 117).

30. See the preface to Hegel, *The Philosophy of History*, iii.

31. Samuel Hearne dedicated his *Journey* (1795) to the "Governor and Committee of the Hudson's Bay Company"; John Long his *Voyages and Travels* (1791) to Sir Joseph Banks, president of the Royal Society. Lewis and Clark's *History* is prefaced by a letter from former President Jefferson explaining the origins and purposes of the expedition and memorializing the by-then-dead Lewis.

32. Lewis and Clark, *History of the Expedition*, 52.

33. See Frantz, *The English Traveller*, 15–19, for an account of the effect of the Royal Society and the new science of the seventeenth century on the conventions of travel reporting. In the eighteenth century, Cook's voyages set the pace in scientific exploration. Cook's entourages included several highly trained men who issued their own reports, supplementary to the master narratives of the expeditions. His voyages were joint ventures of the British Admiralty and the Royal Society. See MacLulich, "The Emergence of the Exploration Narrative," 10–11, 54–55, for discussions of Cook's impact on travel reporting.

34. Lewis and Clark, *History of the Expedition*, xxvii.

35. See also Jackson, *The Letters*, 62–63.

36. Whereas modern anthropology has been much criticized on the grounds that it is complicit with western colonialism, Lewis and Clark were unselfconscious about using ethnographic categories to extend their society's control of others. Nevertheless, as I shall argue, in undertaking to write their reports, they confronted a conflict between the relationships they developed "in the field" and those that were prescribed by the conventions of exploration reporting. In *Time and the Other*, Johannes Fabian argues that there is a split between modern ethnographic research and anthropological theorizing in this respect. Anthropological writing "creates its object" in part through the distancing effects of temporal categories, especially the "denial of coevalness" or "shared time." Ethnography is often forced to operate in shared time through the "cognitive necessity" inherent in research exchanges with the group under study (21–35).

37. Lewis and Clark, *History of the Expedition*, xxvii—-xxviii.

38. Although my term for this rhetoric is "local," suggesting a definition in

Notes

Conclusion

1. See Sayre, *Thoreau and the American Indians*.
2. Marx, *The Machine in the Garden*, 262.
3. Thoreau, *Walden*, 3–4.
4. Hegel, *The Philosophy of History*, 60–61.
5. Thoreau, *Walden*, 322.
6. Cited in Rogin, *Fathers and Children*, 78.
7. For a discussion of narratives recounting overland journeys to the California gold fields, see Fender, *Plotting the Golden West*, 51–128.

Works Consulted

Adams, Percy. *Travelers and Travel Liars.* Berkeley: University of California Press, 1962.

Adams, Stephen, and Donald Ross, Jr. "Thoreau's 'Ktaadn': 'The Main Astonishment at Last.' " *English Language Notes* (March/June 1983): 39–47.

Altick, Richard. *The English Common Reader: A Social History of the Mass Reading Public, 1800–1900.* Chicago: University of Chicago Press, 1957.

Analytical Review; or History of Literature, Domestic and Foreign. London, 1796.

Antelyes, Peter. *Tales of Adventurous Enterprise: Washington Irving and the Poetics of Western Expansion.* New York: Columbia University Press, 1990.

Axtell, James. *After Columbus: Essays in the Ethnohistory of Colonial North America.* New York and London: Oxford University Press, 1988.

——— *The Invasion Within: The Contest of Cultures in Colonial North America.* New York: Oxford University Press, 1985.

Bakeless, John. *The Eyes of Discovery: The Pageant of North America as Seen by the First Explorers.* Philadelphia: Lippincott, 1950.

Bartram, John. *Observations on the Inhabitants, Climate, Soil, Rivers, Productions, Animals, and Other Matters Worthy of Notice Made by Mr. John Bartram, in his Travels from Pensilvania to Onondago, Oswego and the Lake Ontario, in Canada.* London: Whiston and White, 1751.

Batten, Charles L., Jr. *Pleasurable Instruction: Form and Convention in Eigh-*

teenth-Century Travel Literature. Berkeley: University of California Press, 1978.

Beaglehole, J. C. *The Life of Captain James Cook.* Stanford: Stanford University Press, 1974.

Benveniste, Emile. *Problems in General Linguistics.* Trans. Mary Elizabeth Meek. Coral Gables, Fla.: University of Miami Press, 1971.

Bercovitch, Sacvan. "The Ideological Context of the American Renaissance." In *Forms and Functions of History in American Literature: Essays in Honor of Ursula Brumm.* Ed. Winfried Fluck, Jurgen Peper, and Willi Paul Adams. Berlin: Erich Schmidt Verlag, 1981

—— "The Modernity of American Puritan Rhetoric." In *American Letters and Historical Consciousness: Essays in Honor of Lewis P. Simpson.* Ed. J. Gerald Kennedy and Daniel Mark Fogel. Baton Rouge and London: Louisiana State University Press, 1987.

—— "The Problem of Ideology in American Literary History." *Critical Inquiry* 12 (1986): 631–653.

—— *The Puritan Origins of the American Self.* New Haven: Yale University Press, 1975.

Berkhofer, Robert F., Jr. *The White Man's Indian: Images of the American Indian from Columbus to the Present.* 1978. Reprint. New York: Vintage, 1979.

Brebner, John Bartlet. *Explorers of North America.* 1933. Reprint. London: A. and C. Black, 1955.

Brereton, John. *A Brief and True Relation of the Discoverie of the North Part of Virginia. . . .* London, 1602. Reprint. Ann Arbor: University Microfilms International, 1966.

Carver, Jonathan. *The Journals of Jonathan Carver and Related Documents, 1766–1770.* Ed. John Parker. St. Paul: Minnesota Historical Society, 1976.

—— *Travels through the Interior Parts of North-America, in the Years 1766, 1767, and 1768.* London, 1778. Reprint. Philadelphia: Joseph Crukshank, 1784.

Christie, John Aldrich. *Thoreau as World Traveler.* New York: Columbia University Press, 1965.

Clark, William Bedford. "How the West Won: Irving's Comic Inversion of the Westering Myth in *A Tour on the Prairies.*" *American Literature* 50 (1973): 335–347.

Cooper, James Fenimore. *The Deerslayer.* New York: Putnam, 1912.

—— *The Pathfinder.* Ed. Richard Dilworth Rust. Albany: State University of New York Press, 1981.

—— *The Pioneers.* Ed. James F. Beard and James P. Elliott. Albany: State University of New York Press, 1980.

———— *The Prairie.* New York: Putnam, 1912.

Critical Review; or, Annals of Literature. London, 1797 (Series 2).

Crone, G. R., and Skelton, R. A. "English Collections of Voyages and Travels, 1625–1846." In *Richard Hakluyt and His Successors.* Ed. Edward Lynam. London: Hakluyt Society, 1946.

Cronon, William. *Changes in the Land: Indians, Colonists, and the Ecology of New England.* New York: Hill and Wang, 1983.

Daniells, Roy. "The Literary Relevance of Alexander Mackenzie." *Canadian Literature* 38 (1968): 19–28.

DeVoto, Bernard. *Course of Empire.* Boston: Houghton Mifflin, 1952.

Dwight, Timothy. *Greenfield Hill: A Poem.* In *The Connecticut Wits.* Ed. Vernon L. Parrington. New York: Harcourt, Brace, 1926.

Edinburgh Review, or Critical Journal (London) 1 (October 1802–January 1803): 141–158. (Review of Mackenzie's *Voyages from Montreal.*)

Egam, Ferol. *Frémont, Explorer for a Restless Nation.* New York: Doubleday, 1977.

Eggleston, Wilfred. *The Frontier and Canadian Letters.* Toronto: Ryerson Press, 1957.

Emerson, Ralph Waldo. *The Collected Works of Ralph Waldo Emerson.* Vol. 1. Ed. Robert E. Spiller and Alfred R. Ferguson. Cambridge: Harvard University Press, Belknap Press, 1971.

———— *The Collected Works of Ralph Waldo Emerson.* Vol. 3. Ed. Alfred R. Ferguson, Jean Ferguson Carr, and Joseph Slater. Cambridge: Harvard University Press, Belknap Press, 1983.

———— *Complete Works.* 12 vols. Ed. E. W. Emerson. Boston: Houghton Mifflin, 1903–1904.

———— *The Journals and Miscellaneous Notebooks of Ralph Waldo Emerson.* 16 vols. Ed. William H. Gilman, Alfred R. Ferguson, Harrison Hayford, Ralph H. Orth, J. E. Parsons, and A. W. Plumstead. Cambridge: Harvard University Press, Belknap Press, 1960–1982.

Fabian, Johannes. *Time and the Other: How Anthropology Makes Its Object.* New York: Columbia University Press, 1983.

Fender, Stephen. *Plotting the Golden West: American Literature and the Rhetoric of the California Trail.* Cambridge: Cambridge University Press, 1981.

Fleck, Richard F. *Henry Thoreau and John Muir Among the Indians.* Hamden, Conn.: Shoe String Press, Archon Books, 1985

Foster, William. "Samuel Purchas." In *Richard Hakluyt and His Successors.* Ed. Edward Lynam. London: Hakluyt Society, 1946.

Franklin, Wayne. *Discoverers, Explorers, Settlers: The Diligent Writers of Early America.* Chicago: University of Chicago Press, 1979.

Franklin, Wayne. "The Misadventures of Irving's Bonneville: Trapping and Being Trapped in the Rocky Mountains." In *The Westering Experience in American Literature.* Ed. Merrill Lewis and L. L. Lee. Bellingham, Wash.: Bureau for Faculty Research, Western Washington University, 1977.

Frantz, R. W. *The English Traveller and the Movement of Ideas, 1660–1732.* The University Studies of the University of Nebraska, vol. 22. Lincoln: University of Nebraska Press, 1934.

Frémont, John Charles. *The Expeditions of John Charles Frémont.* Ed. Donald Jackson and Mary Lee Spence. Urbana: University of Illinois Press, 1970.

—— *Narrative of the Exploring Expedition to the Rocky Mountains in the Year 1842, and to Oregon and California in the Years 1843–44.* Washington, D.C.: Henry Polkinghorn, 1845.

—— *Narratives of Exploration and Adventure.* Ed. Alan Nevins. New York: Longman, Green, 1956.

Fussell, Edwin. *Frontier: American Literature and the American West.* Princeton: Princeton University Press, 1965.

Galinsky, Hans. "Exploring the 'Exploration Report' and Its Image of the Overseas World: Spanish, French, and English Variants of a Common Form Type in Early American Literature." *Early American Literature* 12 (1977): 5–24.

Gass, Patrick. *A Journal of the Voyages and Travels of a Corps of Discovery, under the Command of Capt. Lewis and Capt. Clarke of the Army of the United States, from the Mouth of the River Missouri through the Interior Parts of North America to the Pacific Ocean, during the Years 1804, 1805 and 1806.* Pittsburgh: Zodak Cramer, 1807.

Giltrow, Janet. "Westering Narratives of Jonathan Carver, Alexander Henry, and Daniel Harmon." *Essays on Canadian Writing* (Summer 1981): 27–41.

Goetzmann, William H. *Exploration and Empire.* New York: Knopf, 1966.

Gove, Phillip Babcock. *The Imaginary Voyage in Prose Fiction.* New York: Columbia University Press, 1941.

Green, Martin. *Dreams of Adventure, Deeds of Empire.* New York: Basic Books, 1979.

—— *The Great American Adventure.* Boston: Beacon Press, 1984.

Hakluyt, Richard. *Voyages.* London: Dent Everyman, 1907. Reprint. London: Dover, 1962.

Handbook of North American Indians. Vol. 6. *Subarctic.* Ed. June Helm. Washington, D.C.: Smithsonian Institution, 1981; vol. 15. Ed. Bruce G. Trigger. 1978.

Harley, J.B. "Deconstructing the Map." *Cartographica* 26.2 (Spring 1989): 1–20.

Harrington, Charles D. "Self-Definition in Literature of Exploration." *Exploration: *Journal of the MLA Special Section on Exploration and Travel* 3 (1975): 1–12.

Hawkesworth, John. *An Account of the Voyages undertaken by Order of His Present Majesty . . . for Making Discoveries in the Southern Hemisphere, and Successively performed by Commodore Byron, Captain Wallis, Captain Carteret, and Captain Cook. . . .* London: W. Strahan and T. Cadell, 1773.

Hazard, Lucy Lockwood. *The Frontier in American Literature.* New York: Crowell, 1927.

Hearne, Samuel. *Journey from Prince of Wales's Fort in Hudson's Bay to the Northern Ocean in 1769, 1770, 1771, 1772.* Ed. Richard Glover. Toronto: Macmillan, 1958.

Hedges, William, L. *Washington Irving: An American Study, 1802–1832.* 1965. Reprint. Westport, Conn.: Greenwood, 1980.

Hegel, Georg Wilhelm Friedrich. *The Philosophy of History.* Trans. J. Sibree. Intro. C. J. Friedrich. New York: Dover, 1956.

Henry, Alexander (the elder). *Alexander Henry's Travels and Adventures in the Years 1760–1776.* Ed. Milton Milo Quaife. Chicago: R. R. Donnelly and Sons, 1921.

—— *Travels and Adventures in Canada and the Indian Territories.* New York, 1809. Reprint, ed. James Bain. Toronto: Morang, 1901.

Herbert, T. Walter, Jr. *Marquesan Encounter: Melville and the Meaning of Civilization.* Cambridge: Harvard University Press, 1980.

Hildebidle, John. *Thoreau: A Naturalist's Liberty.* Cambridge: Harvard University Press, 1983.

Hoag, Ronald Wesley. "The Mark on the Wilderness: Thoreau's Contact with Ktaadn." *Texas Studies in Language and Literature* 24 (1982): 23–46.

Hodgson, Maurice. "The Exploration Journal as Literature." *The Beaver* (Winter 1967): 4–12.

Huggan, Graham. "Decolonizing the Map: Post-Colonialism, Post-Structuralism and the Cartographic Connection." *Ariel: A Review of International English Literature* 20.4 (October 1989): 115–131.

Hulme, Peter. *Colonial Encounters: Europe and the Native Caribbean, 1492–1797.* London and New York: Methuen, 1986.

Innis, Harold A. *The Fur Trade in Canada.* Rev. ed. Toronto: University of Toronto Press, 1956.

—— "Peter Pond and the Influence of Captain James Cook on Exploration in the Interior of North America." *Proceedings and Transactions of the Royal Society of Canada* (3rd series) 22 (1928): 131–141.

Irving, Washington. *The Adventures of Captain Bonneville.* Ed. Robert A. Rees and Alan Sandy. Vol. 16 of *The Complete Works of Washington Irving.* Boston: Twayne, 1977.

Irving, Washington. *Astoria, or Anecdotes of an Enterprize beyond the Rocky Mountains*. Ed. Richard Dilworth Rust. Vol. 15 of *The Complete Works of Washington Irving*. Boston: Twayne, 1976.

——— *The Complete Works of Washington Irving*. Gen ed., Richard Dilworth Rust. Boston: Twayne, 1969–.

——— *The Crayon Miscellany*. Ed. Dalia Kirby. Vol. 22 of *The Complete Works of Washington Irving*. Boston: Twayne, 1979.

——— *The Life and Voyages of Christopher Columbus*. Ed. John Harmon McElroy. Vol. 11 of *The Complete Works of Washington Irving*. Boston: Twayne, 1981.

——— *The Sketch Book of Geoffrey Crayon, Gent*. Ed. Haskell Springer. Vol. 8 of *The Complete Works of Washington Irving*. Boston: Twayne, 1978.

Jackson, Donald. *The Letters of the Lewis and Clark Expedition*. Urbana: University of Illinois Press, 1962.

James, Edwin. *Account of the Exploring Expedition from Pittsburgh to the Rocky Mountains Performed in the Years 1819 and '20, by Order of the Hon. J. C. Calhoun, Sec'y of War, under the Command of Major Stephen H. Long. From the Notes of Major Long, Mr. T. Say, and Other Gentlemen of the Party. Compiled by Edwin James, Botanist and Geologist for the Expedition*. 2 vols. Philadelphia: H. C. Carey and I. Lea, 1823.

Jefferson, Thomas. *The Papers of Thomas Jefferson*. Vol. 9. Ed. Julian P. Boyd. Princeton: Princeton University Press, 1954.

Jehlen, Myra. *American Incarnation: The Individual, the Nation, and the Continent*. Cambridge: Harvard University Press, 1986.

——— "The American Landscape as Totem." *Prospects* 6 (1981): 17–36.

Jennings, Francis. *The Invasion of America*. Chapel Hill: University of North Carolina Press, 1975.

Juricek, John. "American Usage of the Word 'Frontier' from Colonial Times to the Present." *Proceedings of the American Philosophical Society* 110.1 (February 1966): 10–34.

Kellogg, Robert, and Robert Scholes. *The Nature of Narrative*. London: Oxford University Press, 1966.

Kime, Wayne R. "The Completeness of Washington Irving's *A Tour on the Prairies*." *Western American Literature* 8.1–2 (1973): 55–65.

Kolodny, Annette. *The Land Before Her: Fantasy and Experience on the American Frontiers, 1630–1860*. Chapel Hill: University of North Carolina Press, 1984.

——— *The Lay of the Land: Metaphor as Experience and History in American Life and Letters*. Chapel Hill: University of North Carolina Press, 1975.

Kopley, Richard. "The Hidden Journey of *Arthur Gordon Pym*." In *Studies in* the American Renaissance, 29–51. Ed. Joel Myerson. Boston: Twayne, 1982.

———— "The 'Very Profound Under-current' of *Arthur Gordon Pym*." In *Studies in the American Renaissance*, 143–175. Ed. Joel Myerson. Charlottesville: University of Virginia Press, 1987.

Kroeber, Karl. *Romantic Narrative Art*. Madison: University of Wisconsin Press, 1960.

Lamar, Howard S. Introduction to *Account of an Expedition from Pittsburgh to the Rocky Mountains under the Command of Major Stephen Long*, by Edwin James. Philadelphia: H. C. Carey and I. Lea, 1823. Abridged reprint. Barre, Mass.: Imprint Society, 1972.

Lawrence, D. H. *Studies in Classic American Literature*. 1923. Reprint. New York: Viking, 1964.

Lawson-Peebles, Robert. *Landscape and Written Expression in Revolutionary America: The World Turned Upside Down*. Cambridge and New York: Cambridge University Press, 1988.

Lewis, Meriwether, and William Clark. *History of the Expedition under the Command of Lewis and Clark, To the Sources of the Missouri, thence across the Rocky Mountains and down the Columbia River to the Pacific Ocean, performed during the Years 1804–5–6, by Order of the Government of the United States*. 4 vols. Ed. Elliott Coues. New York: Francis P. Harper, 1893.

———— *The Original Journals of the Lewis and Clark Expedition*. 8 vols. Ed. Reuben Gold Thwaites. New York: Dodd, Mead, 1904–1905.

Lewis, R. W. B. *The American Adam: Innocence Tragedy and Tradition in the Nineteenth Century*. Chicago: University of Chicago Press, 1955.

Limerick, Patricia Nelson. *Legacy of Conquest: The Unbroken Past of the American West*. New York: Norton, 1987.

Literary World (New York), no. 124 (June 16, 1849): 515. (Review of Irving's *Bonneville*.)

Logan, John Allen. *Passage Through the Garden: Lewis and Clark and the Image of the American Northwest*. Urbana: University of Illinois Press, 1975.

Long, John. *Voyages and Travels of an Indian Interpreter and Trader*. Vol. 2 of *Early Western Travels, 1748–1846*. Ed. Reuben Gold Thwaites. Cleveland: Arthur M. Clark, 1905.

McElroy, John Harmon. "The Integrity of Irving's *Columbus*." *American Literature* 50 (1978): 1–16.

MacGregor, Alan Leander. " 'Lords of the Ascendant': Mercantile Biography and Irving's Astoria." *Canadian Review of American Studies* 21.1 (Summer 1990): 15–30.

Mackenzie, Alexander. *Journals and Letters of Alexander Mackenzie.* Ed. W. K. Lamb. Cambridge: Hakluyt Society, Cambridge University Press, 1970.

—— *Voyages from Montreal, on the River St. Lawrence, through the Continent of North America, to the Frozen and Pacific Oceans; in the Years 1789, and 1793.* London: 1801.

MacLaren, I. S. "Alexander Mackenzie and the Landscapes of Commerce." *Studies in Canadian Literature* 7 (1982): 141–150.

—— "Creating Travel Literature: The Case of Paul Kane." *Papers of the Bibliographical Society of Canada* 27 (1988): 80–95.

—— "Samuel Hearne's Accounts of the Massacre at Bloody Fall, 17 July 1771." *Ariel: A Review of International English Literature* 22.1 (January 1991): 25–51.

—— "Washington Irving's Problems with History and Romance in *Astoria.*" *Canadian Review of American Studies* 21.1 (Summer 1990): 1–13.

MacLulich, Thomas Donald. "Canadian Exploration as Literature." *Canadian Literature* 81 (1979): 72–85.

—— "The Emergence of the Exploration Narrative in Canada." Ph.D. dissertation, York University, Toronto, 1976.

—— "The Explorer as Hero: Mackenzie and Frazer." *Canadian Literature* 75 (1977): 61–73.

McWilliams, John P. *Political Justice in a Republic.* Berkeley: University of California Press, 1972.

Marx, Leo. *The Machine in the Garden: Technology and the Pastoral Ideal in America.* London: Oxford University Press, 1964.

Meinig, D. W. *Atlantic America, 1492–1800.* Vol. 1 of *The Shaping of America: A Geographical Perspective on 500 Years of History.* New Haven: Yale University Press, 1986.

Melville, Herman. *Moby Dick.* New York: Norton, 1967.

Miller, Perry. *Errand Into The Wilderness.* Cambridge: Harvard University Press, 1956.

—— "The Romantic Dilemma in American Nationalism and the Concept of Nature." In *Nature's Nation.* Cambridge: Harvard University Press, Belknap Press, 1967.

Mitchell, Lee Clark. *Witnesses to a Vanishing America: The Nineteenth-Century Response.* Princeton: Princeton University Press, 1981.

Montgomery, Franz. "Alexander Mackenzie's Literary Assistant." *Canadian Historical Review* 28 (1937): 301–304.

Moulton, Gary E., ed. *The Journals of the Lewis and Clark Expedition.* Vol. 2. Lincoln: University of Nebraska Press, 1986.

Nash, Gary. *Red, White, and Black: The Peoples of Early America.* Englewood Cliffs, N.J.: Prentice-Hall, 1974.

Nash, Roderick. *Wilderness and the American Mind.* New Haven: Yale University Press, 1969.

Nevius, Blake. *Cooper's Landscapes: An Essay on the Picturesque Vision.* Berkeley: University of California Press, 1976.

Novak, M. E. *Economics and the Fiction of Daniel Defoe.* Berkeley: University of California Press, 1962.

O'Gorman, Edmundo. *The Invention of America: An Inquiry into the Historical Nature of the New World and the Meaning of Its History.* Bloomington: Indiana University Press, 1961.

Overland, Orm. "James Fenimore Cooper's *The Prairie:* The Making of an American Classic." Ph.D. dissertation. Yale University, 1969.

Ozouf, Maria. *La Fête Révolutionnaire, 1789–99.* Paris: Gallimard, 1976.

Parker, John, ed. *The Journals of Jonathan Carver and Related Documents, 1766–1770.* St. Paul: Minnesota Historical Society, 1976.

Parkman, Francis. *The Conspiracy of Pontiac and the Indian War after the Conquest of Canada.* 2 vols. 1851. Reprint. Boston: Little, Brown, 1898.

Parry, J. H. *The Age of Reconnaissance.* London: Weidenfeld and Nicolson, 1963.

Paul, Sherman. *The Shores of America: Thoreau's Inward Exploration.* Urbana: University of Illinois Press, 1958.

Pearce, Roy Harvey. *The Savages of America.* Baltimore: Johns Hopkins University Press, 1953.

Peckham, Howard H. *Pontiac and the Indian Uprising.* 1947. Reprint. Chicago: University of Chicago Press, Phoenix Books, 1961.

Pike, Zebulon. *An Account of Expeditions to the Sources of the Mississippi, and Through the Western Ports of Louisiana, to the Sources of the Arkansaw, Kans, La Platte, and Pierre Jaun, Rivers; Performed by Order of the Government of the United States During the Years 1805, 1806, and 1807. And a Tour Through the Interior Ports of New Spain . . . in the Year 1807.* Philadelphia: C. and A. Conrad and Co., 1810.

—— *The Journals of Zebulon Pike.* Ed. Donald Jackson. Norman: University of Oklahoma Press, 1966.

Poe, Edgar Allan. *Collected Works of Edgar Allan Poe.* 3 vols. Cambridge: Harvard University Press, 1969–1978.

—— *The Imaginary Voyages: The Narrative of Arthur Gordon Pym, The Unparalleled Adventure of One Hans Pfaall, The Journal of Julius Rodman.* Ed. Burton R. Pollin. Vol. 1 of *The Collected Writings of Edgar Allan Poe.* Boston: Twayne, 1981.

Poirier, Richard. *A World Elsewhere: The Place of Style in American Literature.* New York: Oxford University Press, 1966.

241

Pollin, Burton R. "Poe's *Narrative of Arthur Gordon Pym* and the Contemporary Reviewers." *Studies in American Fiction* 2.1 (Spring 1974): 37–56.

—— "Pym's *Narrative* in the American Newspapers: More Uncollected Notices." *Poe Studies* 11.1 (June 1978): 8–10.

—— "Three More Early Notices of *Pym* and the Snowden Collection." *Poe Studies* 8.1 (June 1975): 32–35.

Pratt, Mary Louise. "Conventions of Representation: Where Discourse and Ideology Meet." In *Contemporary Perceptions of Language: Interdisciplinary Dimensions, Georgetown Round Table on Language and Linguistics 1982*, 139–155. Ed. Heidi Byrnes. Washington, D.C.: Georgetown University Press, 1982.

—— "Scratches on the Face of the Country; or, What Mr. Barrow Saw in the Land of the Bushmen." *Critical Inquiry* 12.1 (Autumn 1985): 119–143.

Prescott, William H. *History of the Conquest of Mexico.* 3 vols. New York: Harper Brothers, 1855.

Quinn, David B. *North America from Earliest Discovery to First Settlements.* New York: Harper and Row, 1977.

Richetti, John J. *Popular Fiction Before Richardson: Narrative Patterns, 1700–1739.* Oxford: Oxford University Press, 1969.

Ridgely, J. V. "Tragical-Mythical-Satirical-Hoaxical: Problems of Genre in *Pym.*" *American Transcendental Quarterly* 24.1 (Fall 1974): 4–9.

Robinson, Douglas. "Reading Poe's Novel: A Speculative Review of *Pym* Criticism." *Poe Studies* 15.2 (December 1982): 47–54.

Rogin, Michael Paul. *Fathers and Children: Andrew Jackson and the Subjugation of the American Indians.* New York: Knopf, 1975.

Roppen, George, and Richard Somers. *Strangers and Pilgrims: An Essay on the Metaphor of the Journey.* Norwegian Studies in English, vol. 2. Bergen and New York: Humanities Press, 1964.

Rubin-Dorsky, Jeffrey. *Adrift in the Old World: The Psychological Pilgrimage of Washington Irving.* Chicago and London: University of Chicago Press, 1988.

Sayre, Robert F. *Thoreau and the American Indians.* Princeton: Princeton University Press, 1977.

Seelye, John. *Prophetic Waters: The River in Early American Life and Literature.* New York: Oxford University Press, 1977.

Slotkin, Richard. *The Fatal Environment: The Myth of the Frontier in the Age of Industrialization, 1800–1890.* New York: Atheneum, 1985.

—— *Regeneration Through Violence: The Mythology of the American Frontier.* Middletown, Conn.: Wesleyan University Press, 1973.

Smith, Henry Nash. "Symbol and Idea in *Virgin Land.*" In *Ideology and Classic*

American Literature. Ed. Sacvan Bercovitch and Myra Jehlen. Cambridge: Cambridge University Press, 1986.

———— *Virgin Land: The American West as Symbol and Myth*. Cambridge: Harvard University Press, 1950.

Smith, John. *The Generall History of Virginia, New England, and the Summer Isles*. London, 1624. Reprint. Ann Arbor: University Microfilms International, 1966.

Spengemann, William. *The Adventurous Muse: The Poetics of American Fiction, 1789–1900*. New Haven and London: Yale University Press, 1977.

Stafford, Barbara Maria. *Voyage into Substance: Art, Science, Nature, and the Illustrated Travel Account, 1760–1840*. Cambridge: MIT Press, 1984.

Starr, G. A. "Escape from Barbary: A Seventeenth-Century Genre." *Huntington Library Quarterly* 29 (1965): 36–37.

Tallmadge, John. " 'Ktaadn': Thoreau in the Wilderness of Words." *ESQ: A Journal of the American Renaissance* 31.3 (1985): 137–148.

Tanner, Tony. *Scenes of Nature, Signs of Men*. Cambridge and New York: Cambridge University Press, 1987.

Thompson, David. *Travels in Western North America*. Ed. Victor Hopwood. Toronto: Macmillan, 1971.

Thoreau, Henry David. *The Maine Woods*. Ed. Joseph J. Moldenhauer. Princeton: Princeton University Press, 1972.

———— *Walden*. Ed. J. Lyndon Shanley. Princeton: Princeton University Press, 1971.

———— *A Week on the Concord and Merrimack Rivers*. Ed. Carl F. Hovde. Princeton: Princeton University Press, 1980.

———— "A Yankee in Canada." In *Excursions*, vol. 9 of *The Writings of Henry David Thoreau*. Boston: Houghton Mifflin, 1893.

Thwaites, Reuben Gold, ed., *Early Western Travels, 1748–1846*. 32 vols. Cleveland, Ohio: Arthur H. Clark, 1905.

Tichi, Cecelia. *New World, New Earth: Environmental Reform in American Literature from the Puritans through Whitman*. New Haven and London: Yale University Press, 1979.

Turner, Frederick Jackson. *The Frontier in American History*. New York: Holt, 1962.

Turner, Victor. *Dramas, Fields and Metaphors: Symbolic Action in Human Society*. Ithaca: Cornell University Press, 1974.

Tuttleton, James W. "The Romance of History: Irving's *Companions of Columbus*." *American Transcendental Quarterly* 24.1 (Fall 1974): 18–23.

Vaughan, Alden T., and Edward C. Clark. *Puritans Among the Indians: Accounts of Captivity and Redemption, 1676–1724*. Cambridge: Harvard University Press, Belknap Press, 1981.

von Humboldt, Alexander. *Essai Politique sur l'Ile de Cuba.* Paris, 1826.

Waldon, Freda F. "Alexander Henry, Esq. of Montreal; Fur Trader, Adventurer and Man of Letters." Unpublished M.A.thesis. University of London, 1930. (Copies in National Library of Canada, Columbia University Library, Hamilton, Detroit, and Toronto Public libraries.)

Washburn, Wilcomb. E. "The Meaning of 'Discovery' in the Fifteenth and Sixteenth Centuries." *The American Historical Review* 68 (1962): 1–21.

White, Hayden. "The Value of Narrativity in the Representation of Reality." *Critical Inquiry* 7.1 (1980): 5–27.

Williams, Roger. *A Key into the Language of America.* Ed. James Hammond Trumbull. Vol. 1 of *The Complete Writings of Roger Williams.* New York: Russell and Russell, 1963.

Williams, Stanley T. *Life of Washington Irving.* 1935. Reprint. New York: Octagon, 1971.

——— "Washington Irving." In *Literary History of the United States.* Ed. Robert E. Spiller, Willard Thorp, Thomas H. Johnson, Henry Seidel Canby. 3rd ed. New York: Macmillan, 1963.

Williamson, J. A. *The Ocean in English History.* London: Oxford University Press, 1941.

——— "Richard Hakluyt." In *Richard Hakluyt and His Successors.* Ed. Edward Lynam. London: Hakluyt Society, 1946.

Zanger, Jules. "Poe's Endless Voyage: *The Narrative of Arthur Gordon Pym.*" *Papers on Language and Literature* 22.3 (Summer 1986): 276–283.

Index

Adoption, 61

Adventures of Captain Bonneville, 119, 121, 130, 149–160; aesthetic and personal vision in, 153, 157–161; collapse of fur trade in, 150–153; expansionist ideology in, 153; hero in, 154–156; treatment of Indians in, 153–154, 155–156; narrative perspective in, 149–150; compared to *Tour*, 145; virgin land in, 160; *see also* Bonneville, Benjamin

American Renaissance, 11, 115–116

Antelyes, Peter, 116, 120, 153, 161, 224n29, 224n41, 225n43, 226n51

Astor, John Jacob, 145; presence in *Astoria*, 147–148; and Christopher Columbus, 147, 148, 225n51

Astoria, 119, 121, 130, 131, 132, 146–149; compared to *Columbus*, 144; discovery in, 146; landscape in, 148–149; narrative perspective in, 148–149; social conflict in, 149; as source for *Pym*, 168; strategic failure in, 151; territorial claims in, 149

Axtell, James, 216n45

Bakeless, John, 100–101, 102

Bartram, John: attitudes to Indians, 75–76; rendering of landscape, 74–75; *Observations*, 74–77

Bercovitch, Sacvan, 100

Biddle, Nicholas, 84

Bonneville, Benjamin, 145–146; *see also Adventures of Captain Bonneville*

Calhoun, John C., 79

Cannibalism, 61, 169

Captivity narrative, 60–61

Carver, Jonathan, 173; as source for Henry's *Travels and Adventures*, 57

Cheyennes, 92

Chopunnish, 94

Clark, William, *see* Lewis, Meriwether

Colonial discourse: definition of, 10, 57; in Henry's *Travels and Adventures*, 57, 59

Columbus, Christopher: compared to John Jacob Astor, 147, 226n51; *see also Life and Voyages of Christopher Columbus*

Cook, James, 17, 173

Cooper, James Fenimore, 55, 203, 209; handling of colonial conflict, 10–11; conflict over land in plots, 9, 10; *Deerslayer*, 10; and Washington Irving, 119; *Last of the Mohicans*, 4, 10; in D. H. Lawrence, 4; in R. W. B. Lewis, 5–6; Natty Bumppo, 177, 179; *Pathfinder*, 10; *Pioneers*, 8; *Prairie*, 8, 9; in Richard Slotkin, 8
Coppermine River, 32; massacre at, 36–39
Coues, Elliott, 100, 101, 102
Crone, G. R. and R. A. Skelton, 17

Dene, 28; *see also Voyage to the Northern Ocean*
Discovery: aesthetic or personal, 21, 96–99, 102, 106–107, 109–111, 157–161, 189; American sense of, 83; as aspect of colonial discourse, 10; definition of, 19–20; in Hearne, 20; in Irving, 124–125, 125–126, 161; myths of, 28, 30–31, 144, 162–163; in O'Gorman, 12; romantic discourse of, 25, 174, 209; in early United States, 13
Discovery of America: as linguistic event, 25; Thoreau's revision of, 205
Discovery narratives: American, 71–73, 77–84, 185–188; authority of, 24–26, 166–167; coherence of, 26; conflict in, 9; conventions of, 18, 71, 167–173; economic context of, 21; editing of, 19; eighteenth-century, 17; emptiness trope in, 189; and European expansion, 11; as historical narrative, 24; Washington Irving's use of, 118, 120–122; plots of, 82–83, 187; Poe's use of, 121; publication of, 79–80; sense of purpose of, 80; romantic, 203; as quest for self-knowledge, 167, 185; scientific discourse in, 59; and settlement, 82; social standing of author of, 77–78, 80–82; concept of space in, 72; Thoreau's use of, 121–122; tone of, 79; transcendence in, 185–186
Dwight, Timothy, 85

Emerson, Ralph Waldo, 180, 183–185, 203; "The American Scholar," 184, 210; "Fortune of the Republic," 183; on the infinity of nature, 230*n*63; *Nature*, 183–184, 228*n*34; non-narrative style of, 184–185, 228*n*34; and self-discovery in the land, 183–184; "The Transcendentalist," 184
Empty continent, myth of, 7
Ethnography, 220*n*36, 220–221*n*38
Euro-American: definition, 211*n*2
Expeditions, exploratory: equipping of, 80; American sponsorship of, 78–79
Exploration, *see* Discovery
Exploration narrative, *see* Discovery narrative
Explorer: ideal of, 80–82

Fabian, Johannes, 220*n*36, 220–221*n*38
Fender, Stephen, 111, 222*n*61
Franklin, Wayne, 194; definition of discovery, 19–20, 212–213*n*10
Frémont, Jessie Benton, 19
Frémont, John Charles, 16, 18, 19, 102, 107–111, 171, 172, 188; aesthetic and personal responses of, 109–111; social standing of, 78; tone of, 109
Frontier: changing definition of, 73–74, 77
Fur trade, 213*n*11, 213*n*14, 214*n*33; and Samuel Hearne, 28–30; and Alexander Henry, 56–57; as cause of Indian wars, 215*n*34; literature of, 15–16, 17; and Alexander Mackenzie, 42–43
Fussell, Edwin, 165, 168

Gosnold, Bartholomew, 192
Green, Martin, 11–12

Harley, J.B., 216*n*43
Hearne, Samuel, 15, 17, 19, 22, 26–41, 57, 169, 171, 172, 173, 193; biography, 26; as discoverer, 20, 37, 39; relation to land, 83; and northern Indians, 28, 29–30, 36, 48; northern environment, adaptation to, 27; on scientific travel, 214*n*23; *see also Journey to the Northern Ocean*
Hedges, William, 115–116, 117
Hegel, Georg Wilhelm Friedrich, 24, 207
Henry, Alexander, 15, 17, 55–69, 169, 170, 172, 212*n*1; and fur trade, 56–57; national identity of, 57; references to

other travellers, 215–216*n*38; adopted by Wawatam, 63–64; *see also Travels and Adventures in Canada and the Indian Territories*

Higginson, Thomas Wentworth, 191

Hildebidle, John, 228*n*42, 230*n*58

History of the Expedition under the Command of Lewis and Clark, 84–101, 173; aesthetic response in, 96–99; assembly of, 84; as assertion of American power, 87; authority of, 88–89; modes of discovery in, 89–90; ethnography in, 90–92; conflict over land in, 77; reception of, 85

Hoag, Ronald Wesley, 229*n*57, 230*n*61

Hudson's Bay Company, 22–23, 39

Hulme, Peter: on colonial discourse, 10, 57; on cannibalism, 65

Humboldt, Alexander von, 128

Hunt, Wilson Price, 147

Indians: demonization of, 108–109; as local color, 108; obscuring of national distinctions among, 105–106, 107–108; as a "problem," 104–105; Indian removals, 2

Inuit, 36, 38–39

Irving, Washington: as an American in Europe, 117; *Companions of Columbus,* 120; and Cooper, 119; Geoffrey Crayon persona, 113–117, 119; myth of discovery, 144, 162–163; use of discovery narrative, 120–122, 131–132; heroes of sensibility in, 162–163, 203; as historian, 113, 118; attitudes to Indians, 118, 225–226*n*44; "Philip of Pokanoket," 225*n*44; nature of his romanticism, 117–118, 209; use of simile and metaphor, 224–225*n*41; *The Sketch Book,* 115–117, 131, 132, 142; "Traits of Indian Character," 225*n*44; use of travel genres, 114–116; *see also Adventures of Captain Bonneville; Astoria; Life and Voyages of Christopher Columbus; A Tour on the Prairies*

James, Henry: *The Ambassadors,* 179

Jefferson, Thomas, 72, 79, 85, 91

Jehlen, Myra, 219–220*n*28, 228*n*34, 228*n*35, 228*n*36

Journey to the Northern Ocean, 26–41; myth of discovery in, 28, 30–31; guides in, 31–34; conflicting intentions in, 27, 39–41; first journey, account of, 31; second journey, account of, 32–35; plot of, 40; sense of progress in, 33; role of science in, 41; suffering in, 33

Juricek, John, 73

Kime, Wayne, 139

"Ktaadn," 188–201; as discovery narrative, 190, 200; early explorers in, 188; idea of first contact in, 191–192, 194, 198–199, 201; Indians in, 196–197; lumbering in, 195; mythology in, 199, 200; primitive man in, 198–199; time in, 230*n*58; transcendence in, 197–198, 200, 229*n*57; travel in, 194–195; virgin land in, 188–189

Land: as commodity, 209; conflict over, 1, 6, 9, 122; descriptions of, 221*n*44; conceived of as empty, 2, 3, 190, 209; as metaphor of the self, 209; presentation of in John Bartram, 74–75

Land claims: conflicting bases of, 9

Lawrence, D. H., 3–5

Lawson-Peebles, Robert, 221*n*44

Lewis, Meriwether and William Clark, 16, 17, 19, 84–101, 102, 171, 172, 173, 189, 193; as official envoys, 90; as American icons, 86; social standing of, 78; *see also History of the Expedition under the Command of Lewis and Clark*

Lewis, R. W. B., 5–7

Life and Voyages of Christopher Columbus, 113, 118, 121, 122–130, 131, 144; character of Columbus, 126; effects of colonization in, 127–129; discovery in, 124, 125–126; dramatic irony in, 123; hero in, 133; narrative structure in, 129–130; idea of virgin world in, 126–127

Limerick, Patricia, 3, 76

Long, John, 22
Long, Stephen, 16, 78, 102, 173
Louisiana Purchase, 85

Mackenzie, Alexander, 15, 17, 23, 41–55, 57, 89, 171, 173; biography, 41; commercial ambitions of, 42–43; relation to land, 83; and North-West Company, 42; *see also Voyages . . . to the Frozen and Pacific Oceans*
MacLaren, I. S., 19, 45, 213*n*21, 214*n*27
Mandans, 91–92
Manifest destiny, 83
Marx, Leo, 2, 204–205
Matonabbee, 35, 172
Meinig, D. W., 219*n*23
Melville, Herman: Ishmael, 177; *Moby Dick*, 178, 185, 187
Michilimackinac, 66
Miller, Perry, 1
Missouri River, 98
Missouris, 90
Mitchell, Lee Clark, 83, 217*n*4
Moulton, Gary, E., 84
Multnomahs, 94

Narrative, romantic, 115–116
Narrative of Arthur Gordon Pym, 165–182; alienation in, 180; authority in, 166–167, 174–175; baffled narrator in, 173; discovery in, 179; conventions of discovery narrative in, 167–173; references to discovery narratives in, 173; and Emerson, 180; as fact or fiction, 166–167; guide figure in, 170; romantic hero in, 174–177, 185–186; rejection of history in, 177–178; romantic narrative in, 178–179; Other in, 170–171, 181–182; suffering as trope in, 169–170; desire for transcendence in, 180–181
Narrativity, 19, 213*n*17
Nature: nineteenth-century idea of, 2
Navarrete, Martín Leonardo Fernández de, 122
North-West Company, 68

O'Gorman, Edmundo, 12, 228–229*n*44
Osages, 91, 103–104

Ottoes, 90
Overland, Orm, 218*n*12

Parkman, Francis, 104–105
Paul, Sherman, 190–191
Pawnees, 91, 103, 108
Pike, Zebulon, 16, 18, 102–107, 182; aesthetic and personal responses of, 106–107; biography, 102; attitudes to Indians, 103; *Journals*, 173; social standing of, 78
Poe, Edgar Allan: use of the discovery narrative, 121, 165–166; and Emerson, 183; "MS. Found in a Bottle," 176; and the West, 165–166; *see also Narrative of Arthur Gordon Pym*
Pond, Peter, 173
Pratt, Mary Louise, 216*n*43
Prescott, William H., 125

Rich Obadiah, 122
Ridgely, J.V., 167
Rogin, Michael Paul, 2, 3, 208–209
Rubin-Dorsky, Jeffrey, 116–117, 225–226*n*44

Sayre, Robert F., 172
Science: in Hearne's *Journey*, 41; in Lewis and Clark's *History*, 90–92
Shoshones, 93
Sioux, 104
Slotkin, Richard, 8, 212*n*10
Smith, Henry Nash, 7
Smith, John, 192
Spengemann, William, 115, 178–179

Thompson, David, 173
Thoreau, Henry David, 179, 188–201, 203–210; use of the discovery narrative, 121–122, 190, 205–206, 208; and American history, 189–190, 191–192, 199, 204, 208; use of metaphor, 190–191, 204–205, 207; idea of nature, 191; *Walden*, 181, 189, 200, 206–207, 207, 208; *see also* "Ktaadn"
Tour on the Prairies, 114, 115, 121, 130–144; discovery tradition in, 142–144; Henry Ellsworth in, 133, 134; exotic

references in, 137; Indians in, 134, 135, 141, 224n29; mock heroic tone in, 134; narrative persona in, 133, 136–137, 138–140, 225n43; narrator compared to Columbus, 138, 143; treatment of rangers in, 133–136; reception of, 130; romanticism in, 143–144; social class in, 137–138

Travels and Adventures in Canada and the Indian Territories, 55– 70; adoption in, 61, 63–64; authenticity of, 215n35; cannibalism in, 61, 64–65; as captivity narrative, 60, 69; as colonial discourse, 59, 68–69; as discovery narrative, 58, 60; disguise in, 62–65; liminal states in, 65–68; as source for Parkman, 217n48; publication of, 216n39; lack of strategic importance of, 57–58

Turner, Frederick Jackson, 73

Turner, Victor: theory of initiation, 217n51

Twain, Mark, 177, 179

Voyages . . . to the Frozen and Pacific Oceans, 41–55, 173; as adventure, 49–50; author's self-portrayal in, 42; and cartography, 59; conflict in, 46, 49; editing of, 44–45; lack of ethnography in, 54, 60; guides in, 47–48; landscape description in, 52; plot of, 45; purposes in, 42–44; rendering of time in, 47; unity of, 44

Wallawallas, 93

Wawatam, 63, 172

West: conflicting ideas about, 87–88; Irving's treatment of, 161–162

Westering ideology, 85

Williams, Roger, 193

Williams, Stanley T., 130

White, Hayden, 19, 213n17

White man, trope of first sight by, 100